The Discourse of Enclosure

SUNY series in Medieval Studies
Paul E. Szarmach, editor

The Discourse of Enclosure

Representing Women in
Old English Literature

By
Shari Horner

State University of New York Press

Published by
State University of New York Press, Albany

© 2001 State University of New York

All rights reserved

Printed in the United States of America

For information, address State University of New York Press,
State University Plaza, Albany, NY 12246

Production by Christine L. Hamel
Marketing by Fran Keneston

Library of Congress Cataloging-in-Publication Data

Horner, Shari, 1961–
   The discourse of enclosure : representing women in Old English
literature / by Shari Horner.
      p. cm. — (SUNY series in medieval studies)
      Includes bibliographical references and index.
      ISBN 0-7914-5009-0 (alk. paper) — ISBN 0-7914-5010-4 (pbk. : alk.
paper)
      1. English literature—Old English, ca. 450-1100—History and criticism.
2. Women and literature—England—History—To 1500.   3. Feminism
and literature—England—History—To 1500.   4. Women—England—
History Middle Ages, 500-1500.   5. Enclosure (Monasticism)—
England—History to 1500.   6. Women in literature.   I. Title.   II. Series.

PR179.W65 H67 2001
829'.09352042—dc21

                                                                00-049237

10   9   8   7   6   5   4   3   2   1

Cover Illustration: Planet Art.

Contents

Acknowledgments

My work on women in Old English literature began when I was a graduate student at the University of Minnesota, and parts of this book are derived from my dissertation. I would like to thank my dissertation director, Calvin Kendall, for his guidance then and for his support over the many years between that project and this one. Several others supported my work in those years, and I am grateful to Rita Copeland, David Wallace, Oliver Nicholson, Susan Noakes, and the members of the Medieval Studies Research Group at Minnesota for reading and listening to my ideas about female enclosure over and over again.

Jane Chance and Helen Damico deserve special thanks for reading and encouraging my work and for their generous personal and professional support; likewise, Marilynn Desmond read and commented on several versions of this book and I am grateful for her guidance. I wish to thank as well several friends and colleagues who, over the past several years, have contributed to my understanding of Old English literature and feminist theory, and who were always willing to answer my many questions: Rebecca Barnhouse, Anne Clark Bartlett, Susan Bernstein, Virginia Blanton-Whetsell, Patricia Briggs, Mary Dockray-Miller, Jim Landman, David Porter, Anna Roberts, Leslie Stratyner, and Jon Wilcox. At Shippensburg University, the interlibrary loan staff cheerfully provided crucial and timely help.

I am happy to acknowledge the research support I received from the University of Nebraska at Kearney Research Services Council; from Penn State University in the form of a Research Development Grant; and from the National Endowment for the Humanities, which awarded me both a summer stipend and the opportunity to participate in a Summer Seminar on Old English literature, directed by Paul Szarmach.

Professor Szarmach has my deep gratitude and my utmost respect; inspirational as a scholar and mentor, he has generously encouraged this project since that summer in 1995. Along with the anonymous readers of my manuscript for SUNY Press, who offered both motivation and instructive criticism, he has made this a better book, and I am grateful to them all. All errors that remain are, of course, my own.

My husband, Michael Bibby, always believed in this book, even when I sometimes wasn't so sure. His advice has been consistently reliable and rigorous; his personal and intellectual strength sustains me. And although my sons, three-year-old Nicholas and two-month-old Jonathan, are not yet aware that I am even writing this, I hope that someday they will read it. This book is for them all.

Portions of this book, now revised, previously appeared as articles, and I am grateful to University of Chicago Press and the University Presses of Florida, respectively, for allowing me to include the following material:

"Spiritual Truth and Sexual Violence: The Old English *Juliana*, Anglo-Saxon Nuns, and the Discourse of Female Monastic Enclosure." *Signs: Journal of Women in Culture and Society* 19 (1994): 658–675. (c) 1994 by the University of Chicago Press. Reprinted with permission of the University of Chicago Press.

"The Violence of Exegesis: Reading the Bodies of Ælfric's Female Saints." In *Violence Against Women in Medieval Texts*. Ed. Anna Roberts. Gainesville: University Press of Florida, 1998. 22-43. (c) 1998 by the University Press of Florida. Reprinted with permission of the University Press of Florida.

For Michael, always.
And now, for Nicholas and Jonathan.

The Discourse of Enclosure: Inscribing the Feminine in Anglo-Saxon Literature

One of the most venerated early medieval female saints in England, the seventh-century English abbess Æthelthryth of Ely, steadfastly remained a virgin through two marriages, the second of which lasted more than twelve years. Her ability to do so was considered a miracle by her hagiographers; narratives of her life both by Bede (in the eighth century) and by Ælfric (in the tenth) begin by presenting information about this miraculous bodily *integritas*.[1] Eventually, Æthelthryth persuaded her second husband to allow her to join a convent, and she was soon appointed abbess at Ely. In later years, Bede tells us, Æthelthryth developed a "very large tumour beneath her jaw" ("tumorem maximum sub maxilla") (394–395), which, although it was lanced and drained by a physician, eventually caused her death. Bede reports that "[w]hen she died she was buried by her own command in a wooden coffin, in the ranks of the other nuns, as her turn came" ("et aeque, ut ipsa iusserat, non alibi quam in medio eorum iuxta ordinem quo transierat ligneo in locello sepulta") (392–393).

Sixteen years later, her sister Seaxburh, then abbess at Ely, exhumed Æthelthryth's bones in order to translate them into the church. Miraculously, the body was undecayed. The physician, who witnessed the exhumation, reported with amazement that the jaw-wound had healed: "so that instead of the open gaping wound which she had when she was buried, there now appeared, marvellous to relate, only the slightest traces of a scar" ("ita ut mirum in modum pro aperto et hiante uulnere, cum quo sepulta erat, tenuissima tunc / cicatricis uestigia parerent") (394–395). It was widely believed that

1

the saint's virginity during life was responsible for her corporeal purity
after death. As Bede explained, "the divine miracle whereby her flesh
would not corrupt after she was buried was token and proof that she
had remained uncorrupted by contact with any man" ("Nam etiam
signum diuini miraculi, quo eiusdem feminae sepulta caro corrumpi
non potuit, indicio est quia a uirili contactu incorrupta durauerit")
(392–393). The nuns re-clothed the saint in fine linen, transferred
her to a white marble sarcophagus miraculously found for the occa-
sion, and installed her in the church.

In addition to the narratives of Bede and Ælfric, a fascinating
visual record of St. Æthelthryth survives in the tenth-century Benedictional of Æthelwold (Figure 1).[2] Here, her stylized miniature is
accompanied by a benediction for her feast day, which, like the narratives, emphasizes the miracle of Æthelthryth's married virginity
and bodily incorruption:

> Omnipotens unus et aeternus deus pater et filius et spiritus
> sanctus, qui beatae aeðeldryðe animum septiformis gratiae
> ubertate ita succensum solidauit, ut duorum coniugum thal-
> amis asscita immunis euaderet, castamque sibi piissimus
> sponsam perpetim adoptaret, uos ab incentiua libidinum
> concupiscentia muniendo submoueat, et sui amoris igne
> succendat. Amen.

> [May the one omnipotent and eternal God, the Father and
> the Son and the Holy Spirit, who made the will of blessed
> Æthelthryth steadfast and so ablaze with the bounty of
> seven-fold grace that, summoned to the marriage beds of
> two husbands, she avoided them, remaining intact, and
> was taken as a chaste bride in perpetuity by the most just
> one, remove you from the burning desire of lust by pro-
> tecting you, and kindle the fire of his own love. Amen.][3]

By maintaining her bodily *integritas* during marriage, and protecting
the sealed nature of her virginal body, St. Æthelthryth progressed
from earthly to spiritual marriage by taking monastic vows and
becoming a bride of Christ. Because she preserved her virginity in
the face of great odds, Æthelthryth was protected by monasticism,
and she likewise had the power to protect both the Christians who

Figure 1. Saint Æthelthryth. British Library Add. 49598 fol. 90v. By permission of The British Library.

visited her tomb and made use of her relics, and those who heard
(or read) her story. The prayer emphasizes the spatial significance of
her bodily and spiritual *integritas*:

> Quatinus ab huius recediui saeculi cupiditate remoti, uirtu-
> tum omnium lampadibus adornati, eius in caelis mereamini
> habere consortium, quae terreni regis caritatiue contempsit
> thalamum, spretaque lata terrenae cupiditatis uia, artam
> monasticae conuersationis eligere uoluit uitam, ac hodierna
> die uoti compos, caelestem aeterni regis intrare promeruit
> aulam. Amen.

> [So that remote from the desire for this vain world, [and]
> adorned with the lamps of all virtues, you may merit to
> have in heaven the company of her who on account of her
> love, rejected the marriage bed of an earthly king and, having
> spurned the broad path of earthly desire, wished to adopt
> the narrow life of monasticism and on this day, obtaining
> her wish (uoti), deserved to enter the heavenly palace of
> the eternal king. Amen.][4]

As Robert Deshman explains, the layout of the miniature is likewise
spatially significant within the Benedictional: the saint is turned
towards the facing page historiated initial of Christ, who extends his
fingers in blessing back to her. The unified design of the two facing
pages underscores the saint's protected status as a bride of Christ.[5]

Moreover, the miniature depicts St. Æthelthryth as a type of the
Virgin Mary, carrying both a book, which suggests her monastic
vows, and a branch of flowers, which symbolically links her to both
Christ and Mary (Deshman, 123). Her head is framed by a nimbus,
and the detailed folds of her garments encircle her womb. The strong
diagonal lines of the page's frame uniformly direct the eye to this
central image, and the circular motifs of the foliated border that
surrounds the saint echo the visual focus on her womb. The saint
stands within the heavy, elaborate floral frame, and she is circum-
scribed by a background inscription, also within the frame: "Imago
Sanctae Æthelthrythe abbatissae ac perpetuae virginis." The words
themselves enclose her body, with some words actually split down
the middle—as with "ima...go" for example, which frames her head.[6]

The image of Æthelthryth in the Benedictional illustrates the themes of intactness and enclosure that govern both Bede's and Ælfric's accounts of her life. At the most obvious narrative level, the saint's bodily *integritas* during life was proven by the incorruption of her body after death; though married, her body remained sealed, and thus it did not decay. After she joined the convent at Ely, Æthelthryth was apparently strictly cloistered. But beyond the enclosures of body and cloister, the narratives—like the manuscript image—construct many kinds of layers that surround the saint and include multiple images of literal and metaphoric enclosure. Æthelthryth herself saw in her jaw tumor a fitting example of divine justice, for her pleasure in wearing expensive necklaces during her youth. The necklaces represent the "chains" of worldly vanity that fettered her in life; the infected tumor fittingly symbolizes her corrupt behavior; the lancing and eventual disappearance of the tumor demonstrate that the saint has rid herself of such earthly corruption. The scar, perhaps, reinforces the sealed nature of this body and acts as a signal reminder of the humanity of Christ and his saints. In the narratives, as in the manuscript, careful attention is paid to the layers and kinds of clothing that envelop this body: woollen garments during life, and fine linens after death.[7] Originally buried in a wooden coffin (a fact that makes the lack of physical decay after sixteen years all the more miraculous), the saint was later transferred to a marble sarcophagus, described in terms that emphasize the ways it contains her body: "Mirum uero in modum ita aptum corpori uirginis sarcofagum inuentum est, ac si ei specialiter praeparatum fuisset, et locus quoque capitis seorsum fabrefactus ad mensuram capitis illius aptissime figuratus apparuit" ["This sarcophagus was found to fit the virgin's body in a wonderful way, as if it had been specially prepared for her; and the place for the head, which was cut out separately, seemed to be exactly shaped to its size"] (Colgrave and Mynors, 396–397).[8] In short, every detail in both the narratives and the miniature contributes to an overwhelming image of purity, intactness, and enclosure of the saint.

The metaphors, themes, and images of enclosure that govern early medieval narratives such as the Life of St. Æthelthryth are the larger subject of this book. Scholars have long recognized, of course, that medieval religious women were enclosed, that virginity was highly valued, and that these two positions were profoundly interrelated throughout the Middle Ages. But how do the material practices of female monastic enclosure shape or inform the textual operations of early medieval narratives?[9]

The thesis of this book is that many Old English texts construct their female subjects by means of a discourse of enclosure derived from the increasingly restrictive conditions of early medieval female monasticism. As the Life of St. Æthelthryth demonstrates so compellingly, the female subject of early English literature is enclosed by many layers—textual, material, discursive, spatial—all of which image and reinforce the powerful institutions of the Christian church that regulated the female body. Moreover, female bodies were themselves enclosures, a point emphasized by the Anglo-Saxon artist who focused the viewer's eye on Æthelthryth's womb, and by Bede, who, in his hymn to the saint, compared her to the Virgin Mary: "Regis ut aetherei matrem iam, credo, sequaris, / tu quoque sis mater regis ut aetherei" [Royal Mother of Heaven's King your leader now; / You too, maybe, a mother of Heaven's King" (398–399).[10] The discourse of enclosure prescribes, regulates, and thereby normalizes the female subject of early English literature, differentiating her from her male counterparts, and providing a historically and culturally specific matrix through which to view this subject.

In large part, then, this study examines how pre-Conquest English narratives construct femininity. Feminist scholars have skillfully demonstrated the myriad ways that gender is one crucial category for organizing society and culture. Understanding how the usually hidden operations of gender accomplish this organization has been a primary project for recent feminist social and literary historians.[11] Most importantly, gender is historically variable and contingent; definitions of masculinity or femininity are not universal constructs but dependent upon shifting local, temporal, and cultural specificities.[12] As Susan Crane has usefully explained in a discussion of later medieval literature, "Gender emerges not as the fixed expression of binary sex difference but as a socially instituted construct that interacts with other constructs of class, faith, and so on. . . . Like all social representations gender has a history, and literature has a prominent role in that history of asserting and modifying what it means to live in gendered identity."[13] The discourse of enclosure offers a particularly valuable model for examining how the social institutions of female monasticism and Old English literature interact. The point is not that female monasticism and literature exist in a cause-and-effect relationship, but rather that both construct and are in turn constructed by the social and religious discourses at work within early English culture.

The "gendered self," according to Judith Butler, only appears fixed or stable, because it is "produced by the regulation of attributes along culturally established lines of coherence" (*Gender Trouble*, 24). These "regulatory practices" produce gender identity: "There is no gender identity behind the expressions of gender; that identity is performatively constituted by the very 'expressions' that are said to be its results" (25). This formulation of gender as a "doing" or "performing" is crucial for understanding how texts and cultures continually construe the categories of masculine and feminine, thereby normalizing these constructions. Thus gender must be understood as a repeated set of culturally established acts; the repetition produces the appearance of a stable gendered self. In the same way, the culturally established "expressions" of gender mandated by the terms of female religious enclosure produce the seemingly stable gender identities of women in Old English literature. Analyzing the discursive operations of enclosure will clarify the means by which those subjects emerge within literary texts.

For the early medieval church, "enclosure" signified the legislated isolation and separation of both male and female religious from society; the boundaries of the cloister were as important for containing those within (active enclosure) as for keeping the rest of the world out (passive enclosure).[14] As Jane Schulenburg has shown, although the rules of the cloister were theoretically intended for both male and female religious, these rules were applied much more rigorously to women. Moreover, although the universal practice of enclosure for female religious was not decreed until 1298 (by Pope Boniface VIII), the need for female religious enclosure was emphasized by patristic writers and monastic rules from the earliest centuries of Christianity.[15] The first monastic rule written specifically for nuns, that of Caesarius of Arles in the sixth century, states as its first general principle:

> Si qua relictis parentibus suis saeculo renuntiare et sanctum ovile voluerit introire, ut spiritalium luporum faucibus deo adiuvante possit evadere, usque ad mortem suam

de monasterio non egrediatur, nec in basilicam, ubi ostium esse videtur.

[If anyone, having left her parents, wishes to renounce the world and enter the holy fold, in order to evade, with God's help, the jaws of spiritual wolves, let her never leave the monastery until her death, not even into the church, where the door can be seen.][16]

Here Caesarius initiates a favorite theme: the need to avoid the dangers posed by the potential penetration-points into the enclosure, specifically doors and windows. Towards the end of the rule, he elaborates on this theme:

Ante omnia propter custodiendam famam vestram nullus virorum in secreta parte in monasterio et in oratoriis introeat, exceptis episcopis, provisore et presbytero, diacono, subdia-cono, et uno vel duobus lectoribus, quos et aetas et vita com-mendat, qui aliquotiens missas facere debeant. Cum vero aut tecta retractanda sunt, aut ostia vel fenestrae sunt con-ponendae, aut aliquid huiusmodi reparandum, artifices tan-tum et servi ad operandum aliquid, si necessitas exegerit, cum provisore introeant; sed nec ipsi sine scientia aut per-missione matris. Ipse vero provisor in interiorem partem monasterii nisi pro his utilitatibus, quas superius conpre-hendimus, numquam introeat, et aut numquam aut difficile sine abbatissa aut alia honestissima teste: ut sanctae secre-tum suum, sicut decet et expedit, habeant.

[Above all, for the safeguarding of your reputation, let no man come into the private part of the monastery or into the oratory, with the exception of bishops, the provider and a priest, deacon, subdeacon, and one or two readers, commended by their age and life, who must celebrate masses from time to time. And when the buildings must be remodeled, or doors and windows must be constructed; or any repairs of this sort are needed, such artisans and workers as are necessary to do the work may come in with the provider, but not without the knowledge and permission of the mother. And the provider may never enter the inner part of the monastery except for those reasons which we have explained above, and never without the abbess or at least some other very respectable witness, so that the holy women have their private place as is fitting and expedient.][17]

Caesarius's regulations show both his concern with the physical space of the convent, and his recognition that it will be impossible to isolate the nuns completely from the world. This being the case, he is at pains to regulate as strictly and specifically as possible the potential access points to the enclosure.

As Schulenburg has skillfully documented, from 500 to 1100 the rules for female claustration became increasingly rigid; even in Anglo-Saxon England, where abbesses and female religious had enjoyed relatively more autonomy than their continental counterparts, the freedom and power exercised by early Anglo-Saxon abbesses, such as those described by Bede, were severely constrained by the disciplinary reforms of the tenth century monastic revival (see "Strict Active Enclosure," 65–67). The *Regularis Concordia*, the general principles of Benedictine regulation drafted by Æthelwold in the mid-970s, makes special provision for the unbroken enclosure of nuns:

Hoc etenim Dunstanus, egregius huius patriae archiepiscopus, praesago afflatus spiritu, ad corroborandum praefati synodalis conuentus conciliabulum, prouide ac sapienter addidit: ut uidelicet nullus monachorum, uel alicuius altioris gradus uir uel inferioris, secreta sanctimonialium audax ingredi lustrando praesumeret; et hi qui spiritualis imperii prioratum ad disciplinae utilitatem non ad saecularis tyrannidem potentatus super eas exercent. . . .

[Now in order to confirm the deliberations of the aforesaid Synodal Council, Dunstan, the noble archbishop of our country, moved by the spirit of prophecy, providently and wisely added these further instructions: that no monk, nor indeed any man whatever his rank, should dare to enter and frequent the places set apart for nuns; and that those who have spiritual authority over nuns should use their powers not as worldly tyrants but in the interests of good discipline.][18]

The *Regularis Concordia* thus demonstrates a more profound concern with the separation of the sexes than is found in the Benedictine Rule. In addition to this physical segregation, the governance of monks and nuns is likewise divided by gender, according to the provisions of the *Regularis Concordia*. The strict gender segregation laid out here is clearly meant to reinforce the provision that King Edgar and Queen Edith, respectively, will oversee the monks and nuns, in order to guarantee that no scandal results from close interaction.[19] Yet while the rules for governance by the king and queen would seem to establish a "separate but equal" system, the gender segregation outlined above reveals inequity. No similar warning prohibits women from entering male space; rather, the female space is the sacred and impenetrable domain.[20]

The archaeological evidence for medieval English nunneries shows that the concerns of both Caesarius and the author of the *Regularis Concordia* were manifested in the physical layout of the nuns' cloister. Roberta Gilchrist has recently shown that archaeological remains from the later Middle Ages reveal that male and female cloisters differed in ways that were specifically related to their gender functions:

> [T]he number of levels of permeability (stages of access from the precinct) was higher for nunneries than monasteries. . . . The nunneries also had a higher degree of segregation from their precincts than the monasteries. In other words, it was more difficult to gain access to the nuns' cloisters from their surrounding precincts. The greater enclosure of religious women was guarded by a higher number of physical, as well as ideological, barriers.[21]

The material evidence of those medieval monasteries and convents which have been excavated, Gilchrist suggests, confirms the extent to which medieval female religious were strictly confined within gendered space:

> Contrary to the idealised image proposed by contemporary feminists, . . . medieval nuns were contained within a private domain, not dissimilar to that of their secular counterparts, which emphasised their chaste fidelity as Brides of Christ.[22]

Thus the physical evidence supports the ideology of female enclosure set out in monastic rules such as that of Caesarius and confirms for us that Caesarius's strict regulations were in fact matched by religious women's daily life in ways that were not matched by the experiences of religious men.

The Anglo-Saxon law-codes of King Alfred support both the ideal and the reality of strict enclosure as well, by emphasizing the criminality of those who would transgress the claustral boundary. Alfred's Law 8 makes the following provision:

> Gif hwa nunnan of mynstere ut alæde butan kyninges lefnesse oððe biscepes, geselle hundtwelftig scill', healf cyninge, healf biscepe 7 þære cirican hlaforde, ðe ðone munuc age.

> [If anyone takes a nun from a nunnery without the permission of the king or bishop, he shall pay 120 shillings, half to the king, and half to the bishop and the lord of the church, under whose charge the nun is.][23]

Alfred 18 stresses the taboo associated with violating the female religious body by doubling the fine for assaulting a nun:

> Gif hwa nunnan mid hæmeðþinge oððe on hire hrægl oððe on hire breost buan hire leafe gefo, sie hit twybete swa we ær be læwdum men fundon.

> [If anyone lustfully seizes a nun, either by her clothes or by her breast, without her permission, he shall pay as compensation twice the sum we have fixed in the case of a woman belonging to the laity.][24]

Just as Alfred's Laws are clearly designed to regulate physical interactions and behaviors, the spiritual guidelines established by Aldhelm in the *de Virginitate* regulate the spiritual well-being of female religious. Significantly, Aldhelm's advice to the nuns of Barking frames spiritual guidance in distinctly corporeal terms. The female readers to whom the *de Virginitate* is addressed are expected to keep both body and soul firmly enclosed and protected from any kind of penetration:

Idcirco virginibus Christi . . . contra horrendam rabidis molar-
ibus et venenosis genuinis inermes quosque ac virginitatis
lorica spoliatos pudicitiaque parma exutos atrociter discer-
pere nituntur, lacertosis viribus dimicandum est et quasi
adversus ferocissimas barbarorum legiones, quae manipula-
tem tironem Christi testudinem strofosae fraudis ballista
quatere non cessant. . . .

[Virgins of Christ . . . must . . . fight with muscular energy
against the horrendous monster of Pride and at the same
time against those seven wild beasts of the virulent vices,
who with rabid molars and venomous bicuspids strive to
mangle violently whoever is unarmed and despoiled of the
breastplate of virginity and stripped of the shield of modesty;
and they must struggle zealously with the arrows of spiritual
armament and the iron-tipped spears of the virtues as if
against the most ferocious armies of barbarians, who do not
desist from battering repeatedly the shieldwall of the young
soldiers of Christ with the catapult of perverse deceit.][25]

Aldhelm's language here is typically sensational, but nonetheless
emphasizes the ways in which the protection and enclosure of the
female religious body are at once spiritual and corporeal. The virtues
of virginity and modesty require a physical sort of protection against
penetration, and the battle is strenuous and constant.[26]

A vivid (if idealized) description of strict female enclosure can
be found in the eighth century Life of St. Leoba. At Wimbourne, the
double monastery in which Leoba's parents placed her as a girl, the
monks and nuns were strictly separated by monastic regulations:

Quorum ab initio fundationis suae utrumque ea lege disciplinae ordinatum est, ut neutrum illorum dispar sexus ingre-
deretur. Numquam enim virorum congregationem femina
aut virginum contubernia virorum quisquam intrare permit-
tebatur, exceptis solummodo presbiteris qui in aecclesias
earum ad agenda missarum officia tantum ingredi solebant
et consummata solemniter oratione statim ad sua redire.
Feminarum vero quaecumque saeculo renuntians earum
collegio sociari voluerat, numquam exitura intrabat, nisi

causa rationabilis vel magnae cuiuslibet utilitatis existens eam cum consilio emitteret. Porro ipsa congregationis mater, quando aliquid exteriorem pro utilitate monasterii ordinare vel mandare necesse erat, per fenestram loquebatur et inde decernebat quaecumque ordinanda aut mandanda utilitas rationis exigebat.

[From the beginning of the foundation the rule firmly laid down for both was that no entrance should be allowed to a person of the other sex. No woman was permitted to go into the men's community, nor was any man allowed into the women's, except in the case of priests who had to celebrate Mass in their churches; even so, immediately after the function was ended the priest had to withdraw. Any woman who wished to renounce the world and enter the cloister did so on the understanding that she would never leave it. She could only come out if there was a reasonable cause and some great advantage accrued to the monastery. Furthermore, when it was necessary to conduct the business of the monastery and to send for something outside, the superior of the community spoke through a window and only from there did she make decisions and arrange what was needed.][27]

Tetta, the abbess in charge of both monks and nuns, rigorously preserved this separation of the sexes:

Rigorem etiam disciplinae . . . tanta sollicitudine tenuit, ut numquam feminarum ad clericos pateretur accessum. Virgines vero, cum quibus ipsa indesinenter manebat, adeo immunes a virorum voluit esse consortio, ut non tantum laicis aut clericis, verum etiam ipsis quoque episcopis in congregationem earum negaret ingressum.

[She maintained discipline with such circumspection . . . that she would never allow her nuns to approach clerics. She was so anxious that the nuns, in whose company she always remained, should be cut off from the company of men that she denied entrance into the community not merely to laymen and clerics but even to bishops.][28]

This description suggests the extent to which an abbess, or any female religious, may have internalized the severe, even violent warnings given by a writer like Aldhelm. The need to defend "with muscular energy . . . the breastplate of virginity and . . . the shield of modesty" becomes not only a way to organize thinking about the female body, but also a way to regulate that body, to confine and restrict it in terms that simultaneously protect and liberate it.

Early medieval women often *desired* isolation and enclosure, in order to achieve a higher level of spirituality, as is evidenced in their letters and biographies.[29] The Anglo-Saxon nun Bugge, for example, who corresponded with the archbishop Boniface in the early eighth century, wished to make a pilgrimage to Rome in order to join her "sister" Wethburg, an anchorite there. Although the voyage would seem to suggest a *lack* of enclosure, its ultimate end was the freedom for spiritual reflection that Wethburg found within her cell.[30] The Life of Leoba, as we have seen, explains that the strict abbess Tetta, who showed such profound concern with gender segregation, "gave her instruction by deed rather than word . . . whenever she said that a certain course of action was harmful to the salvation of souls she showed by her own conduct that it was to be shunned" (trans. Talbot, 107). The author of the vita, Rudolph, writes that Leoba "used to recall with pleasure" the abbess's strict discipline (107). The late Anglo-Saxon *Life of Christina of Markyate* details at length a young woman's struggle to escape the demands of her family and focus on her spiritual life by retiring from the world, first in an anchorhold and later in a convent.[31] Thus physical enclosure could lead to a state of higher spiritual well-being, and a freedom from earthly demands.

The non-literary manifestations of female enclosure seen here correspond to a discourse of enclosure that we can see in Old English literary representations of women. This correspondence suggests that "enclosure" is a broad organizing system of thought: in other words, the material practices of female monastic enclosure inform or structure representations of women in literary texts. This discursive system defines, limits, regulates, and authorizes the feminine with Old English literature. Thus the statements and images found in literary texts—such as poems, homilies, or hagiography—are as much an integral part of this system as the non-literary texts—such as monastic rules, episcopal letters, or convent architecture—that legislate female enclosure.

Enclosure operates as what Michel Foucault calls a "discursive formation:" the systematic "dispersion" and reunification of many kinds of themes, statements, and concepts at work in disparate cultural fields.[32] Foucault's model is useful for understanding the circulation of "enclosure" as a theme circulating among the various kinds of statements and texts—secular, religious, Latin, vernacular, popular, learned, imaginative, regulative—that this study examines. The pervasiveness of enclosure as a condition of both monastic ideology and literary representation suggests that it is a broad cultural model that normalizes and prescribes the roles and possibilities of expression of and by medieval women. We have seen that this is a gendered social model in that it works to contain women more than men; we shall also see that it is a gendered literary practice.

The surge in feminist medievalist scholarship of the 1980s and 1990s has included, not surprisingly, greatly increased interest in the spiritual and bodily practices of medieval women, and the institutions in which those practices found expression or suppression.[33] Prompted especially by Caroline Walker Bynum's *Holy Feast and Holy Fast*,[34] scholars have recognized that these practices differed from those of medieval men in ways that are deeply inflected by gender. Moreover, recent feminist and cultural studies scholarship has been centrally concerned with "deviations" from normative institutional practices, with ways that institutional practices were subverted, rejected, or rewritten to meet more precisely the needs of individuals who fell outside of "normal" boundaries.[35]

One such practice, which has attracted particular attention in recent years, was anchoritism, in which men and women withdrew from the world to devote their lives to the solitary contemplation of God. Although both sexes became anchorites, the practice seems to have been particularly appealing to women, and later medieval evidence not only reveals the particular histories of a number of female anchoresses, but also includes a body of texts written specifically for these female readers.[36] Feminist scholars have successfully recuperated the *Ancrene Wisse* and the related devotional texts of the Katherine Group and the Wooing Group from their place as philological specimens for dialect study, and instead have begun to mine these works for information about the social and cultural histories of women, spirituality, literacy, the body, gender, marginality, and power.[37] The recent publication of a number of textbooks and translations of medieval women's spiritual and devotional literature signals the new canonicity of such scholarship and of texts such as *Ancrene Wisse*.[38]

While anchoritism and monastic enclosure are two very different phenomena, they share a number of defining characteristics. Most importantly, both anchoritism and monastic enclosure seek to confine the female religious body, to isolate that body from society, and to protect it from invasion or penetration, whether literal or spiritual.[39] Both practices achieve this separation spatially, of course, but also symbolically: the female religious is confined within the walls of her cell or cloister, and in addition she herself symbolizes the *integritas* of that space, as her virginal body remains impenetrable and sacred. As the representative of the Virgin Mary, moreover, the female religious body itself comes to symbolize not only the "walls" of an enclosure, but that which is enclosed within, and the womb itself represents the innermost level of enclosure. Thus the female religious in monasticism and anchoritism is both enclosed and enclosure; the symbolic and literal layers of these practices both confine and define her.

Yet as recent scholarship has repeatedly demonstrated, both anchoritism and female monasticism flourished in England, according to extant records, primarily *after* the Norman Conquest, thus postdating the Anglo-Saxon period. Most historians, therefore, have chosen to begin their studies of these movements and of medieval "women's" literature in the twelfth century, admittedly a point at which written records become more plentiful.[40]

But what do we find if we back up, chronologically? What social and cultural formations can we trace in the centuries between those studied, for example, by Peter Brown in *The Body in Society: Men, Women, and Sexual Renunciation in Early Christianity* (whose analysis extends only through the fifth and sixth centuries) and Caroline Walker Bynum in *Holy Feast and Holy Fast* (who briefly considers the roots of her subject in antiquity before moving to a discussion of the high Middle Ages)? My study will demonstrate that the ideologies, as well as the material practices, of female monastic enclosure are already at work in the vernacular literature of Anglo-Saxon England. Women in Old English literature are typically understood by scholars today as being strong, independent, eloquent, sometimes martial figures; and to be sure, they are all of these at times. However, I believe that we can identify in the literature a simultaneous and

marked tendency to circumscribe and confine the female figures of
early English literature that is analogous to early medieval cultural
constraints on female religious. Even when Anglo-Saxon literary
imagery portrays its women as autonomous or militaristic, it works
simultaneously to promote the ideals of monastic enclosure.[41] Because
the monastery was the primary site of literacy and textual production
in the early Middle Ages, female monasticism provides an especially
relevant context for understanding the textual representations of
women.[42] This study will trace the structure, language, and imagery
of female enclosure through Old English poetry and late Anglo-
Saxon prose, and will suggest that this literature offers significant
precursors to the corporeal practices and cultural themes of anchoritism and female monastic enclosure so prevalent in literature of the
later Middle Ages.

One starting point for my analysis comes from Judith Bennett's
recent appeal to feminists to read across traditional period divisions
in re-writing the history of women:

> . . . we should develop a 'way of seeing' women's history
> that better recognizes continuity and that, indeed, takes
> continuity as its chief problematic. . . . [T]his emphasis on
> continuity demands an attention to the mechanisms and
> operations of patriarchy in the history of women. . . . [A]
> study of patriarchy simply fits our historical evidence
> much better than the paradigm of great transition; the
> balance of continuity over change in such areas as women's
> work requires an approach that can better accommodate a
> history of small shifts, short-term changes, and enduring
> continuities.[43]

My study of the discourses of enclosure in early English literature
responds to Bennett's charge to take "continuity" as one of its chief
problematics. That is, across a wide range of secular and religious
literature, poetry and prose, spanning perhaps 300 years, I wish to
suggest that we can trace continuities in the cultural representations
of women and in the category of the feminine throughout much of
Anglo-Saxon culture, and that Old English literature anticipates
views of gender and femininity found in later medieval texts. Such
continuities of representation exist, governed by the shifting but

nonetheless remarkably stable discourses and ideologies of female monastic enclosure.

There are dangers in studies of continuity, of course: in particular, the danger of seeming to erase or elide genuine differences in the genres, cultures, or historical periods in question. Thus I will not attempt to write a smoothly diachronic history of women and enclosure in early medieval literature. Rather, I will look at four distinct moments in Anglo-Saxon literary history, in order to offer close readings of texts produced in and by those moments and to expose the thematic and discursive links between them. I do not mean to suggest any essential truths that cannot be dismantled or deconstructed; I will suggest, however, that the discourses of enclosure running through this literature are deeply embedded in early English literary representations of women and gender.

The four chapters in this book follow a number of related trajectories. The chapters move from secular to religious literature, beginning with the Old English elegies and concluding with Ælfric's homilies and hagiography; they encompass (depending on how we date them) early oral-derived poetry and late scholarly prose.[44] They find their subject matter in the narratives of Germanic migration cultures and Latin church culture, thus to some extent following the path of what Stephanie Hollis has called the "conversionary dynamic" of Anglo-Saxon England, as it increasingly assimilated the ideology of Roman Christianity to its pre-Christian Germanic-heroic ethos. Moreover, the texts studied below range from the firmly canonical *Beowulf* to the lesser-known Old English female elegies and saints' lives, texts that feminist inquiry has only begun to bring to scholarly light. Throughout these diverse textual practices, I suggest, the construction of femininity in Anglo-Saxon literary culture remains remarkably stable; the enclosure of women is one of the defining conceptual frameworks of Anglo-Saxon literary texts. I will not suggest that traditional texts such as *Beowulf* directly reflect the practices of medieval monasticism. Rather, the conditions and ideology of female enclosure permeate a wide range of early medieval cultural practices, and we can trace their operations across a surprisingly diverse body of literature.

My first chapter examines the anonymous Old English "female" elegies, the only two poems in Old English known to have a female first-person narrator. I locate these poems within the contexts of female monasticism, arguing that the cultural imperative of female enclosure finds expression in these texts. Unlike the speakers of such "male" elegies as "The Seafarer" or "The Wanderer," the female speakers are literally enclosed within a variety of physical or natural barriers. These speakers seem to chafe at their physical confinement, complaining of their circumstances and reflecting on the physical pleasures they can no longer enjoy. Their laments resonate with the themes and images seen in the literature of early English monasticism, including letters written by Anglo-Saxon nuns, cut off from their loved ones, and often living in lonely, isolated, and even perilous conditions. In remarkably similar ways, both the letters and the female lyrics evoke the worldly longing and the suffocating frustration of women who are physically enclosed. Although the circumstances of production of the female lyrics are by no means clear, I argue in this chapter that the culture of female monasticism provides a plausible and historically specific framework through which to view these texts. Unlike the male elegiac speakers, the female speakers of "The Wife's Lament" and "Wulf and Eadwacer," unable to move literally beyond the isolation of female enclosure, move inward to explore instead their own physical desires and inner emotions, even as the elegies themselves give expression to those desires beyond the confines of female enclosure.

This cultural framework of female monasticism can provide new—and perhaps unexpected—ways of reading female characters in a variety of Old English texts. Just as the ideology of female enclosure suggests a clearer understanding of the female elegies, motifs and tropes of enclosure are equally valuable for understanding the narrative and textual constructions of women and femininity in *Beowulf,* a poem decidedly unconcerned with actual female monasticism. If the female elegies offer us a look inside the enclosure itself, *Beowulf* offers a series of tantalizing glimpses of the dangers of uncontrolled femininity, before the dominant models of female containment are authorized by *Beowulf* himself. My second chapter examines the women of *Beowulf* by arguing for a metaphoric extension of the ideology of female enclosure to the conventional critical model of the Old English peace-weaver—the woman given in marriage to secure peace between hostile tribes. The function of the peace-weaver has been the subject of much discussion in recent feminist analyses of Old English poetry, although this figure has not usually been linked to the views of femininity inherent in Christian monasticism. Yet structurally and thematically, the role of the peace-weaver has profound connections to the enclosed female religious. The model of female enclosure pervades the poem, as the women in *Beowulf* are defined in terms of the desirability of containment—seen in the "conventional" figures of Hildeburh, Wealhtheow, and Hygd—and the dangers of escape—suggested by Grendel's Mother and Modthryth, both of whom are finally contained. My reading of the women's stories told in *Beowulf* demonstrates that the enclosure model works on multiple levels. The peace-weaver exemplifies a kind of social and often physical (if not monastic) enclosure. Just as significantly, however, through narrative frames and ring compositions, the poem itself circumscribes each separate account of peace-weaving; in other words, the poem's structure reinforces its meaning. As it operates in *Beowulf*, I suggest, the discourse of enclosure exposes the poem's rhetorical practices. The stories of women in *Beowulf* develop cumulatively, each validating the cultural functions of enclosed femininity through both imaginative and structural patterning.

In the texts discussed in my first two chapters, Christian ideology figures implicitly, only discernible in the female elegies and in *Beowulf* once those poems are situated alongside contemporary discourses of female monastic enclosure. Chapters Three and Four take up explicitly Christian texts, Cynewulf's Old English poetic version of the Latin life of St. Juliana, and Ælfric's *Lives of Saints*, respectively. In my readings of these saints' lives, I suggest that enclosure works on two distinct levels, just as the female body within early medieval monastic culture must be both enclosed *and* enclosure. Female saints, in emulating the Virgin Mary, are both contained and "containers," a condition that is signalled by the lives' insistence on the saints' virginal and impenetrable bodies.

Both chapters investigate the ways that the discourse of enclosure constructs saints' bodies as texts, revealing spiritual truth only to initiated Christian readers and denying literal or corporeal meaning to unskilled, pagan readers. Again we see that this textualization of the female saint's body is deeply dependent upon metaphors of containment and release, and on the desirability of *integritas* and the dangers of penetrating the boundaries of female enclosure. In *Juliana*, the saint herself demonstrates proper Christian reading practices, even as her body remains indecipherable to her pagan torturers. Such scenes of reading, with their dual insistence on the saint's virginity and *stabilitas*, I suggest, offer practical models of resistance for Anglo-Saxon female monastic readers in the age of Viking invasions. Finally, Ælfric's development of the corporeal metaphors of reading *lichamlice* (literally, carnally) and *gastlice* (spiritually) and his concern with how best to read the "naked words" of Scripture, inform his Lives of female virgin martyrs and provide for us an internal critical model for understanding the torture and display of virginal female bodies.

All four chapters apply the cultural and ideological models of early medieval monastic enclosure to texts which—with the possible exception of *Juliana*—have not previously been associated with female monasticism. I align "The Wife's Lament" and "Wulf and Eadwacer," *Beowulf*, *Juliana*, and the Lives of Saints Agatha, Agnes, Lucy, and Eugenia with many contemporary Anglo-Saxon texts which did originate or derive from female monastic culture. I hope to demonstrate the prevalence of the cultural model of enclosure within Anglo-Saxon literary culture through my analysis of these texts. This study is not meant as a comprehensive survey of the workings of enclosure within the Old English corpus, but instead seeks to understand how the discourse of enclosure constructs an Anglo-Saxon notion of the feminine within a variety of culturally significant texts. The discourse of enclosure allows us to see continuity across these texts. By suggesting ways of reading the cultural manifestations of enclosure in literature that predates that which is usually the focus of scholarship on medieval female monasticism, monastic enclosure, and anchoritism, I hope my book will open the way for future studies of continuity between the literary culture of Anglo-Saxon England and the later Middle Ages.

NOTES

1. The accounts of St. Æthelthryth can be found respectively in *Bede's Ecclesiastical History of the English People*, ed. and trans. Bertram Colgrave and R.A.B. Mynors (Oxford: The Clarendon Press, 1969), 390–401; and W.W. Skeat, ed., *Ælfric's Lives of Saints*, EETS o.s. 114 (Oxford: Oxford University Press, 1900; rpt. 1966): 432–441. My citations are from the Colgrave and Mynors edition, with translations *en face* and page numbers provided parenthetically.

For recent analyses of various medieval versions of Æthelthryth's life, see Jocelyn Wogan-Browne, "Rerouting the Dower: The Anglo-Norman

Life of St. Audrey by Marie (of Chatteris?)," in *Power of the Weak: Studies on Medieval Women*, ed. Jennifer Carpenter and Sally-Beth MacLean (Urbana: University of Illinois Press, 1995), 27–56; Christine Fell, "Saint Æðelþryð: A Historical-Hagiographical Dichotomy Revisited," *Nottingham Medieval Studies* 38 (1994): 18–34; and Susan J. Ridyard, *The Royal Saints of Anglo-Saxon England* (Cambridge: Cambridge University Press, 1988). On married virginity in the middle ages, see Dyan Elliot, *Spiritual Marriage: Sexual Abstinence in Medieval Wedlock* (Princeton: Princeton University Press, 1993).

2. Robert Deshman, *The Benedictional of Æthelwold* (Princeton: Princeton University Press, 1995): 121–124 and plate 28.

3. Text and translation quoted in Deshman, *Benedictional*, 122.

4. Text and translation from Deshman, 122.

5. Deshman notes that in the Benedictional, the symbolism of the nimbi encircling the heads of Saints Æthelthryth and Mary Magdalene, when they appear together in an image depicting a choir of virgins, "placed them in a special relation to the Virgin Mary at the Incarnation and suggested that their preeminence among the virgins resulted from their particularly faithful emulation of the *virgo virginum*" (151). The nimbus—as a type of shield—is symbolically linked to the preservation of virginity; as Deshman explains, "Standing crowned with the protective 'shield' of God's favor in the heavenly choir, [Æthelthryth] manifestly exemplifies the happy fate awaiting those whom God shields from sin in this life" (151).

6. According to Deshman, "More than any preceding work, the Benedictional achieved the systematic synthesis of picture and frame into a single composition" (243). He demonstrates that within the Benedictional, the frames and figures work to synthesize meaning; the frames often develop or further articulate the imagery of the figures. I suggest that this is the case with St. Æthelthryth; the combination of frame and figure serves to emphasize the bodily integrity of the saint. On the aesthetic uses of frames in Anglo-Saxon visual and literary art, see Pauline Head, *Representation and Design: Tracing a Hermeneutics of Old English Poetry* (Albany: SUNY Press, 1997).

7. See Christine Fell, "Saint Æðelþryð," 24.

8. Ælfric makes the correspondence between body and sarcophagus even more explicit: "Wæs eac wundorlic . þæt seo ðruh wæs geworht þurh godes foresceawunge hire swa gemæte . *swylce heo hyre sylfre swa ge-sceapen wære* . and æt hire hæfde wæs aheawen se stan . gemæte þam heafde þæs halgan mædenes . [It was also wonderful that through God's providence the coffin was made for her so perfectly, *just as she herself was shaped*, and at her head the stone was hewn perfectly fitting the head of the holy maiden.] (Skeat 438; emphasis added; translation mine).

9. A number of feminist scholars have recently begun to address this question in terms of anchoritic enclosure in the later middle ages. See Jocelyn

G. Price, "'Inner' and 'Outer': Conceptualizing the Body in *Ancrene Wisse* and Aelred's *De Institutione Inclusarum*," in *Medieval English Religious and Ethical Literature*, ed. Gregory Kratzmann and James Simpson (Cambridge: D.S. Brewer, 1986), 192–208; Sarah Beckwith, "Passionate Regulation: Enclosure, Ascesis, and the Feminist Imaginary," *South Atlantic Quarterly* 93.4 (1994): 803–824; and Elizabeth Robertson, *Early English Devotional Prose and the Female Audience* (Knoxville: University of Tennessee Press, 1990).

10. See Fell, "Saint Æðelþryð," 24. It is interesting to note that this passage of Bede's displays a sort of rhetorical circularity.

11. Joan Wallach Scott, *Gender and the Politics of History* (New York: Columbia University Press, 1988), 27. See also Judith Bennett, "Feminism and History," *Gender and History* 1.3 (1989): 251–272.

12. A concept articulated most compellingly by Judith Butler, *Gender Trouble* (New York: Routledge, 1990), 24–25, 140–141.

13. *Gender and Romance in Chaucer's* Canterbury Tales (Princeton: Princeton University Press, 1994), 7. See also Joan Wallach Scott, *Gender and the Politics of History*, 28–50.

14. For an excellent history of active enclosure (that is, the prohibition against leaving the cloister) in the early middle ages, see Jane Tibbetts Schulenburg, "Strict Active Enclosure and its Effects on the Female Monastic Experience," in *Distant Echoes: Medieval Religious Women*, Vol. 1, ed. John A. Nichols and Lillian Thomas Shank (Kalamazoo: Cistercian Publications, 1984), 51–86. Schulenburg's article skillfully surveys both primary and secondary sources on the topic of enclosure, and is essential reading for all who are interested in the backgrounds and history of medieval monastic enclosure of women. See also Emile Jombart and Marcel Viller, "Clôture," *Dictionnaire de Spiritualité, ascétique, et mystique, doctrine et histoire*. Vol. 2 (Paris: Beauchesne, 1953), cols. 979–1007; and E. Renoir, "Clôture Monastique," *Dictionnaire d'Archéologie Chrétienne et de Liturgie*. Vol. 3 (Paris: Librairie Letouzey et Ané, 1914), cols. 2024–2034.

15. Schulenburg, "Strict Active Enclosure," 52–53.

16. Caesarius of Arles, *Regulae Monasticae*, in *Opera Omnia*, Vol. II: *Opera Varia*, ed. D.G. Morin (Maretioli, 1942), 102. Trans. Emilie Amt, ed., *Women's Lives in Medieval Europe: A Sourcebook* (New York: Routledge, 1993), 221–222.

17. Caesarius, article 36, p. 111; trans. Amt, 228.

18. Dom Thomas Symons, ed. and trans., *Regularis Concordia: Anglicae Nationis Monachorum Sanctimonialiumque* [The Monastic Agreement of the Monks and Nuns of the English Nation] (London: Thomas Nelson and Sons, Ltd., 1953), 4–5. See also the recently edited interlinear Latin and Old English edition: Lucia Kornexl, ed., *Die Regularis Concordia und Ihre Altenenglische Interlinearversion* (Munich: Wilhelm Fink Verlag, 1993); the text cited above is found on pp. 8–9.

19. This gendered system of governance is described in *Regularis Concordia*, 2.

20. By the late eighth century, the Second Council of Nice (787) prohibited the further establishment of double monasteries, a system of monks and nuns living separately but jointly under the rule of (typically) an abbess. Again, the rules set out by this council show unequal treatment of male and female space. As Mary Bateson has shown, one of the Council's main tenets dictated that "No monk may enter a house of nuns"; moreover, "No monk may sleep in a house of nuns." Quoted in Mary Bateson, "Origin and Early History of Double Monasteries," *Transactions of the Royal Historical Society* n.s. 13 (1899): 163–164. Again, there is no provision made for nuns entering monks' quarters; clearly the intention is to protect the female space. Stephanie Hollis effectively summarizes the status of women under these changing conditions: "As a consequence of steady pressures towards the segregation and enclosure of female religious which rendered abbesses dependent on their bishop for transactions with the world at large, abbesses' authority over their establishments passed ultimately to the bishops, a development accompanied by a decline in the prestige of abbesses and their communities." (*Anglo-Saxon Women and the Church* [Woodbridge, Suffolk: Boydell, 1993], 77).

21. Gilchrist, *Gender and Material Culture: The Archaeology of Religious Women* (London and New York: Routledge, 1994), 166. See also Gilchrist's article, "The Spatial Archaeology of Gender Domains: A Case Study of Medieval English Nunneries," *Archaeological Review from Cambridge* 7.1 (1988): 21–28.

22. Gilchrist, "The Spatial Archaeology of Gender Domains," 26–27.

23. Text and translation from F.L. Attenborough, ed. and trans., *The Laws of the Earliest English Kings* (Cambridge: Cambridge University Press, 1922), 68–69. See the discussion of this law in Christine Fell, *Women in Anglo-Saxon England* (Oxford: Blackwell, 1984), 123–124.

24. Text and translation from Attenborough, 72-73. I have argued elsewhere that the Old English phrase "mid hæmeðþinge," translated here by Attenborough as "lustfully," carries the connotation of forced or violent sexual assault, even rape. See "The Language of Rape in Old English Literature and Law: Views from the Anglo-Saxon(ist)s," in *Sex and Sexuality in Anglo-Saxon England: Essays in Memory of Daniel G. Calder*, ed. Robert Bjork, Carol Braun Pasternack, and Lisa Weston (in preparation).

25. Rudolph Ehwald, ed. *Aldhelmi Opera*. Monumenta Germaniae Historica Auctorum Antiquissimorum Vol. XV (Berlin: Weidmann, 1961), 239–240. Translation from Michael Lapidge and Michael Herren, eds. and trans., Aldhelm: The Prose Works (Cambridge and Totowa: Brewer/Rowman and Littlefield, 1979), 68.

26. On medieval ideals of "militant" virginity, see John Bugge, Virginitas: *An Essay in the History of a Medieval Ideal* (The Hague: Martinus Nijhoff, 1975); and Jane Tibbetts Schulenburg, "The Heroics of Virginity: Brides of Christ and Sacrificial Mutilation," in *Women in the Middle Ages and Renaissance: Literary and Historical Perspectives*, ed. Mary Beth Rose (Syracuse: Syracuse University Press, 1986), 29–72.

27. G. Waitz, ed. *Vita Leobae Abbatissaie Biscofesheimensis Auctore Rudolfo Fuldensi*. Monumenta Germaniae Historica. Scriptores 5, part 1 (Hannover, 1887; rpt. Stuttgart: Anton Hiersemann, 1992), 123. Trans. C.H. Talbot, *The Life of Leoba, by Rudolph, Monk of Fulda*, in *Medieval Women's Visionary Literature*, ed. Elizabeth Alvilda Petroff (Oxford: Oxford University Press, 1986), 107.

28. Waitz, ed., 123; trans. Talbot, 107.

29. Of course, letters and especially biographies can be highly ideological documents; I do not mean to suggest that texts which were produced by women themselves, or were closely connected to women, were somehow exempt from the ideological influence of enclosure—very likely just the opposite.

30. For the correspondence between Bugge and Boniface addressing this issue, see M. Tangl, ed., *Die Briefe des Heiligen Bonifatius und Lullus*. 2nd ed. Monumenta Germaniae Historica. Epistolae Selectae I (Berlin: Weidmann, 1955), 21–26; 47–49; and Ephraim Emerton, ed. and trans., *The Letters of Saint Boniface* (New York: Norton, 1940, 1976), 36–40; 56–57.

On the medieval desire for the anchoritic life, especially concerning the freedom to be found within the cell, see Ann K. Warren, *Anchorites and Their Patrons in Medieval England* (Berkeley: University of California Press, 1985), 7–18; 100–102.

31. C.H. Talbot, ed. and trans. *The Life of Christina of Markyate: A Twelfth Century Recluse* (Oxford: The Clarendon Press, 1959). Rpt. Medieval Academy Reprints for Teaching 39 (Toronto: University of Toronto Press, 1998).

32. Michel Foucault, *The Archaeology of Knowledge*, trans. A.M. Sheridan Smith (New York: Pantheon Books, 1972), 31–39.

33. Two recent essay collections, in fact, are devoted to medieval bodies, in both theory and practice (although neither includes an essay on Old English literature): Linda Lomperis and Sarah Stanbury, eds., *Feminist Approaches to the Body in Medieval Literature* (Philadelphia: University of Pennsylvania Press, 1993); and Miri Rubin and Sarah Kay, eds., *Framing Medieval Bodies* (New York: St. Martin's Press, 1994). Much of the current work has been inspired by the essays collected in Michel Feher, et al., eds., *Fragments for the History of the Human Body*, 3 Vols. (New York: Urzone, 1989). See also the annotated bibliography at the end of Volume 3: Barbara Duden, "A Repertory of Body History," 471–578.

34. Caroline Walker Bynum, *Holy Feast and Holy Fast: The Religious Significance of Food to Medieval Women* (Berkeley: University of California Press, 1987).

35. Two important recent books, which draw on the work of such contemporary social theorists as Julia Kristeva, Mikhail Bakhtin, Michel de Certeau, and Pierre Bourdieu (among others), are Karma Lochrie, *Margery Kempe and Translations of the Flesh* (Philadelphia: University of Pennsylvania Press, 1991); and Laurie A. Finke, *Feminist Theory, Women's Writing* (Ithaca: Cornell University Press, 1992).

36. On the literature of anchoritism, see especially Robertson, *Early English Devotional Prose and the Female Audience.*

37. In addition to Robertson, see the following articles by Jocelyn Wogan-Browne, "Saints' Lives and the Female Reader," *Forum for Modern Language Studies* 27 (1991): 314–332; "Chaste Bodies: Frames and Experiences," in *Framing Medieval Bodies*, ed. Rubin and Kay, 24–42; and (as Jocelyn G. Price) "'Inner' and 'Outer': Conceptualizing the Body in *Ancrene Wisse* and Aelred's *De Institutione Inclusarum.*" See also Catherine Innes-Parker, "Sexual Violence and the Female Reader: Symbolic 'Rape' in the Saints' Lives of the Katherine Group," *Women's Studies* 24 (1995): 205–217; and Beckwith, "Passionate Regulation: Enclosure, Ascesis, and the Feminist Imaginary."

38. A surprisingly rich collection of classroom editions of primary sources in Middle English and in translation has recently been published; see especially *Anchoritic Spirituality:* Ancrene Wisse *and Associated Works*, trans. Anne Savage and Nicholas Watson (New York and Mahwah: Paulist Press, 1991), which translates *Ancrene Wisse* in its entirety, as well as the works of the Katherine and Wooing Groups. See also *Ancrene Wisse: Guide for Anchoresses*, trans. Hugh White (London: Penguin, 1993); and *Medieval English Prose for Women: Selections from the Katherine Group and* Ancrene Wisse, ed. and trans. Bella Millett and Jocelyn Wogan-Browne (Oxford: Clarendon Press, 1990), which provides facing page translations.

39. For the ways that anchoritism is specifically a practice of the body and is linked to medieval ideologies of the female body, see Elizabeth Robertson, "The Rule of the Body: The Feminine Spirituality of the *Ancrene Wisse*," in *Seeking the Woman in Late Medieval and Renaissance Writings: Essays in Feminist Contextual Criticism* (Knoxville: University of Tennessee Press, 1989), 109–134; and Price, "'Inner' and 'Outer.'"

40. This is not to say that female monastic enclosure and female anchoritism did not exist in Anglo-Saxon England; quite the contrary. But the records are admittedly sparse. Nevertheless, the evidence of the Boniface correspondence, of the Life of Leoba, and of the Life of Christina of Markyate, which discusses both practices, signals that both models of female enclosure were firmly established in early medieval England.

41. Early (i.e., late 1970s and early 1980s) feminist scholarship of Old English literature tended to posit one of two possible (and opposing) female roles in Old English literature: either women were active, heroic, even militaristic, or they were the hopelessly passive pawns of men. For the first view, see Helen Damico, *Beowulf's Wealtheow and the Valkyrie Tradition* (Madison: University of Wisconsin Press, 1984), and Alexandra Hennessey Olsen, "Cynewulf's Autonomous Women: A Reconsideration of *Elene* and *Juliana*," in *New Readings on Women in Old English Literature*, ed. Helen Damico and Alexandra Hennessey Olsen (Bloomington: University of Indiana Press, 1990), 222–232. Jane Chance, in *Woman as Hero in Old English Literature* (Syracuse: Syracuse University Press, 1986) tends toward the "passive" view, but sees a potential for female power through "heroic chastity" (*passim*); one problem with this model, however, is that it requires female characters to find this power by renouncing their "female-ness," their sexuality. For complete endorsements of the "passive" view, see Alain Renoir, "A Reading Context for *The Wife's Lament*," in *Anglo-Saxon Poetry: Essays in Appreciation*, ed. by Lewis E. Nicholson and Dolores Warwick Frese (Notre Dame: Notre Dame University Press, 1975), 224–241; and Anne L. Klinck, "Female Characterisation in Old English Poetry and the Growth of Psychological Realism: *Genesis B* and *Christ I*" *Neophilologus* 63 (1979): 597–610. For a useful critique of this view, see Gillian Overing, *Language, Sign, and Gender in* Beowulf (Carbondale: Southern Illinois University Press, 1990), 77–78.

More recently, feminist scholars have sought to dismantle the binary oppositions found in previous scholarship, and to understand "women" and "femininity" in Old English literature more as complexly layered productions of Anglo-Saxon literary culture. See John P. Hermann, "Why Anglo-Saxonists Can't Read: Or, Who Took the Mead out of Medieval Studies?" *Exemplaria* 7 (1995): 9–26, for a brief discussion of the two "generations" of feminist critics. For good overviews of feminist Anglo-Saxon scholarship, see Helen Bennett, "From Peace Weaver to Text Weaver: Feminist Approaches to Old English Literture," in *Twenty Years of the 'Year's Work in Old English Studies'*, ed. Katherine O'Brien O'Keeffe, *OEN Subsidia* 15 (1989), 23–42; and Clare A. Lees, "At a crossroads: Old English and Feminist Criticism," in *Reading Old English Texts*, ed. Katherine O'Brien O'Keeffe (Cambridge: Cambridge University Press, 1997), 146–169. In addition, I find the following articles especially useful: Karma Lochrie, "Gender, Sexual Violence, and the Politics of War in the Old English *Judith*," in *Class and Gender in Early English Literature*, ed. Britton J. Harwood and Gillian R. Overing (Bloomington: Indiana University Press, 1994), 1–20; and Helen Bennett, "The Female Mourner at Beowulf's Funeral: Filling in the Blanks/ Hearing the Spaces," *Exemplaria* 4 (1992): 35–50. My own argument here does not support either the "active" or "passive" model of Old English femininity, but rather seeks to understand how both models operate, and how both are informed by the cultural contexts of early medieval female monasticism.

42. For a broad overview of Anglo-Saxon female literacy, see my dissertation, "Women's Literacy and Female Textuality in Old English Poetry" (University of Minnesota, 1992), 12–58.

43. Judith Bennett, "Medieval Women, Modern Women: Across the Great Divide," in *Culture and History, 1350–1600: Essays on English Communities, Identities, and Writing*, ed. David Aers (New York and London: Harvester Wheatsheaf, 1992), 164.

44. Nearly all the terms I use here, even such basic ones as "secular" and "religious" or "early" and "late" and even—in the case of Ælfric— "poetry" and "prose" are matters of ongoing debate among Anglo-Saxonists. My categories are not attempts to resolve these debates, but rather used for the sake of convenience as I attempt to summarize broad patterns and prevailing critical views. The dating of all the poetry in my study is open to question, although the dates of the manuscripts (ca. A.D. 1000) are generally agreed upon. On the dating controversies, see Donald G. Scragg, "The Nature of Old English Verse," in *The Cambridge Companion to Old English Literature*, ed. Malcolm Godden and Michael Lapidge (Cambridge: Cambridge University Press, 1991), 55–58. On *Beowulf* see Roy Michael Liuzza, "On the Dating of *Beowulf*" in Beowulf: *Basic Readings*, ed. Peter S. Baker (New York and London: Garland, 1995), 281–302; and the essays in Colin Chase, ed. *The Dating of* Beowulf (Toronto: University of Toronto Press, 1981; rpt. 1998).

CHAPTER 1

Looking Into Enclosure in the Old English Female Lyrics

The only two poems in Old English to feature a first-person female speaker are known by the titles "Wulf and Eadwacer" and "The Wife's Lament."[1] These "female" elegies exhibit the cultural and physical restrictions on religious women discussed in my introduction. Although they are usually linked to poems that appear deeply inflected by Christianity, such as "The Wanderer" or "The Seafarer," the female elegies have traditionally not been seen to exhibit the cultural influences of the Christian church. In fact, these poems fit more neatly into the culture of female monasticism than has been realized in previous scholarship. The elegies illustrate the tension between the silenced and enclosed female religious of Anglo-Saxon England, and an active feminine speaking subject that a character like Wealhtheow in *Beowulf* can only suggest. The speakers of "The Wife's Lament" and "Wulf and Eadwacer" offer the possibility of a female voice, but they are nevertheless firmly constrained within social and spatial boundaries. They move figuratively, if not literally, beyond enclosure, to write a space for themselves as subjects, to create texts, even though (or because) each is unable to move beyond the earth-cave and the fen-surrounded island that she inhabits involuntarily.

Much of the critical discussion about these poems has centered on the question of gender, since several critics (one as recently as 1987) have found it unlikely that an Old English poem would feature a female persona. They have thus explained away the grammatical forms that gender these speakers, usually citing scribal error.[2] In general, however, critics agree that these speakers are women. Beyond that, the poems are frustratingly enigmatic. Both speakers

29

share a longing for past pleasures, paired with a lament for present misery. Both are physically confined. Unlike those elegies known to have male speakers, such as "The Wanderer" or "The Seafarer," the female elegies do not pair earthly sorrow with the future hope of Christian (or spiritual) consolation; rather, as one critic has recently written about "The Wife's Lament," each speaker "seems irrevocably trapped in her present."[3] And unlike the speakers in the male elegies, the female speakers do not attempt to deny or surmount the pleasures and pains of the body in the material world; rather, their mental journeys are strictly focused on their physical circumstances, past and present.

Unable to go wandering or seafaring, the female speakers of the elegies instead use another form of creative power: they "weave" their own stories into texts. They loosen (but do not shed) the bonds of enclosure, as they signify beyond conventionally gendered borders. Because their physical containment restricts action but not speech or thought, their journeys turn inward, insisting upon (and thereby linking) the physical and the personal. They thereby anticipate devotional literature written for enclosed female religious of the twelfth and thirteenth centuries, which, as Elizabeth Robertson has shown, developed a feminine spirituality grounded in the body. This devotional tradition, comprising works such as *Ancrene Wisse*, *Hali Meidhad*, and *Sawles Warde*, builds upon the popular medieval (mis)conception of the Aristotelian view that saw woman as flawed or imperfect man. Intended for female readers (though written by male authors), this literary tradition linked the categories of woman and body: "From a medieval perspective, therefore," Robertson writes, "a woman's spiritual nature was defined by her inescapable corporeality."[4]

The female elegies themselves are grammatically gendered feminine. Yet just as significantly, an "inescapable corporeality" similarly distinguishes each text. Moreover, within each poem the cultural manifestations of female enclosure in Anglo-Saxon England produce a discourse of enclosure which in turn produces and *genders* each speaker. We can understand the "self" or "subject" of these elegies as the individual identity produced through a given set of linguistic, discursive, and gendered properties or behaviors. The subject speaks or otherwise enacts these "attributes"—or more precisely, is enacted by them.[5] The elegies are powerful examples of the cultural construction of gender in Old English texts, made all the more powerful because they are anonymous.[6] Analyzing the operations of the discourse of enclosure in the elegies will help to clarify the means by which those feminine subjects emerge within the poems.

Judith Butler's formulation of gender performance is particularly useful for the analysis of the feminine subjects of these anonymous elegies, because it permits us to bypass questions of authority and authorship and to examine instead the ways in which the repeated "acts" of gender in the poems produce their feminine speaking subjects. Butler argues that gender is not a stable or fixed category, but is instead a repeated set of culturally and socially established acts, and this repetition constitutes the appearance of a stable gendered self. She writes: "There is no gender identity behind the expressions of gender; that identity is performatively constituted by the very 'expressions' that are said to be its results" (*Gender Trouble*, 25). The seemingly stable gender identities of the female elegiac speakers are, I suggest, likewise the products of culturally established "expressions" of gender mandated by the terms of female religious enclosure.

As we have seen, the discourse of enclosure marks the female body as both an object to be enclosed and itself an enclosure, both prohibited from movement and impenetrable. Of all the Old English elegies, only the two female elegies exhibit these restrictions against their speakers; the male elegiac speakers, in contrast, are defined by their free, unfettered physical movement (even though they are exiled).[7] The Wanderer, in the elegy of that name, walks the paths of exile, and like the *hlaford* in "The Wife's Lament," or like Wulf, the Wanderer's body is not enclosed; though exiled, he is not imprisoned. Thus although we might reasonably argue that the Wanderer endures a kind of spiritual or metaphysical "imprisonment" by being exiled, he is not physically contained. In a poem such as "Deor," in which a man *is* fettered (Weland the smith), readers can be reassured of metaphysical, if not actual release, voiced in the refrain, "þæs ofereode, þisses swa mæg." In the same poem, however, Beadohild's physical condition, pregnancy, is inescapable; she cannot expect the same kind of physical release from the ties that bind her that Weland can.

The concept of enclosure in the male elegies is therefore antithetical to enclosure in the female elegies. In vivid contrast to the female speakers, who let their imaginations wander since their bodies cannot, the speaker in "The Wanderer" wishes rather to enclose or imprison his "traitorous" mind, to fetter his thoughts, which dwell too often on his earthly misery:[8]

. . . ic to soðe wat

þæt bið in eorle   indryhten þeaw
þæt he his ferð-locan   fæste binde
healde his hord-cofan   hycge swa he wylle (11b–14).

[I know truly that it is a noble custom in a man to bind fast his 'soul-enclosure,' protect his heart, whatever he may think.]

Though the speaker of "The Wanderer" may appear to be expressing a non-gender-specific desire, the cultural convention he refers to here is in fact gendered masculine. In the "male" elegies, that is, though the speakers obviously lament their past and present circumstances, they also display the belief that such lamenting is inappropriate, and they attempt to silence themselves, to reject a focus on worldly suffering. As Robert E. Bjork has shown, the Wanderer restricts his own self-expression because his culture mandates such restraint.[9] What Bjork calls "the imagery of silence," in which the Wanderer specifically wishes to bind up his thoughts, is likewise echoed in the Old English *Maxims*: "Thought must be held in, hand controlled, the pupil must be in the eye, wisdom in the breast, where the thoughts of a man are."[10] This insistence on "tightlipped stoicism" is a cultural imperative that not only constrains the Wanderer, but that also reassures him: all customs, conventions, and boundaries— whether social, cultural, or material—remain comfortingly in place (Bjork, 122).

In "The Seafarer," too, the speaker wishes to control his errant thoughts, but not before they have roamed widely over the seas, not unlike the speaker himself. As John C. Pope has argued, what begins as a literal voyage for the Seafarer leads him to contemplate a spiritual or allegorical voyage, as his soul "leaves" his body and "roams widely," returning to urge the body onwards:[11]

Forþon nu min hyge hweorfeð   ofer hreþerlocan,
min modsefa   mid mereflode

ofer hwæles eþel   hweorfeð wide,
eorþan sceatas,   cymeð eft to me
gifre ond grædig,   gielleð anfloga,
hweteð on hwælweg   hreþer unwearnum
ofer holma gelagu   (58–64a).

[Therefore now my mind roams over my breast-enclosure, my spirit roams widely with the sea, over the whale's home, over the earth's surfaces, and comes again to me, ravenous and greedy, the lone-flier yells, urges the heart on the whale-way irresistibly, over the lake of the waters.]

Yet the transformation that occurs (apparently allegorically) over the course of "The Seafarer" ensures considerable movement for the speaker, since even the spiritual journey he longs for will mean a release of both body and spirit. As Rosemary Woolf explains, "[i]t is from the dead life, transient on land, that the Seafarer wishes to escape by embarking on his sea-voyage."[12]

For the Seafarer, the thoughts of the heart do not have to be locked away, but rather redirected. Once he elects this allegorical voyage, the elegy moves into its turn of Christian consolation, and he regains control of those wandering thoughts:

Stieran mon sceal strongum mode,   ond þæt on staþelum
    healdan,
ond gewis werum,   wisum clæne (109–110)

[A man must control {his} strong spirit, and hold it within bounds, and {must} be prudent with men and pure in {his} ways.][13]

Even here, with this appeal to stability, there is forward movement as the speaker recognizes that although his thoughts might not be successfully repressed, they can be controlled and propelled in a desirable direction.

Like the Wanderer, then, the Seafarer directs his thoughts away from worldly discomforts, towards a metaphysical or spiritual release.[14] At the end of "The Seafarer," the speaker's language is still deeply focused on movement:

Uton we hycgan   hwær we ham agen,
ond þonne geþencan   hu we þider cumen (117–118)

[Let us think where we may have a home, and then think
how we might go there.]

Both male speakers embrace the traditionally gendered hierarchies
of early Christian thought: they reject the physical (the feminine) in
favor of the spiritual (the masculine).[15] The Wanderer, to be sure,
laments the loss of physical treasures and comforts, but he emphasizes their transience, and that poem ends, like "The Seafarer," with
the speaker repressing his anxious, material thoughts and turning
his attention to a more spiritual plane. The elegies do not provide
this option to the female speakers. But while female physical enclosure prohibits action, it permits speech; the desires of the female
speakers turn inward as they expose and explore memories of their
physical lives that the Wanderer would have locked away. And, just
as they lack the consolatory turn seen in the male elegies, the female
elegies willingly express both emotion and physical discomfort. The
narrative emphasis on physical enclosure, paired with such "interiority," genders the speakers of "Wulf and Eadwacer" and "The Wife's
Lament" feminine.[16] While my analysis of these poems will not
attempt to prove female authorship, or even a precise monastic provenance, it will offer a new context for reading them. The social,
cultural, and material conditions of early medieval female monasticism can clarify many of the lexical, rhetorical, and cultural ambiguities of the female elegies. Above all, we shall see that reading the
elegies within a monastic context situates these speakers within the
literary and social history of Anglo-Saxon women.

MONASTIC TEXTUALITY AND THE FEMALE VOICE

Textual evidence from the early Middle Ages, specifically the extant
writings of Anglo-Saxon nuns, can inform our understanding of the
two Old English female elegies. Scholars have recently demonstrated
the relatively high levels of literacy among Anglo-Saxon religious
women and among their counterparts on the continent.[17] This
literacy is evidenced primarily by Latin letters written to and by the
nuns. Yet even this "textual travel" was eventually restricted. As Peter

Dronke has shown, a capitulary issued by Charlemagne in 789 prohibited not just the nuns' movement outside the cloister, but even
their communication. As cited by Dronke, the capitulary reads, in
part:

> [N]o abbess should presume to leave her convent without
> our permission, nor allow those under her to do so . . . and
> on no account let them dare to write *winileodas*, or send
> them from the convent.[18]

Unfortunately, no *winileodas*, or "songs for a friend," survive, and so
we cannot gain a precise picture of the kinds of texts the nuns were
prohibited from composing and sending to their "friends."

Dronke, however, argues that "Wulf and Eadwacer" may provide a glimpse of the genre, and he links the two female elegies to
extant Latin letters by Anglo-Saxon nuns, suggesting that the female
elegies and the nuns' letters may derive from analogous (if not identical) personal, social, or material circumstances.[19] Like the nuns'
letters, the Old English female elegies may suggest evidence of female
literary practices and traditions; certainly the thematic similarities are
profound. He translates a letter from the nun Berthgyth written to
her brother, perhaps in the 770s:

> Why is it, my brother,
> that you have let pass so long a time,
> that you have delayed to come?
> Why do you not want to remember
> that I am alone upon this earth,
> and no other brother will visit me,
> or any kinsman come to me? . . .
> Oh brother, oh my brother,
> how can you afflict the mind of me, who am naught,
> with constant grief, weeping and sorrow,
> day and night, through the absence of your love?[20]

Dronke argues that "the language comes close to that of the . . .
[*winileodas*] . . . . The evocation of solitude and tears and longing has
precise parallels in the two extant Anglo-Saxon women's love-
laments . . . in the naked emotions expressed, though not of course

in the poems' narrative situations."[21] Dronke's sensitive comparisons between Berthgyth's letters and "Wulf and Eadwacer," however, are unnecessarily undercut by his last point, since we simply cannot know the "narrative situations" of the Old English poems.

We do know, however, that the locus of women's literary activity in early medieval England was the convent. Numerous examples of this "feminine textuality"—the copying of books, the composing of Latin verse, the studying of Scripture—can be found throughout the letters known as the Boniface correspondence.[22] That the Old English female elegies may have been produced for or within such a community of female scholars is no doubt unverifiable, but must remain a strong likelihood.[23]

The women whose letters are preserved in the Boniface correspondence were nuns who sometimes lived as missionaries among hostile strangers, and who typically were cut off from friends or surrounded by only a small community. The nun Egburg, writing to Boniface (ca. 716–718), occupies an isolated position strikingly similar to that of the two Old English female speakers. She focuses her letter on her physical or worldly unhappiness. She regrets the departure of her sister, Wethburg, who has left for Rome to become a *reclusa*, or anchorite. Egburg contrasts her sister's more happy enclosure with her own undesired position: "Illa arduam et arctam iam greditur callem; ego autem adhuc in infimis lege carnali ceu quadam compede prepedita iaceo" ("She treads the hard and narrow way, while I lie here below, bound by the law of the flesh as it were in shackles").[24] Her words evoke the double bond of female claustration: within her physical or spatial isolation, she is likewise bound by *lege carnali*, "the law of the flesh," her own body. Her expressions anticipate the admonitions to anchoresses that we see in the twelfth and thirteenth centuries, warning against the dangers of the world outside the cell; Egburg, though she knows it is improper, misses the comforts and companions of *this* world. We shall see that the female lyrics likewise evoke this articulation of worldly longing, and the suffocating frustration of bodily and spatial enclosure expressed in the correspondence of the unhappy nun.

The Boniface correspondence also includes letters illustrating the increasingly insistent demand for strict female enclosure. As Stephanie Hollis has shown, a number of Boniface's female correspondents desired to travel to Rome on pilgrimage, and Boniface was not altogether opposed to the prospect of female journeying—the journey, after all, led them to a more spiritual and contemplative life.[25] Some, like Wethburg, traveled to Rome only to be enclosed there as anchorites.[26] The correspondence as a whole contains numerous examples of female pilgrimage, and of both male and female monastics alike choosing pilgrimage as the avenue towards a greater *stabilitas*. Gillian Overing and Clare Lees have recently suggested that a common theme of loneliness or "alienation of women from kin" links the women's letters of the Boniface correspondence: "It is hard to escape the conclusion that women, exiled from their kin for whatever reasons, seek the solace of real exile and the life of the ascetic, or *peregrinus*."[27] Yet I would argue that the women also seek permanence and stability, just as Boniface urges. Female pilgrimage in these examples is a temporary condition leading to the greater *stabilitas* to be found in some actual or symbolic enclosure, whether anchorhold or kinship structure.

Boniface is modestly ambivalent about his capacity to advise another of his correspondents, Bugge, about the suitability of her own proposed pilgrimage to Rome. He writes:

Notum sit tibi, soror carissima, de illo consilio, quo me indignum per litteras interrogasti, quod ego tibi iter peregrinum nec interdicere per me nec audenter suadere presumo.

[I desire you to know, dearest sister, that in the matter about which you wrote asking advice of me, unworthy though I am, I dare neither forbid your pilgrimage on my own responsibility nor rashly persuade you to it.][28]

Yet the purpose of pilgrimage for Bugge, according to Boniface, must always be the desire for greater *stabilitas*, for separation from worldly matters in favor of the contemplative life. Boniface goes on to advise Bugge:

Si enim sollicitudinem, quam erga servos Dei et ancillas et monasterialem vitam habuisti propter adquirendam quietem et contemplationem Dei dimisisti, quomodo debes nunc secularium hominum verbis et voluntatibus servire cum labore et tediosa sollicitudine? Melius enim mihi videtur, si

propter seculares in patria libertatem quietem mentis habere
nullatenus possis, ut per peregrinationem libertatem contem-
plationis, si volueris et possis, adquiras; quemadmodum
soror nostra Uuiethburga faciebat. Quae mihi per suas litteras
intimavit, quod talem vitam quietem invenisset iuxta limina
sancti Petri, qualem longum tempus desiderando quaesivit.

[If, for the sake of rest and divine contemplation, you have
laid aside the care for the servants and maids of God and
for the monastic life which you once had, how could you
now subject yourself with labor and wearing anxiety to the
words and wishes of men of this world? It would seem to
me better, if you can in no wise have freedom and a quiet
mind at home on account of worldly men, that you should
obtain freedom of contemplation by means of a pilgrimage,
if you so desire and are able, as our sister Wiethburga [*sic*]
did. She has written to me that she has found at the shrine
of St. Peter the kind of quiet life which she had long sought
in vain.][29]

Wethburg's pilgrimage to Rome was merely a means to an end—
not, perhaps, unlike the journey of the speaker described in "The
Wife's Lament." Clearly the pilgrimage's most important results for
the Anglo-Saxon nuns were the freedom from earthly concerns and
the possibility of an inwardly focused contemplative life.

Later, Boniface's ambivalence about the desirability of female
pilgrimage is resolved. In a letter to Archbishop Cuthbert of Canterbury, he writes:

... bonum esset et honestas et pudicitia vestrae ecclesiae et
aliquod velamentum turpitudinis, si prohiberet synodus et
principes vestri mulieribus et velatis feminis illud iter et
frequentiam, quam ad Romanam civitatem veniendo et
redeundo faciunt, quia magna ex parte pereunt paucis
remanentibus integris. Perpauce enim sunt civitates in
Longobardia vel in Francia aut in Gallia, in qua non sit
adultera vel meretrix generis Anglorum. Quod scandalum
est et turpitudo totius aecclesiae vestrae.

[. . . it would be well and favorable for the honor and purity of your church, and provide a certain shield against vice, if your synod and your princes would forbid matrons and veiled women to make these frequent journeys back and forth to Rome. A great part of them perish and few keep their virtue. There are very few towns in Lombardy or Frankland or Gaul where there is not a courtesan or a harlot of English stock. It is a scandal and disgrace to your whole church.][30]

As Hollis has aptly commented on this passage, "Boniface's apprehension of rampant female sexuality at large and needing to be brought under control heralds a legislative movement towards the enclosure of monastic women on the continent."[31] One crucial difference between the type of pilgrimage Boniface describes here and that described in the letters from Egburg and to Bugge is his emphasis on the nature of the women's journeys. The pilgrimages described in the earlier letters had, as their goal, the eventual enclosure of the female traveller. In his letter to Archbishop Cuthbert, however, Boniface specifically complains of the frequency of female pilgrimage, which does not result in the containment of the pilgrims, but which results instead, apparently, in the "dangerous" spread of English female sexuality along the pilgrimage route.

The seriousness of transgressing the rules of enclosure is documented in a letter from Lull excommunicating the abbess Switha for allowing two of the nuns in her charge to leave the enclosure.[32] As Christine Fell has suggested, Switha's fault in allowing the women to leave the enclosure was two-fold: not only were the nuns accused of being wandering and disobedient, *vagas et inobedientes* (Tangl, 266), faults that Lull seems to consider even worse than unchastity, but Switha acted on her own authority in allowing the nuns to leave the cloister, by not securing Lull's permission in advance: *sine licentia et consilio meo* (Tangl, 265; see Fell, 37). Lull's anger at the women's transgression demonstrates his strong desire to keep them strictly enclosed, and to assert his own authority over their—and especially the abbess's—activities. He effectively removes the abbess's authority over the nuns, placing all members of the convent under his own control.[33]

These accounts of the Anglo-Saxon nuns affiliated with the
Boniface mission suggest that nuns may have chafed under strict
enclosure; they may have wanted more freedom to move beyond the
cloister, or at least freedom to regulate their own movements. The
abbess Switha, in the example above, lacks the supervisory control
practiced by early Anglo-Saxon abbesses such as Hild. Certain sources
suggest that unlike Wethburg, the Anglo-Saxon anchorite in Rome
(but perhaps like Switha's nuns), not all women submitted voluntarily
to exile or claustration. The twelfth century saw the rise of the genre
of *planctus monialis*, the lament of the unhappily or unwillingly pro-
fessed nun. The oldest known example of the genre survives in a
twelfth-century manuscript, but the bitter tone and intense loneliness
found in the *planctus* glance backward to the letters of nuns such as
Berthgyth and Egburg, even as they point forward to the unhappy
nuns of the later Middle Ages:

> Heu misella!
> nichil est eterius
>   tali vita!
> Cum enim sim petulans
>   et lasciva,
>
> Sono tintinnabulum,
> respeto psalte[rium],
> gratum linquo somnium
> cum dormire cupere[m]
>   —heu misella!—
> pernoctando vigilo
> [cum] non velle[m];
> iuvenem amplecterer
> quam libenter!
> . . . .
> Ago trabe circulum,
> pedes volvo per girum,
> flecto capu[d] supplicum,
> [non] ad auras tribut,
>   heu misella!
>
> Manus dans, [in] c[or]di[bu]s
>   rumpo pec[tus]

linguam [te]ro dentibus
   verba promens.

Woe is me, nothing is more degrading than such a life! for,
though I am made for love and play,
   I have to ring the chapel-bell, to chant the psalter over
and over, to leave my dear dreams when I long to sleep—
woe is me—and stay awake all night against my will. How
gladly I would fly into a lover's arms!
. . . .
   I pace the floor, walking round and round, I bow my
head submissively, not raising it heavenwards, woe is me;
giving in, my heart bursts with grief, but as the words come
out I bite my tongue.[34]

This lament presents many of the themes and concerns that plagued
both Boniface and the female speakers of the elegies: the female
sexual desire to transgress the claustral boundary; the emphasis on
past pleasures and the dissatisfaction with present circumstances;
the loneliness and solitude of pacing within one's confinement; the
desire to spill the "word-hoard" and express emotion. The *planctus*
speaker's movements as she chants the psalter and paces in her cell
in the early hours before dawn are, in fact, sharply evocative of the
activities described by the speaker in "The Wife's Lament." As
Daichman writes, "There is almost unbearable sorrow in the lament
of the nun, but there is also anger at the memory of all she has been
forced to leave behind, therefore, no matter how mournful the
song, the longings of the flesh still come through; 'cupiditas' will
not be vanquished by 'caritas'" (69).[35] She might well be describing
the speaker of either female elegy.

   It was not rare for medieval English girls or women to be forced
into the cloister for religious, legal, social, or political reasons, typically either as child oblates (cf. Rudolph's Life of Leoba), or—in the
case of older girls or women—to benefit male relatives or dissatisfied
husbands. As Barbara Yorke has recently written, "some royal women
were undoubtedly disposed of against their will and it is not always
clear whether all those who retired from the position of queen really
wanted to do so."[36] Eileen Power described later medieval convents
as a "'dumping ground' for unwanted and unwilling girls";[37] similarly,

Yorke suggests that Anglo-Saxon convents "provided convenient places in which male relatives could place female kin whom they wanted removed from active life" (Yorke, 102). On the other hand, Anglo-Saxon law codes confirm the benefits of the convent for the Anglo-Saxon widow with similar family troubles. According to Hollis, "the church offered an alternative form of protection if [the widow's] own family were dead or otherwise unable to aid her in maintaining possession of property against her husband's relatives."[38] Such practices resonate in the Old English female lyrics. In "The Wife's Lament," for example, not only does the woman suffer exile on account of the secret plotting of relatives, but the poem carries the impression of a woman speaking from beyond the grave, a position that was at least symbolically accurate.[39]

Stephanie Hollis suggests an imaginative connection between the elegies and monasticism, by linking "Wulf and Eadwacer" to the decline of the Anglo-Saxon system of double monastic houses governed by an abbess:

> Inasmuch as the monasteries were the seminal site for the construction of generic alterity, the undying lament of the woman in *Wulf and Eadwacer* will serve with particular aptness as an elegy for the double monastery: 'Wulf is on one island, I am on another . . . unalike are we'.   (300)

In spite of the intriguing possibilities of this connection, however, the female speaker and Wulf do not share "separate but equal" status; rather, the contexts of monastic regulation of female movement, and the increasingly strict demands for female enclosure, traced above, suggest ways that the culture of female monastic enclosure may condition the female elegies. Involuntarily enclosed, the speakers of "Wulf and Eadwacer" and "The Wife's Lament" offer a tantalizing glimpse inside enclosure, even as they seek to break down the walls of their confinement by focusing narrative attention not on their spiritual release but on their physical containment.

"Wulf and Eadwacer"

The presence of the Old English female elegies in the Exeter Book invites the possibility that monastic language, imagery, or ideology may be deeply embedded within popular, seemingly secular poems about women's laments for their lost lords.[40] The speaker of "Wulf and Eadwacer," isolated on her fen-surrounded island, images the strictly enclosed female religious of the early Middle Ages. The physical fact of her enclosure is described within the poem, but more importantly, because she protests against this condition, and because she suggests the barest possibility of escape, the enclosed condition acts as the force that shapes her identity. At nineteen lines, the poem is brief and enigmatic enough to merit quoting in full:

> Leodum is minum   swylce him mon lac gife;
> willað hy hine aþecgan,   gif he on þreat cymeð.
>   Ungelic is us.
> Wulf is on iege,   ic on oþerre.
> Fæst is þæt eglond,   fenne biworpen.   (5)
> Sindon wælreowe   weras þær on ige;
> willað hy hine aþecgan,   gif he on þreat cymeð.
>   Ungelice is us.
> Wulfes ic mines widlastum   wenum dogode;
> þonne hit wæs renig weder   ond ic reotugu sæt,   (10)
> þonne mec se beaducafa   bogum bilegde,
> wæs me wyn to þon,   wæs me hwæþre eac lað.
> Wulf, min Wulf,   wena me þine
> seoce gedydon,   þine seldcymas,
> murnende mod,   nales meteliste.   (15)
> Gehyrest þu, Eadwacer?   Uncerne earne hwelp
> bireð wulf to wuda.
> þæt mon eaþe tosliteð   þætte næfre gesomnad wæs,
> uncer giedd geador.[41]

> It is to my people as if one gave them a gift.
> They intend to kill him if he comes into [their] troop.
>   It is different with us.
> Wulf is on one island, I am on another.
> Enclosed is that island, surrounded by fen.
> Bloodthirsty men are there on that island.
> They intend to kill him if he comes into [their] troop.
>   It is different with us.
> I thought with hope of my Wulf's long journeys;

when it was rainy weather and I sat lamenting
then the warrior enclosed me in his arms (in branches?)
It was pleasant for me (till?) then, yet it was also hateful
    to me.
Wulf, my Wulf! My hopes of you
have made me sick—your rare visits—
mournful in mind, not lack of food.
Do you hear, Eadwacer? Our pitiful whelp
Wulf bears to the woods.
One may easily rend that which was never joined:
Our song together.[42]

The act of "writing" a poem, of voicing resistance to the structures of enclosure, creates this elegy's gendered self. The poem is both narrative text and woven textile (a metaphor the speaker herself employs in the penultimate line), and thus her creative act is both subjective and material.[43] Just as it links the creative acts of textile and textual production, the poem displays the dual impulses of popular and monastic traditions. This duality pervades the female Old English elegies: the *winileodas* famously prohibited by Charlemagne in the Capitulary of 789 seem closely linked not only to the nuns' letters in the Boniface correspondence, but also to the language and imagery of the Old English female elegies.

    In "Wulf and Eadwacer," the speaker clearly delineates her space from Wulf's, her (apparent) lover, but her descriptions of the islands are impossibly obscure. Because the antecedents are ambiguous, it is difficult to determine which island is secure and surrounded by a fen, and which island contains bloodthirsty men, lying in wait for Wulf. We can determine, however, that like the Anglo-Saxon missionary nuns, the speaker in "Wulf and Eadwacer" is cut off from her loved one by "congregations of waters" (in Dronke's phrase).[44] Her isolated enclosure helps us to make some distinctions: "þæt eglond", refers to its immediate antecedent ("oþerre"); in other words, when she refers to that "latter" island, she means "her" island, as the fen-enclosed space. It is clear, moreover, that bloodthirsty men are pursuing Wulf "on ige." I would argue that Wulf and the "bloodthirsty men" *must* be on the same island, because there would be little danger to Wulf if he were separated from his enemies by a fen. The "difference" alluded to in the refrain refers to the speaker's unwilling separation from both Wulf and the rest of her people. It is a difference not only of space or proximity, but also social status, degree, perhaps rank.[45] The lexically similar forms "iege" and "ige" contrast with the speaker's "eglond" to further support this delineation of what becomes essentially an opposition of public (masculine) and private (feminine) space.

The speaker in this lyric refuses to equate female enclosure with silence. Her concerns are physical—analogous to those contemporary Anglo-Saxon religious women whose letters reveal the same passionate longing for loved ones on earth. At exactly its midpoint, the poem captures the tension between the silence of female enclosure and the vocal expression of worldly desire. The poem moves in lines 1–9 from ambiguous and abstract spatial references ("aþecgan," "iege/eglond/ige," "wælreowe weras," etc.) to the very specific and con-crete images of lines 10–11—rainy weather, weeping, physical vio-lence—before moving back out towards the ambiguous and abstract imagery of the whelp, the song, and the Wulf/wolf. Much as Alain Renoir has demonstrated the sharply telescopic movement of Grendel's approach to Heorot, here in "Wulf and Eadwacer" we move steadily from broad references to the islands inward to the speaker's immediate physical space and her innermost emotions.[46] We have seen already that the poem makes careful spatial distinc-tions ("Wulf is on one island, I am on another"). In lines 10–11, the speaker makes analogous temporal distinctions by means of a when-then clause ("þonne . . . þonne"). In line 10, the verb form "reotugu" denotes not a silent or passive lament, but an active vocal expres-sion, perhaps even best translated as "wailing," as her voice breaks through her enclosed solitude.[47] Immediately, though, her lament is silenced, and here we see one of the poem's greatest mysteries, for who is "se beaducafa" who encloses the speaker in his arms: Wulf or Eadwacer? If we read him as Wulf, the simultaneous joy and pain she feels suggest that her physical pleasure in Wulf's presence is paired with her emotional suffering in anticipating his absence—a perfectly logical reading.

If, however, "se beaducafa" is Eadwacer, he silences her lament through his action of enclosing her, perhaps "pinioning" her, in his arms. In this reading, Eadwacer performs a dual violence on the speaker. He possibly rapes her ("bogum bilegde," if we translate, "surrounded me with his arms") or at least forces her into enclosed exile (if we translate, "enclosed me with branches"), and he tries to muffle her lament for Wulf. The verb "bilegde" (from *belecgan*, to surround) evokes the Old English verb *belucan*, "to enclose, to lock up." Both rape and enclosure are masculine attempts to regulate and silence the feminine articulation of passion, of self, and of sexuality. Even the poem's erratic meter—within only nineteen lines, four a-verses are unaccompanied by the usual b-verses—suggests a break from the strict confining structure of Old English metrics.[48] The opposition between female voicing and male silencing culminates in the temporally ambiguous line: "wæs me wyn *to þon*, wæs me hwæþre eac lað" [it was joyful for me *up to that point* (till then?); yet it was also hateful to me (line 12, emphasis added)]. Again, as in lines 3, 4, and 8, the carefully balanced phrasing ("wæs me . . . wæs me. . . .") underscores the strict juxtaposition between pleasurable and hateful feelings. If, following Peter Baker, we translate "to þon" as "till then" or "up to that point" we must view the phrase in temporal terms, in terms of "before" and "after."[49] The joy the speaker experienced came from the freedom to articulate her longing for Wulf and not, as many critics assume, from any sexual pleasure she receives from Eadwacer's violence.[50] I suggest, moreover, that her pleasure also derives from her self-expression. She felt joy *up to* the moment Eadwacer surrounded her with his arms, while the subsequent violence was hateful to her because it stripped her of the ability to mourn for Wulf. When Eadwacer silences her, he destroys the one consolation she has: giving voice to her unhappiness and longing for Wulf. Analogously, the female writers of the Boniface correspondence seem to derive a similar kind of "textual" pleasure in expressing to their correspondents their loneliness and isolation.

"Eadwacer," like the name Wulf ("outlaw"), signifies both a proper name, and an epithet descriptive of his function in the poem: "ead" (wealth, riches, happiness) and "wacer" (guardian, watcher).[51] In his possible rape and more certain silencing of the speaker, Eadwacer in effect prohibits her expression of joy; he is the guardian ("wacer") of her happiness ("ead"), who tries to limit the possibility both of earthly love and of female creative expression.

The poem's ending provides the speaker's clearest articulation of a female creativity that exceeds the boundaries of the literal and emotional enclosure imposed upon her by her physical environment and by Eadwacer. In lines 16–19, the irregular use of single half-lines, like the erratic meter of line 13a ("Wulf, min Wulf"), dismantles the confining structures of metrical correctness. We have seen that the affective, intensely emotional nature of the poem echoes a letter sent by a similarly sorrowful Anglo-Saxon nun: "Quare non vis cogitare, quod ego sola in hac terra et nullus alius frater visitet me, neque propinquorum aliquis ad me veniet? . . . O frater, o frater mi. [Why do you not want to remember that I am alone upon this earth, and no other brother will visit me, or any kinsman come to me? . . . O brother, O my brother]."[52] The strikingly parallel forms, "Wulf min Wulf" and "O frater, o frater mi" interrupt the rhetorical and structural demands of each text to articulate intense longing.

An even more tangible connection exists between the language of the poem and another text that may have been found in the library (or at least the cultural memory) of the Anglo-Saxon female religious: the Old English version of the gospel according to St. Matthew. The textile metaphors found in the poem's final lines ("tosliteð . . . gesomnad") echo the Old English glosses of Matthew 19:6, "ne ge-twæme nan mann. Þa ðe god gesomnode." Similarly, the Latin text of the Lindisfarne Gospels is glossed thus in the Northumbrian dialect: ["þæt forgon god gegeadrade monn ne to-slite/to-sceaða/suindria"].[53] The passage is, of course, known today for its use in the marriage service: "therefore what God hath joined together, let no man put asunder." The direct evocation of the language of marriage to describe the speaker's longed-for relationship with Wulf is particularly poignant, because it forcefully contrasts her relationships with each of the men. She refuses to name her relationship with Eadwacer as marriage (whatever the nature of that relationship might be), instead inverting the familiar language of the institution to represent a relationship that can only be torn asunder.

The "hwelp" of line 16b, which evidently belongs jointly (as indicated by the dual pronoun "uncerne") to the speaker and Wulf, presents an additional crux. Critics are generally split over whether the speaker is referring to a child she had, either by Wulf or Eadwacer (perhaps as the result of the rape?), or whether the "hwelp" is figurative, a metaphor for her relationship (probably with Wulf).[54] The poem explicitly links the "hwelp" and the "giedd": both are governed by the dual possessive pronoun "uncer" and both nouns represent the results of female creative processes found within domestic and monastic female spheres—namely, childbirth and weaving. In taking the "hwelp" from her, Wulf removes the only material sign of their relationship. The visible product of their love, the child, is replaced by something more ephemeral: the "giedd," the text of their relationship.

The textile metaphors "tosliteþ" and "gesomnad" represent the "giedd" as a fabric, a woven textile whose threads can be torn: "þæt mon eaþe tosliteð," one may easily slit, "þætte næfre gesomnad wæs," that which was never seamed (18). As Jane Chance has pointed out, the metaphor "directly inverts that normally characterizing the role of woman."[55] In other words, the text(ile) woven by this peaceweaver is not a relationship, but an actual text, the song of their relationship. Like Philomela, the speaker of "Wulf and Eadwacer" weaves her own violent history into a narrative tapestry. The feminine self constructed by the elegy is defined by female monastic experience, not the heroic world; the fabric she weaves is not for the greater glory of God but for the expression of that feminine self-hood, of her own worldly happiness and sorrow. Her final textile metaphors point to the fragility of borders and enclosures and open the possibility of rupture, even as the act of creating a narrative has permitted this speaker to move beyond the confines of prescriptive femininity.

"The Wife's Lament"

In a popular modern English translation of "The Wife's Lament," the speaker describes her situation in an unusual way: "My new lord commanded me into a convent / Of wooden nuns . . . I was forced to live in a nuns'-nest of leaves."[56] The imagery of the translation seems at first reading to be merely poetic: the "wooden nuns" represent trees in a forest, and the "nuns'-nest of leaves" is a nicely alliterating and seemingly archaic description of underbrush. Yet this language introduces an element into the poem that is not usually found there by modern readers, since the poem's original language has not been seen to include religious imagery.

This translation (unwittingly, I suspect) enters the speaker into the realm of Anglo-Saxon female monasticism. The Old English original too, I suggest, shows evidence of this cultural sphere. Regardless of whether the speaker of the poem literally entered a convent, we know that she is exiled and alone. My analysis of "The Wife's Lament" suggests that the poem's language constructs its feminine speaking subject by encoding the imagery and language of early medieval female monasticism. Again, the poem uses the discourse of enclosure to inscribe gender in an otherwise anonymous text.

To summarize briefly the situation in "The Wife's Lament": most critics now agree that the speaker is a woman.[57] She has been exiled as a result of secret plotting by her lord's relatives; she now lives confined to an "earth-cave" under an oak tree, within a grove, surrounded by thorny branches—contained, in other words, by at least three layers of barriers. She spends her time lamenting her circumstances, and she ends by acidly describing the fate of those who must wait for or depend upon a loved one. Like "Wulf and Eadwacer," the poem remains ambiguous, and like that poem, "The Wife's Lament" articulates—and resists—the culturally produced gender roles imposed by monasticism.

The first line of the poem locates it within the Germanic context of the traditional Old English elegy of exile: "Ic þis giedd wrece   bi me ful geomorre" [I recite this song about my very mournful self]. The speaker emphasizes her *present* suffering, before shifting to the past—her unhappiness was caused by her lord's departure "ofer yþa gelac" [over rolling waves] (7a). As I have suggested, the only means of release or escape for an Anglo-Saxon woman was through self-expression, through creating a text, and thereby a textual self. "The Wife's Lament" documents an emotional journey, which—unlike the literal and spiritual journeys seen in "The Wanderer" or "The Seafarer"—remains firmly grounded in the body. Thus the speaker explicitly expresses a *feminine* self; at no time does she desire to "progress to manhood."[58] Like the speaker in "Wulf and Eadwacer," this speaker resists the monastic ideology that would require her to reject her physical desires. Confined physically and earth-bound through her female body, she instead opens her *hord-cofa*, releasing those thoughts that the Wanderer would have suppressed.

Consistently, "The Wife's Lament" uses language with distinct monastic overtones, as the speaker (or poet) employs a discourse available for the expression of female sorrow within the culture of female monasticism. In the Boniface correspondence, for example, both male and female letter-writers frequently use secular terms to describe non-conjugal relationships. Likewise, in this elegy, the term *hlaford*, lord (6a), is usually understood to refer to the speaker's husband:

Ærest min hlaford gewat   heonan of leodum
ofer yþa gelac;   hæfde ic uhtceare
hwær min leodfruma   londes wære (lines 6–8)

[First my lord departed hence from his people, across the
rolling waves; I had grief at dawn {as to} where my lord
{literally "people-leader"} might be on earth].

Certainly the terms "hlaford" and "leodfruma" imply a social hier-
archy (and "leodfruma" seems decidedly secular). Yet "hlaford" is
used elsewhere in Old English to describe an ecclesiastical leader or
a spiritual lord—and, of course, God.[59] Such a definition extends the
term's semantic range beyond the usual "husband," encompassing
the possibility of both a secular and religious relationship; if we read
the lord to be the speaker's husband, we might equally read him as
her spiritual guardian. The poem does not precisely define the
woman's status, so that the most we can know is that she is separated
from a beloved man who holds some social power over her and
with whom she has made a pledge: "ful oft wit beotedan / þæt unc
ne gedælde" [very often we two vowed that nothing would separate
us] (21b–22a).

Among male and female religious, vowed spiritual friendships
often resemble conjugal relationships. Boniface, to name the most
prominent example, desired to be buried in the same grave as the
nun Leoba because of the deep spiritual relationship that they shared
during their lives, and that he wanted to perpetuate after their
deaths.[60] Earlier, Leoba had written to request Boniface's spiritual and
literal protection; her father was dead, and her mother seriously ill:

Ergo unica filia sum ambobus parentibus meis; et utinam,
licet sim indigna, ut merear te in fratris locum accipere,
quia in nullo hominum generis mei tanta fiducia spei
posita est mihi quanta in te. . . . quin immo vere dilectionis
ligatura reliquum nodetur in [a]evum. Hoc, frater amande,
enixius efflagito, ut tuarum orationum pelta muniar contra
hostis occulti venenata iacula.

[I am the only daughter of my parents and, unworthy though
I be, I wish that I might regard you as a brother; for there is

no other man in my kinship in whom I have such confidence as in you. . . . May the bond of our true affection be knit ever more closely for all time. I eagerly pray, my dear brother, that I may be protected by the shield of your prayers from the poisoned darts of the hidden enemy.][61]

Clearly Leoba believed that her relationship with Boniface, though based on a spiritual friendship, might offer her a more substantial kind of worldly support (a belief which was confirmed when he later requested that she join him in Germany).[62] Similarly, the relationship between Christina of Markyate and Abbot Geoffrey seems almost cozily domestic:

Visitat de hinc vir misericordie deditus amplius locum. virginis frequentat colloquium. providet domui. et dispositor efficitur agendorum. Intendit ille virgini ministrare subsidia. Desudat illa virum accumulare virtutibus.

[Henceforward the man devoted to good works visited [Christina's] place even more: he enjoyed the virgin's company, provided for her house, and became the supervisor of its material affairs. Whilst he centred his attention on providing the virgin with material assistance, she strove to enrich the man in virtue. . . .][63]

For Christina, as it was for Leoba, such a relationship is both spiritual and pragmatic, since the "hlaford"/abbot/bishop provided real protection and material support.

In "The Wife's Lament," the speaker's assertion, "Ða ic me feran gewat folgað secan" (9), has been interpreted to mean that she sought financial support, or protection, or her husband (who would presumably provide both). "Folgað" is usually understood as "the service due by a retainer to his lord."[64] It contains in particular the sense of "official" service, that given or owed to some sanctioned institution. Again, the term has monastic overtones: one meaning of *folgian* is "to follow the monastic profession."[65] The service sought by the wife puzzles many readers, because it seems unusual for a woman to adopt the heroic language of a retainer. Yet in fact she takes language from a Christian monastic code that includes men and women both;

Aldhelm, to name just one example, describes the nuns of Barking as "soldiers of Christ," and Leoba's language in the letter cited above carries definite martial overtones. Like the nuns of Barking, the Old English speaker has perhaps sought "folgað" to serve her lord, either secular or divine; reading the poem within a Christian context permits a multiplicity of readings.

Reading this elegy as a repeated set of acts signifying a female monastic subject can illuminate other puzzling aspects of the speaker's experience. We know, for example, that she felt "uhtceare," usually translated as "grief just before dawn" and later she says, "þonne ic on uhtan   ana gonge," [then in the (pre)dawn I walk alone] (35). The time she describes is that of matins, the earliest of the canonical hours, just before dawn. Typically at *uhta*, matins, the order sang *uhtsang*, the matins service.[66] "The Wife's Lament," then, can be read as a kind of *uhtsang*: the speaker's mournful lament emulates the conventional matins service and recalls the lamenting nun of the twelfth-century *planctus monialis*. She sings "under actreo," under an oak tree; "treow," of course, is a common Old English poetic metaphor for the cross. The speaker's language can be read as the cultural expression of female monasticism. Like a nun at matins singing the office under the cross (and thus lamenting her Lord), this speaker laments the loss of her lord, under a tree, at the hour of matins.

The most visually arresting image evoked by the speaker within her inverted expression of gendered monastic discourse is her enclosure itself, the "earth-cave" she inhabits. She differentiates this dwelling from her previous worldly life; the earth-cave ("wic wynna leas," a joyless dwelling, 32a) contrasts with her memory of the pleasant dwellings ("wynlicran wic," 52a) she shared with her lord. We need not read the earth-cave as totally disagreeable, since the enclosure has provided her with a refuge from the man's plotting relatives. Likewise, monastic enclosure provided Anglo-Saxon nuns with protection—theoretically, at least—from similarly hostile relatives or even from invading armies. The earth-cave may be literally a natural or man-made cave or tumulus of the sort inhabited by St. Guthlac. Certainly "grave" or tumulus imagery is appropriate for a nun, dead to the world socially and restricted from it physically.[67]

"The Wife's Lament" (like "Wulf and Eadwacer") weaves together images and words connecting the narrator to her "hlaford." The speaker links herself semantically to her lord's emotional and physical circumstances throughout the poem. She is "geomorre" [mournful, 1b], with "hyge geomor" [mournful mind, 16b]; the man is likewise "geomormod" [sad-minded, 42b]. While the woman must endure "feor ge neah . . . fæhðu" [far and near . . . the hostility, 25b–26] on account of her beloved, the man is "ful wide fah / feorres folclondes" [very widely outlawed in far countries, 46b–47a]. In her "wic wynna leas," the woman is surrounded by mountains and briar walls; while she imagines the man, remembering his "wynlicran wic," sitting "under stanhliþe, storme behrimed" [under a rocky cliff, frost-covered from a storm, 48].[68] The repeated words and images intricately weave the similar situations of the woman and man throughout the text. My weaving metaphor is deliberate: in linking the worlds of popular vernacular elegy and monastic textuality, the two female lyrics demonstrate the intersection between popular and learned cultures that would likely mark the work of a literate Anglo-Saxon woman.

Although only a handful of critics have been willing to read any elements of Christianity into "The Wife's Lament," the poem's preservation in the Exeter Book places it within a Christian monastic environment and opens up the possibility that the text may encode (and even reject) monastic ideals within a popular poem apparently about a woman's lament for her lord.[69] Alain Renoir has argued that "a mediaeval English poet may possibly have chosen to let his [*sic*] female protagonist draw upon popular Christian doctrine while relating her misadventures." He reads "The Wife's Lament" as a poem of "Christian inversion" in which her "husband" is brought from a previously exalted and powerful position to a lowly one and suggests that this process seems to illustrate a "familiar New Testament assertion," namely the verse from Luke 1:52: "deposuit potentes de sede. . . .": "He hath put down the mighty from their seat, and hath exalted the humble." According to Renoir, regardless of whether the Anglo-Saxon poet intentionally inserted Christian doctrine into the poem, likely readers of the Exeter Book would have been aware of allusions to Christian doctrine: "anyone attempting to read it through from beginning to end must perforce become attuned to all kinds of allusions to Christian lore and doctrine."[70]

Unfortunately, Renoir does not extend his analysis to its fullest potential, because his discussion omits the context in which the passage from Luke occurs. The verse Renoir cites is embedded in the

Magnificat, the song sung by Mary at the Visitation: "My soul doth magnify the Lord" (Luke 1:46–55). In other words, "The Wife's Lament" can be seen to illustrate a biblical passage which falls within a song sung by a woman; of course, the Old English poem, too, is sung by a woman. The comparison to the biblical verse becomes much more powerful when its context is made explicit. The woman singing the Old English poem embodies—even as she revises—the image of Mary singing the *Magnificat*.

Even read this way, the poem maintains its ambiguity: as a parallel to Mary, a woman singing within a monastic setting would command respect, in imitating the pinnacle of virginity (and images of Mary, of course, suggest the possibility of escape from the curse of Eve, the woman's corrupt body). Yet this woman seems to lament a beloved man on earth, and to focus particularly on physical concerns. Can the poem be read as Christian allegory at all? Can the "hlaford" be Christ, the speaker a "sponsa Christi"? If we read it this way, the poem becomes one ideal of expression from a female monastic community, the kind of environment that might produce such a Christian allegory. Yet the poem also inverts that expression, since it reveals a dissatisfaction with monastic enclosure and a longing for earthly love. Singing a riddling song whose answer may even be the *Magnificat*, the woman narrator links herself at once to Mary—the socially sanctioned image of female creativity—and to the world. Her form admits—insists upon—both kinds of interpretation.

My analysis of the Old English female lyrics has sought to decode what Marilynn Desmond has called "the gender of the text."[71] I have sought to demonstrate how these lyrics, in Judith Butler's terms, "do" gender by analyzing ways that gender positions within the poems are discursively produced. By considering how a monastic discourse of enclosure regulates representation in these poems, I suggest in particular that the performance of gender enacted by the speakers derives from—enacts—historically specific religious and cultural attitudes found in early medieval Christianity regarding the feminine and the female body, although in a significantly different way from the performances of gender we shall see in the following chapters. The deployment of these discourses within the elegies engenders their speaking subjects. The discourse of enclosure shows specifically how the gendered subject position within the text is, in Butler's words, "an identity tenuously constituted in time, instituted in an exterior space through a *stylized repetition of acts* [emphasis in original]."[72] In the next chapter, I turn from a consideration of female enclosure within monasticism to female enclosure within a decidedly secular text: *Beowulf*. Nonetheless, we shall see that the cultural imperatives of female enclosure govern the representation of women in *Beowulf* in ways very similar to the Old English elegies: the women of *Beowulf* are, like the female elegiac speakers, confined both socially and physically. In *Beowulf*, however, we can trace an even more pervasive pattern of female enclosure, as the poem's carefully structured narrative frames and ring compositions serve as methods of "textual" enclosure. Throughout this and subsequent chapters, we shall continue to see the literal and figurative ways in which Old English literature contains and circumscribes femininity. As canonical and exemplary texts, respectively, *Beowulf* and the Old English female saints' lives will reveal an even more markedly "stylized repetition" in their enactments of the feminine.

NOTES

1. Like all Old English poems, the titles of these poems are modern editorial conventions, and are not found in the original manuscript. All my citations from Old English poetry (except *Beowulf*) come from *The Anglo-Saxon Poetic Records*, ed. George Philip Krapp and Elliot Van Kirk Dobbie, Volume III: The Exeter Book (New York: Columbia University Press, 1936). Citations to line numbers are provided parenthetically within my text. Unless otherwise noted, translations are my own.

2. For example, Jerome Mandel, *Alternative Readings in Old English Poetry* (New York: Peter Lang, 1987), argues against a female speaker. Most of the criticism supporting a male speaker appeared in the early to mid 1960s, and was effectively refuted by Angela Lucas, "The Narrator of *The Wife's Lament* Reconsidered" *Neuphilologische Mitteilungen* 70 (1969): 282–297. For critical surveys of this "gender" question, see Marilynn Desmond, "The Voice of Exile: Feminist Literary History and the Anonymous Anglo-Saxon Elegy" *Critical Inquiry* 16 (1990): 572–590; and Patricia Belanoff, "Women's Songs, Women's Language: *Wulf and Eadwacer* and *The Wife's Lament*, in *New Readings on Women in Old English Literature*, ed. Damico and Olsen, 193–203. One recent reader sees *The Wife's Lament* as a riddle, arguing that the solution, "sword," preserves the grammatical gender. See Faye Walker-Pelkey, "*Frige hwæt ic hatte*: 'The Wife's Lament' as Riddle," *Papers on Language and Literature* 28 (1992): 242–266. As recently as 1985, one reader argued for animal, rather than human, characters in the poem, suggesting

that the narrator is a female wolf, and the poem's events concern her wolf-family. See Peter Orton, "An Approach to *Wulf and Eadwacer*," *Proceedings of the Royal Irish Academy* 85 (1985): 223–258. For a comprehensive critical summary and thorough bibliography, as well as texts and facsimiles of all the elegies, see Anne L. Klinck, *The Old English Elegies: A Critical Edition and Genre Study* (Montreal: McGill-Queen's University Press, 1992).

3. Martin Green, "Time, Memory, and Elegy in *The Wife's Lament*," in *The Old English Elegies: New Essays in Criticism and Research*, ed. Martin Green (Rutherford: Fairleigh Dickinson University Press, 1983), 129. I disagree with Green, however, when he argues that "The Wife's Lament" displays "[t]he picture of absolute passivity and hopelessness, of a person suspended in time" (129). While the speaker may lack hope, she is not passive; the act of voicing her sorrow, of creating a poem, contradicts that possibility.

4. Elizabeth Robertson, "The Rule of the Body: The Feminine Spirituality of the *Ancrene Wisse*," in *Seeking the Woman in Late Medieval and Renaissance Writings: Essays in Feminist Contextual Criticism*, ed. Sheila Fisher and Janet E. Halley (Knoxville: University of Tennessee Press, 1989), 112. Robertson applies her argument in much greater length to a variety of early Middle English "women's" texts in *Early English Devotional Prose and the Female Audience* (Knoxville: University of Tennessee Press, 1990).

5. Butler, *Gender Trouble*, 24–25. Similarly, see Elspeth Probyn: "the self is an ensemble of techniques and practices enacted on an everyday basis [that] entails the necessary problematization of these practices. The self is not simply put forward, but rather it is reworked in its enunciation." *Sexing the Self: Gendered Positions in Cultural Studies* (New York: Routledge, 1993), 2.

6. See Desmond, "The Voice of Exile."

7. Martin Green approaches this issue from a slightly different direction, arguing that *all* "the speakers of the elegies are in one way or another seeming isolates, cut off from human society. The Wanderer treads weary ways and navigates ice-cold seas without companionship. The Seafarer evokes the pains of winter weather suffered on night watch on a ship sailing perilously close to rocky cliffs; if he has any companions, he does not mention them. The speaker in *Wulf and Eadwacer* is on a fen-bound island, separated from Wulf. . . . Perhaps the most terrifying picture of isolation is in *The Wife's Lament*, whose speaker sits . . . in a cave under an oak-tree in a dim valley, aware that elsewhere in the world there are people together while she is *ana* 'alone,'" Introduction to *The Old English Elegies*, ed. Martin Green, 13. Yet Green overlooks, I would argue, the obvious differences in the supposedly parallel situations he establishes: that the two male speakers not only travel, display movement, but that they apparently do so voluntarily. The two female speakers are not only enclosed, but more importantly they are enclosed against their will.

8. On "The Wanderer's" image of the *hord-cofa*, breast-coffer, see Sarah Lynn Higley, *Between Languages: The Uncooperative Text in Early Welsh and Old English Nature Poetry* (University Park: Penn State University Press, 1993), 241, and Eric Jager, "Speech and the Chest in Old English Poetry: Orality or Pectorality?" *Speculum* 65 (1990): 845–859.

9. "*Sundor æt Rune*: The Voluntary Exile Status of The Wanderer" *Neophilologus* 73 (1989), 120.

10. Cited in Bjork, "*Sundor æt Rune*," 122.

11. John C. Pope, "Second Thoughts on the Interpretation of 'The Seafarer,'" *Anglo-Saxon England* 3 (1974): 75–86; rpt. in *Old English Shorter Poems*, ed. Katherine O'Brien O'Keeffe (New York: Garland, 1994), 213–229; see especially 218–219.

12. Rosemary Woolf, "*The Wanderer, The Seafarer*, and the Genre of *Planctus*," in *Anglo-Saxon Poetry: Essays in Appreciation*, ed. Lewis Nicholson and Dolores Warwick Frese (Notre Dame: Notre Dame University Press, 1975), 204.

13. I am adapting Sarah Higley's useful translation of "on staþelum healdan," from *Between Languages*, 262.

14. I wish to anticipate briefly here my argument in chapter four: in Ælfric's *Lives of Saints*, the female saints claim to want to have their bodies bound or tortured; binding their bodies, the saints assert, will free their souls. In "The Wanderer" and "The Seafarer," the argument is slightly different: *denying* the body frees the soul to go on its spiritual journey. The saints are not exactly denying their bodies, but rather making use of them. In the female elegies, in contradistinction, bodily pain and physical enclosure cause the speakers to focus on their bodies and on their physical circumstances, with no expectation of future consolation or release; instead, dwelling on that discomfort *is* their release.

15. On these traditional gendered hierarchies in patristic thought and in medieval literature more generally, see Robertson, *Early English Devotional Prose*, 32–43; and Ian Maclean, *The Renaissance Notion of Woman: A Study in the Fortunes of Scholasticism and Medical Science in European Intellectual Life* (Cambridge: Cambridge University Press, 1980).

16. Interestingly, the female elegies lack resolution and closure, unlike the male elegies; Helen Bennett ascribes this difference to the metonymic expressions of the female speakers, as opposed to male elegiac discourse, which she sees as metaphoric. See Bennett's recent article, "Exile and the Semiosis of Gender" in *Class and Gender in Early English Literature: Intersections*, ed. Britton Harwood and Gillian Overing (Bloomington: University of Indiana Press, 1994), 43–58.

17. On the literacy of Anglo-Saxon women see Christine Fell, *Women in Anglo-Saxon England* (Oxford: Blackwell, 1984), 109ff; Stephanie Hollis,

Anglo-Saxon Women and the Church, passim; and Patrick Wormald, "The Uses of Literacy in Anglo-Saxon England and its Neighbors," *Transactions of the Royal Historical Society* 5th ser. 27 (1977), 95–114. For the literacy of continental women see Suzanne Fonay Wemple, *Women in Frankish Society: Marriage and the Cloister 500–900* (Philadelphia: University of Pennsylvania Press, 1981), 175–188; and Rosamond McKitterick, *The Carolingians and the Written Word* (Cambridge: Cambridge University Press, 1989).

18. Cited in Peter Dronke, *The Medieval Lyric* (London: Hutchinson, 1968), 91.

19. Peter Dronke, *Women Writers of the Middle Ages* (Cambridge: Cambridge University Press, 1984), 31.

20. To underscore the connections between the letter and contemporary Latin and vernacular poetic practice, Dronke has versified Berthgyth's letter:

> Quid est, frater mi,
> quod tam longum tempus intermisisti,
> quod venire tardasti?
> Quare   non vis cogitare,
> quod ego sola   in hac terra
> et nullus alius frater visitet
> me, neque propinquorum aliquis ad me veniet? . . .
> O frater, o frater mi,
> cur potes mentem parvitatis meae
> adsiduae merore,
> fletu atque tristitia
> die noctuque
> caritatis tuae absentia   adfligere?

Dronke, *Women Writers of the Middle Ages*, 289, n. 111. Berthgyth's letters are found in M. Tangl, ed., *Die Briefe des Heiligen Bonifatius und Lullus*, 2nd ed. Monumenta Germaniae Historica. Epistolae Selectae I (Berlin: Weidmann, 1955), 282, 284–287.

21. Dronke, *Women Writers of the Middle Ages*, 31.

22. See Christine Fell, "Some Implications of the Boniface Correspondence," in *New Readings on Women in Old English Literature*, ed. Helen Damico and Alexandra Hennessey Olsen, 29–43.

23. The connections between the Boniface correspondence and the elegies have only rarely been examined. One excellent comparison can be found in Ursula Schafer, "Two Women in Need of a Friend: A Comparison of *The Wife's Lament* and Eangyth's Letter to Boniface," in *Germanic Dialects: Linguistic and Philological Investigations*, ed. Bela Brogyanyi and Thomas Krommelbein (Amsterdam and Philadelphia: John Benjamins, 1986), 491–

524. Schafer examines thematic correspondences; she does not address the issue of authorship or provenance.

24. M. Tangl, ed., *Die Briefe des heiligen Bonifatius und Lullus*, 20. Translation from Ephraim Emerton, ed. and trans., *The Letters of Saint Boniface* (New York: Norton, 1940, 1976), 35.

25. There is good evidence for female pilgrimage in the early Anglo-Saxon period; for example, Bede discusses the pilgrimage of both men and women to Rome in his *Ecclesiastical History*, Book V, Chapter 7. As Boniface's remarks indicate, however, female pilgrimage is intended to lead solely to greater *stabilitas*.

26. See Hollis, p. 145, n. 137. See also Dorothy Whitelock, "The Interpretation of 'The Seafarer,'" in *Old English Literature: Twenty-Two Analytical Essays*, ed. Martin Stevens and Jerome Mandel (Lincoln: University of Nebraska Press, 1968), 198–211. Whitelock reminds us that "[a]ccording to her Life by Rudolph, Leoba was enjoined by Boniface before his last journey never to desert the land of her *peregrinatio*" (210)—another example of the security that pilgrimage was to ensure.

27. Clare A. Lees and Gillian R. Overing, "Birthing Bishops and Fathering Poets: Bede, Hild, and the Relations of Cultural Production" *Exemplaria* 6.1 (1994): 59.

28. Tangl, 48; Emerton, 56.

29. Tangl, 48; Emerton, 56.

30. Tangl, 169; Emerton, 140.

31. Hollis, 150; see also Schulenburg, "Strict Active Enclosure," 56–58, for a survey of enclosure legislation.

32. For discussion of this event, see Schulenburg, 68–69; Fell, "Some Implications," 36–37; and Hollis, 106, 285. The letter from Lull to Switha is found in Tangl, pp. 265–266.

33. See also Hollis, 285.

34. The Latin text of the *planctus* and Peter Dronke's modern English translation are both cited in Graciela Daichman, *Wayward Nuns in Medieval Literature* (Syracuse: Syracuse University Press, 1986), 67–69.

35. To cite just one example for comparison purposes, Alain Renoir describes the speaker of *The Wife's Lament* in strikingly similar terms:

> she has been condemned to solitary exile in a dismal grove where she recalls the loving vows which she previously exchanged with [her lord]. As she sadly contemplates the wretched earth-cave in which she must now dwell in desperate solitude, she contrasts her fate to that of happier lovers and bemoans the sorrow that relentlessly gnaws at her heart ("A Reading Context for *The Wife's Lament*," 237–238).

He could as well be describing the speaker of the *planctus*, "grieving deeply on behalf of her companions" [condolens gemitibus—/que consocialibus] (Daichman, 69).

36. "'Sisters Under the Skin'? Anglo-Saxon Nuns and Nunneries in Southern England" *Reading Medieval Studies* 15 (1989), 102.

37. Eileen Power writes that some male relatives used "the nunnery as a 'dumping ground' for unwanted and often unwilling girls, whom it was desirable to put out of the world, . . . a means as sure as death itself and without the risk attaching to murder." The advantage to this was "to gain possession of their inheritance; for a nun, dead in the eyes of the law which governed the world, could claim no share in her father's estate." *Medieval English Nunneries (ca. 1275–1535)* (Cambridge: Cambridge University Press, 1922), 29–30. Cf. John Boswell, *The Kindness of Strangers: The Abandonment of Children in Western Europe from Late Antiquity to the Renaissance* (New York: Pantheon, 1988). Boswell shows that, in the early middle ages, children—regardless of religious vocation—were legally required to remain permanently in the monasteries to which their parents had "donated" them: "by the opening of the seventh century, oblation was well established and defined . . . . According to both civil and ecclesiastical law, the child could never leave the monastery, and the parents took a vow never to endow the child with any property or inheritance" (234). For an interesting discussion of "wandering" nuns breaking their claustral vows in the later middle ages, see Daichman, 3–30.

38. *Anglo-Saxon Women and the Church*, 80.

39. In a related vein, Overing and Lees write:

The narrative process of isolating (in cloister or on pedestal) the female saint obscures . . . her relationships with other women, which in turn obscures the possibility of reconstructing women's experience of kinship" ("Birthing Bishops and Fathering Poets," 62).

I would suggest that this process of isolation is not restricted to the female saints, but works in much the same way for the isolated speakers of the female elegies.

For an argument advancing the view that the speaker of *The Wife's Lament* is not simply exiled but is in fact dead, see Elinor Lench, "'The Wife's Lament': A Poem of the Living Dead," *Comitatus* 1 (1970): 3–23; and Raymond P. Tripp, Jr., "The Narrator as Revenant: A Reconsideration of Three Old English Elegies" *Papers on Language and Literature* 8 (1972): 339–361.

40. The Exeter Book, evidently a monastic compilation, contains both secular and religious poetry, much of which appears to be deliberately grouped together sequentially. Although the relationship between the Christian poetry

of The Exeter Book and the female elegies has not, to my knowledge, been studied in detail, the correspondences may well have been obvious to the book's original readers and/or compilers. See Alain Renoir, "Christian Inversion in *The Wife's Lament,*" *Studia Neophilologica* 49 (1977), 19–24, for speculation regarding these correspondences. For a discussion of The Exeter Book's "verse sequences," see Carol Braun Pasternack, *The Textuality of Old English Poetry* (Cambridge: Cambridge University Press, 1995), 177–179.

41. *Anglo-Saxon Poetic Records*, ed. Krapp and Dobbie, Vol. 3, 179–180.

42. In general, my translation strives to be literal, rather than poetic. I am indebted to Peter Baker's excellent analysis of the ambiguities of the poem's language: "The Ambiguity of Wulf and Eadwacer," *Studies in Philology* 78 (1981), 39–51, and to his "classroom edition" of the poem: *"Wulf and Eadwacer*: A Classroom Edition," *Old English Newsletter* 16.2 (1983), appendix 1–8.

43. For the speakers of both elegies as "mock scopas," creating their own stories, see Chance, *Woman as Hero*, 81–94.

44. *Women Writers of the Middle Ages*, 32.

45. As pure speculation, I would offer the possibility that the difference alluded to by the speaker in her refrain may refer to her own physical presence in a convent. As Hollis suggests, the speaker is above all marked by her alterity, a difference that may refer to social status as well as to gender.

46. See Renoir's essay, "Point of View and Design for Terror in *Beowulf*" (*Neuphilologische Mitteilungun* 63 [1962]: 154–167), which shows how the poem moves our perspective almost filmically from a spectator's view of Grendel's far-off approach to an extreme close-up shot of his eyes, even inside his head.

47. Peter Baker, "The Ambiguity of *Wulf and Eadwacer,*" 47.

48. Similarly, the poem breaks with poetic conventions in other ways; for example, the speaker shifts from speaking *about* Wulf in the third person, to addressing him in second person (line 13). My thanks go to Leslie Stratyner for reminding me of this point. For a cogent structural and metrical analysis, see Ruth P.M. Lehmann, "The Metrics and Structure of *Wulf and Eadwacer,*" *Philological Quarterly* 48 (1969): 151–165.

49. Peter Baker, "The Ambiguity of *Wulf and Eadwacer,*" 48.

50. Marilynn Desmond makes a similar point about *The Wife's Lament*, 587.

51. Peter Baker, "The Ambiguity of *Wulf and Eadwacer,*" 49. For the argument that the poem presents only two main characters, see Stanley Greenfield, *"Wulf and Eadwacer*: All Passion Pent" *Anglo-Saxon England* 15 (1986): 5–14. Two recent articles argue that Wulf is the speaker's son: Marijane Osborne, "The Text and Context of *Wulf and Eadwacer,*" in *The Old English Elegies: New Essays in Criticism and Research*, ed. Martin Green

(Rutherford: Fairleigh Dickinson University Press, 1983), 174–189; and Dolores Warwick Frese, "*Wulf and Eadwacer:* The Adulterous Woman Reconsidered," *Notre Dame English Journal* 15.1 (1983): 1–22; reprinted in Damico and Olsen, *New Readings on Women in Old English Literature*, pp. 273–291.

52. Dronke, *Women Writers of the Middle Ages*, 30–31; text in Tangl, 282.

53. W.W. Skeat, ed. *The Gospel According to Saint Matthew* (Cambridge: Cambridge University Press, 1887), 152. See also James Spamer, "The Marriage Concept in *Wulf and Eadwacer*," *Neophilologus* 62 (1978): 144.

54. Perhaps the speaker is imprisoned *because* of her pregnancy; the story of the pregnant nun of Watton told by Aelred of Rivaulx in the twelfth century is oddly reminiscent of the Old English poem. In Aelred's account, the nuns imprisoned the pregnant woman, and the monks tracked down the guilty man. When the baby was due, it miraculously disappeared, taken from the nun in a dream by the archbishop. The patterns of pregnancy and separation are strikingly similar. See the discussion in Sharon Elkins, *Holy Women of Twelfth-Century England* (Chapel Hill and London: University of North Carolina Press, 1988), 106.

55. *Woman as Hero*, 88.

56. Burton Raffel, trans., *Poems from the Old English* (Lincoln: University of Nebraska Press, 1964), 36, lines 15–16, 27. I am indebted to Roy White for bringing this translation to my attention.

57. Good literal translations illustrating the general view of the wife's position can be found in Nora Kershaw [Chadwick], *Anglo-Saxon and Norse Poems* (Cambridge: Cambridge University Press, 1922), 33–35; and Jane L. Curry, "Approaches to a Translation of the Anglo-Saxon *The Wife's Lament*" *Medium Ævum* 35 (1966): 187–198. Recent feminist studies of the elegy have, I believe, put to rest earlier theories that the speaker is male. For overviews, see Chance, *Woman as Hero in Old English Literature*; Desmond, "The Voice of Exile," and Belanoff, "Women's Songs, Women's Language: *Wulf and Eadwacer* and *The Wife's Lament*."

58. As women are urged to do by such patristic commentators as Ambrose and Jerome; see chapter 3, below.

59. Bosworth-Toller, *An Anglo-Saxon Dictionary with Supplement*, s.v. *hlaford*.

60. See Hollis, 271–300. The image of the "hlaford" departing over the seas is also reminiscent of the Boniface mission; as the letter to Boniface from Leoba makes clear, he departed for Germany leaving Leoba behind in England (although she joined him years later).

61. Tangl, 53; Emerton, 60.

62. See Rudolph of Fulda's *The Life of St. Leoba*, in *Medieval Women's Visionary Literature*, ed. Elizabeth Alvilda Petroff (New York: Oxford University Press, 1986), 106–114.

63. C.H. Talbot, ed. and trans., *The Life of Christina of Markyate: A Twelfth Century Recluse* (Oxford: The Clarendon Press, 1959; rpt. Toronto: University of Toronto Press, 1998), 155. The translation is Talbot's.

64. R.F. Leslie, *Three Old English Elegies* (Manchester: Manchester University Press, 1961), 53.

65. Bosworth-Toller, *An Anglo-Saxon Dictionary with Supplement*, s.v. *folgian*.

66. See Bosworth-Toller, *An Anglo-Saxon Dictionary with Supplement*, s.v. *uhta, uhtceare, uhtsang*.

67. See note 39, above. On the *eorðscræf*, see Karl Wentersdorf. "The Situation of the Narrator in the Old English *Wife's Lament*" *Speculum* 56.3 (1981): 592–516, and Emily Jensen, "*The Wife's Lament's Eorðscræf*: Literal or Figurative Sign?" *Neuphilologische Mitteilungen* 91 (1990): 449–457.

68. For an excellent structural analysis of the poem's patterns and repetitions, see Robert Stevick, "Formal Aspects of *The Wife's Lament*," *JEGP* 59 (1960), 21–25.

69. In addition to Renoir, cited below, the following critics have argued for an allegorical reading of "The Wife's Lament" (though none of these critics reads the poem in terms of female monasticism): M.J. Swanton, "'The Wife's Lament' and 'The Husband's Message': A Reconsideration" *Anglia* 82 (1964): 269–290; W.F. Bolton, "'The Wife's Lament' and 'The Husband's Message': A Reconsideration Revisited" *Archiv* 205 (1969): 337–351; and A.N. Doane, "Heathen Form and Christian Function in 'The Wife's Lament'" *Mediaeval Studies* 28 (1966): 77–91.

70. All citations from Alain Renoir, "Christian Inversion in *The Wife's Lament*," *Studia Neophilologica* 49 (1977), 23.

71. Marilynn Desmond, "The Voice of Exile," 577.

72. *Gender Trouble*, 140.

CHAPTER 2

Voices From the Margins: Women and Textual Enclosure in *Beowulf*

In an article published in 1960, Paull F. Baum speculated (jokingly) that *Beowulf* was written by a woman, perhaps an educated abbess such as Hild.[1] According to Baum, "feminine authorship would account for many things in the poem" (358), including its relative lack of graphic violence, its sympathy for underdogs (including women), its moderate descriptions of victory celebrations ("with none of the grosser indulgences"), and its "extraordinary amount of talking and the tendencies to 'digress'" (359). Baum himself seems not to subscribe to this theory, but asserts that such speculations "do no harm if they are not taken too seriously" (359).

Though his language seems laughable today and his speculation is, at any rate, unverifiable, Baum's theory of female authorship for *Beowulf* nonetheless creates a useful starting point for thinking about the women of *Beowulf*. Based on twentieth-century essentialist views of femininity, his suppositions that women are typically unconcerned with gore and battles, sympathetic to other women's plights, and given to talking too much—simply because they are women—are of course cultural constructions; yet they reflect the belief that women behave certain ways due to biology rather than to social conditioning. Recent feminist theory has taught us that such essentializing notions are not only wrong-headed but counterproductive, because they obscure the cultural conditions that produce "women" and "men" (themselves constructed categories) within a given culture. Thus analyzing the women—or men—of *Beowulf* according to modern standards will produce an unsatisfactory understanding, partial at best, of how Anglo-Saxon culture viewed its women and men. Rather than evaluate (as Baum unwittingly suggests) the gender dynamics of the poem according to anachronistic guidelines, we would do better to approach such an analysis by reconstructing (as much as possible) the cultural, social, and historical contexts in which the poem was written.[2]

In this chapter, I will consider how models of female enclosure operate in *Beowulf*. Unlike Baum, I will not speculate on either the sex or provenance of the author. In examining the ways that *Beowulf* contains its female characters, I do not mean to suggest any literal or historical connection between the poem and female monasticism, though of course the poem has long been recognized to document, however implicitly, a Christian world-view.[3] Yet because *Beowulf* is foundational for any study of Old English literature, its female characters are regularly the standards by which other women in Old English literature are examined. Thus it is important to investigate the extent to which the cultural and rhetorical trope of enclosure shapes and defines the women of *Beowulf*.

In my readings of "The Wife's Lament" and "Wulf and Eadwacer," I suggested that the enclosure model functions on a physical, material level by literally confining and isolating those female speakers. This model serves to maintain monastic imperatives including regulating the female body and its desires; reducing the threats of female sexuality and female authority; and attempting (though not successfully) to silence the female voice. In this chapter I shall argue that the control of women in *Beowulf* is analogous to that of women in early medieval monastic culture, and that reading the poem's women in terms of enclosure reveals the broad cultural theme of female containment—and its corollary, the danger of escape—that mark much of early English literature. We shall see that the women in *Beowulf* are enclosed literally (within physical space); textually (within the poem's narrative structures); and symbolically (within the poem's cultural conceptions of femininity and within kinship structures). Even the text itself works to maintain control of its female characters in terms of both plot and structure. Within the poem, women's stories frame and are framed by each other, functioning intratextually to construct a *Beowulfian* concept of conventional femininity.

It is important to note at the outset that a study of the discourse of female enclosure in *Beowulf* will not simply reconfirm traditional models of Anglo-Saxon femininity as passive and long-suffering.[4] Instead, examining *how* the stories of women are told and retold will offer insight into the rhetorical practices of the poem. Feminist

scholars such as Chance, Damico, and Overing have demonstrated
that the women of *Beowulf* are not incidental but integral—indis-
pensable—to the poem's plot, narrative structure, and meaning.
Examining the tellings and retellings of these women's stories, I will
suggest, allows us to better understand the poem's constructions of
(and the limits it imposes on) femininity. The rhetorical model of
female enclosure is, I will argue, fundamentally linked to the poem's
narrative operations.

Recent studies of *Beowulf*—long examined for its oral properties—
demonstrate that the poem is, to a significant extent, conditioned
by a textual or literate consciousness.[5] Late twentieth-century readers
have increasingly seen *Beowulf* as a story about story-telling, a text
that both constructs and contains many other kinds of texts—histories, sermons, lyrics, and so forth—told for the edification and
entertainment of the poem's internal and external audiences alike.
John Niles summarizes the correspondences between orality and
literacy that likely shaped the *Beowulf* audience's response to the
poem:

> [T]he society to which *Beowulf* pertains was using writing,
> and not just oral poetry, to express an ideology capable of
> persuading people to be governed and rulers to govern
> well. . . . They were familiar with the use of poetry in English
> as a vehicle for Christian doctrine and a means of reinventing
> the Germanic past.[6]

Similarly, the stories told within *Beowulf*, while orally transmitted
by its various characters, imply a familiarity or resonance with other
medieval textual traditions. Certain of these stories in fact resonate
with the early medieval ideology of female enclosure. *Beowulf's* rein-
vention of the Germanic past through poetry, as Niles puts it, means
that we need not automatically assume that female enclosure is a
Christian "overlay" added to the poem. Instead, the enclosure of
women (possibly a tradition preserved from the poem's Germanic
past, but certainly a feature of late Anglo-Saxon religious life) offers
us a more complex way of reading the poem's treatment of women
within the context of late Anglo-Saxon Christianity. *Beowulf's* stories
of women build upon and echo each other, so that these "texts"
function intratextually to inform and revise themselves. According

to Fred Robinson, this continual retelling is an integral feature of the poem: "That the poet was emphasizing that his poem is a retelling is suggested by the fact that he includes so much retelling within *Beowulf*. Repeatedly we are asked to listen to one account of an event and to compare it with another."[7]

Beowulf's stories about women form one cohesive set of "retellings." To show that the interdependent narrative threads of these stories all stem from the same source, I will suggest an analogy to a traditional medieval textual practice: each retelling functions as a gloss or commentary on the previous one and signals an interpretive act on the part of the teller. Like glosses on a manuscript page, the poem's stories about women are marginal yet integral to its meaning. To anticipate my argument briefly: we shall see that the originary story of Hildeburh, evidently familiar to the poem's internal and external audiences, represents the scop's version of the traditional "peace-weaver" narrative (discussed below). This is the first telling within the poem (and although the Finn episode seems elliptical to us, it must have been well-known to the *Beowulf* audience). After the scop completes his song, Wealhtheow picks up the narrative and rewrites it, mingling Hildeburh's story with her own and revealing her dissatisfaction with the story's inevitable outcome. Following the intervention of Grendel's Mother, the narrator rewrites the story again in his linked accounts of Hygd and Modthryth. Finally, Beowulf himself concludes the story-telling with predictions about Freawaru that indict the peace-weaving system. Thus the poem contains (encloses) its female characters (and femininity more generally) as it tells and retells their stories. Out of the "text" of Hildeburh an intratextual system develops that both glosses and interprets the roles available to women in the poem. The tropes and thematics of female enclosure govern femininity in *Beowulf* as much as in the female elegies or in more overtly religious literature.

The dominant critical model for women in *Beowulf* has typically been the peace-weaver, *freoðuwebbe*.[8] The metaphor refers to a woman's arranged marriage to a member of a hostile tribe, as a means of securing peace between feuding factions. Such peace might be the result of either childbearing or verbal diplomacy. In either event, the peace-weaver is framed symbolically between two groups of men, confined by a strict kinship system, enclosed by and exchanged between the groups. Ironically, as Chance and Overing have shown, the peace-weaver inevitably fails; the peace rarely lasts for long and peace-weaving often produces death.[9] Yet at the same time, peace-weaving is productive—if only temporarily. Both childbirth and diplomacy (even if short-lived) are creative acts: the peace-weaver produces a "text" that rewrites history, either her own or that of the two tribes. Among the products of peace-weaving are the new stories that develop out of what is already known.

I return, then, to the analogy of the medieval gloss and the textual operations of the commentary tradition. In Martin Irvine's definition, the medieval gloss "is essentially an interpretive supplement, a set of expressions that attempts to disclose some latent or suppressed meaning in an earlier set of expressions."[10] The gloss supplements the source text by providing "an interpretation that is itself a text" (193). The textual activity of glossing works two ways: a gloss looks back to, indeed is dependent upon, the source text, from which it derives its meaning. And it looks ahead, insofar as it creates new meaning, a new interpretation of the source. In Michael Clanchy's useful description, "[t]he successive series of glosses around a central text show, like tree rings, the proliferation of written record over generations of scholars."[11]

The etymological links between weaving and textuality have long been recognized.[12] According to Mary Carruthers:

> The Latin word *textus* comes from the verb meaning 'to weave' and it is in the institutionalizing of a story through *memoria* that textualizing occurs. Literary works become institutions as they weave a community together by providing it with shared experience and a certain kind of language. . . . Their meaning is thought to be implicit, hidden, polysemous and complex, requiring continuing interpretation and adaptation. . . .
>
> In the process of textualizing, the original work acquires commentary and gloss; this activity is not regarded as something other than the text, but is the mark of textualization itself.[13]

Within *Beowulf*, a story such as the Finn episode provides precisely the sort of institutionalizing effect Carruthers identifies: it knits the community at Heorot together through its shared knowledge of the events at Finnsburg. We can trace the process of textualization as the story of Hildeburh—the peace-weaver's story—threads its way through the stories of women told throughout the poem. Each woman's story glosses (that is, reinterprets) the original peace-weaving narrative of the Finn episode. The poem's feminine texts offer a series of readings and rewritings that find closure, finally, through the hero's own indictment of the system they narrate.

AT THE CENTER: HILDEBURH AS FOUNDATIONAL TEXT

Hildeburh, the originary site of feminine textuality in *Beowulf*, is arguably the most fully enclosed woman in Old English literature. She is not technically a player in the main plot of the poem, but is instead a character in a lay sung by Hrothgar's scop during the victory banquet following Beowulf's defeat of Grendel. Her tragic story is so fragmentary and elliptical that we can only assume it was well-known to the poem's internal and external audiences. The scop tells of the legend of Finnsburg, specifically of a breakdown in the alliance formed between the Danes and the Frisians. Hildeburh, the daughter of the former Danish king and sister to the present king, was given in a peace-weaving marriage to Finn, king of the Frisians. When a violent quarrel broke out between the two sides, Hildeburh's brother and son (by Finn) were killed. She ordered a joint funeral pyre for her brother and son, and we are told that she mourned their deaths with song. Following a temporary peace settlement, the hostilities erupted again, Finn was killed, and Hildeburh was transported (along with the other battle spoils) back to her people, the Danes. As the scop finishes his song, festivities at Heorot resume.

The lay begins and ends by focusing closely on Hildeburh; it is obviously her story, and she frames the narrative. At the same time, she is framed by it: this episode of approximately 90 lines (1067–1159) locates Hildeburh at its beginning (1071–74), its midpoint (1114–18), and its end (1157–59).14 Her story is also enclosed (framed) by the two appearances of Wealhtheow, lines 612b–641 and 1162b–91. As Pauline Head has recently demonstrated, framing devices (or ring structures) in Old English literature and art act as interpretive aids to readers or viewers, enabling more nuanced readings of the text within the frame:15

Frames participate in the construction of the reading process. The decorative borders of Anglo-Saxon manuscript
illuminations relate to the images they contain in ways
that complicate interpretation. . . . [T]hey draw attention to
themselves (so that the reader lingers in enjoyment of them
and is aware of the text as something that has been crafted),
and then, often, they overlap with the image, suggesting
that the limit they have traced can be transgressed. The
framing devices of Old English poetry construct a similar
reading process, drawing attention to themselves and over-
lapping semantically with the passage they have defined.
Like all frames, those of Old English poetry guide the reader's
interpretation of the text (mediate between the readers and
text), telling her or him that this linguistic unit exists within
a larger context, yet is in some way distinct from its surroundings (so they also mediate between general and specific).[16]

The Finn episode, then, draws attention to itself by both enclosing
(framing) and being enclosed by (framed by) Hildeburh; this complex structural enclosure is further framed by the two appearances
of Wealhtheow, which, as Head's discussion suggests, overlap with
and guide our interpretation of Hildeburh's story.

Hildeburh's reported speech ordering the funeral pyre occurs at
the precise midpoint of the episode, that is, 45 lines into this 90 line
passage. Though we do not hear her voice, and though many critics
have found her to be hopelessly passive throughout the episode, the
moment at which she orders the funeral pyre is, rather, a moment of
intense narrative, textual, and sensory power. She orders a visual symbol of the destroyed peace accord, and the pyre signals not only the
breakdown in the alliance at Finnsburg, but also the impossibility of
creating peace out of hostility. She, as much as Beowulf will do later,
indicts the system through this gesture.[17] And like the speakers of the
female elegies, she mourns with songs ("geomrode giddum") from
deep within the confines (literal and textual) of her enclosure.

Whereas the speakers of the female elegies, however, found means
of self-expression within their enclosures, Hildeburh's voice is silenced
within the poem, because the litotes introducing her actually removes
the possibility of her speech:

Ne huru Hildeburh   herian þorfte
Eotena treowe;   unsynnum wearð
beloren leofum   æt þam lindplegan
bearnum ond broðrum. . . .   (1071–1074b)

[Nor indeed had Hildeburh need to praise the faith of the
Frisians; she was blameless, deprived of her loved ones, her
son and her brother, at the shield-play.]

The rhetorical figure plays its usual part in providing emphasis
through understatement, yet in this case it also silences Hildeburh,
denying the audience the opportunity to hear her condemnation
of the Frisians. Nevertheless, the narrator absolves her of responsibility for the failed alliance by describing her as "unsynnum,"
blameless; although critics have tended to see Hildeburh as a
"failure" at peace-weaving (Overing, 85), the breakdown in peace
between the Danes and the Frisians is not attributed to her within
the poem.

When Hildeburh does speak, however, as reported by the scop,
she orders the ritual that displays the failed peace:

Het ða Hildeburh   æt Hnæfes ade
hire selfre sunu   sweoloðe befæstan
banfatu bærnan,   ond on bæl don
eame on eaxle.   (1114–1117a)

[Then Hildeburh commanded her own son {to be} entrusted
to the flames on Hnaef's pyre, put on the pyre by his uncle's
side, their bodies {to} burn.]

Symbolically she continues to weave together the two sides of her
family in an alliance—though here the alliance, on the funeral pyre
of her brother and son, is a gruesome parody of the peaceful alliance
her marriage was to have ensured. The burning bodies on the pyre
are described in bloody and graphic terms:

                     . . . hafelan multon,
bengeato burston,   ðonne blod ætspranc,
lað bite lices.   (1120b–1122a)

[Their heads melted, their wounds burst open, the blood sprang out from their bodies' wounds.]

By joining her son's body to that of her brother, Hildeburh symbolically "writes" the violent and deadly results of the hostilities between the two tribes. Not only is the body of her son a kind of "text" she has produced through the creative processes of peace-weaving, but the pyre, too, is her production, her text. When Hildeburh orders the funeral pyre, she performs her own textualizing act. The pyre serves as her commentary or gloss on a peace-weaving system that is, as Overing and others have noted, destined to self-destruct.[18]

The Finn episode is intensely physical. The funeral pyre requires us to focus on the burning bodies of Hildeburh's son and brother. Similarly, Hildeburh's peace-weaving role highlights the functions of her body within the narrative: her social roles as wife and mother are also necessarily physical ones. The narrative asks that we think about Hildeburh in spatial and sensory terms: symbolically framed by groups of men, she views the bodies of her dead relatives "under swegle" [under the sky] (1079a). When she mourns at the funeral pyre, she is not silently weeping, but rather audibly lamenting with songs, "geomrode giddum" (1118a). At the end, she is physically removed from Finn's hall: when the Danes finally seek revenge for Hnaef's death, Finn is killed "ond seo cwen numen" [and the queen taken, 1153b]. The Danes take Finn's treasures for themselves, and Hildeburh, too, is carried back to the Danes' homeland as part of the spoils:

> Sceotend Scyldinga   to scypon feredon
> eal ingesteald   eorðcyninges,
> swylce hie æt Finnes ham   findan meahton
> sigla searogimma.   Hie on sælade
> drihtlice wif   to Denum feredon,
> læddon to leodum.   (1154–1159a)

[The warriors of the Scyldings carried to the ship all the king's house-property, such as they could find at Finn's home, jewels and precious gems. They carried the noble woman to the Danes on a sea-journey, led her to (her?) people.]

The verb "feredon" (carried) describes the Danes' actions in transporting both the treasures and the woman, thus marking Hildeburh as a valuable commodity, one of Finn's treasures. This final mention of Hildeburh either requires us to view her as an object, similar to treasure, or at least reminds us that the Danes view her as such. Either way, she remains firmly under male control, so that leaving Finnsburg to return to her own people does not free her from either physical or social containment.

Even the elements of Hildeburh's name signal her confined social position: "hild" signifies "battle"; "burh" or "burg" means "fortified place" (Klaeber 437). The battle that results when the peace-weaving alliance fails (that is, the battle between the two male kinship groups that frame her) is contained within her very body. She embodies the unsuccessful peace, both as the mother of a dead son who was born of that alliance, and as the agent (the peace-weaver) who originally bound the hostile sides together. As a peace-weaving mother, her body once enclosed the "text" of that peace, and that body, "burh," becomes the site of the battle, "hild"—she is the fortified place where the tribes met and fought. Hildeburh's is the first story we are told in *Beowulf*, and the most deeply embedded structurally. It is, in a sense, the foundation (the fortified place) of feminine textuality in the poem. As a peace-weaver, Hildeburh is enclosed between two groups of men. She is likewise enclosed textually, within the lay of Finnsburg, and framed by Wealhtheow's two appearances. Hildeburh's fragmentary story presumably does not originate with the scop; in retelling the canonical text, he glosses, provides commentary, on that story. His emphasis on the Hildeburh's role may suggest his awareness of one important female listener, Wealhtheow.[19]

FRAMING THE TEXT: WEALHTHEOW RESPONDS

H. Ward Tonsfeldt has shown that the Finn episode is a tightly structured ring composition, with events extending outward in either direction from the central moment when Hildeburh orders the funeral pyre.[20] His schematic opens and closes with the narrator's warning, at lines 1017 and 1163, that the peace between Hrothgar and Hrothulf, his nephew, will be short-lived, and this warning is amplified through the account of the tragic events at Finnsburg. Yet extending this ring structure outward (beyond Tonsfeldt's schematic) reveals that the narrator's warnings, and the story of Hildeburh at Finnsburg, are further enclosed by the two appearances of Wealhtheow, at lines 612–641 and 1162–1232. As we have seen, frame structures in Old English poetry act as interpretive aids, guiding readers' understanding of both the framed text and the frame itself. When Wealhtheow frames the narrative of Hildeburh at Finnsburg, we can see a semantic overlap: the story of Hildeburh may anticipate what Wealhtheow (or any peace-weaver) can expect to be her own fate. But Wealhtheow does not simply replicate Hildeburh's role—she revises it, offering her own interpretation of events at Heorot filtered through her perception of events at Finnsburg.

Wealhtheow's first appearance, lines 612–641, establishes normative peace-weaving behavior, and thus conventional femininity for the poem. Her ceremonial cup-bearing serves to solidify relations between Hrothgar, his retainers, and Beowulf, and she passes the cup to each man in a strictly choreographed scene.[21] Her movements figuratively bind the men and their retainers together. Beowulf's treatment of Wealhtheow suggests that her role is not simply ceremonial, however; in response to her greeting and exhortation he offers his binding resolution to defeat Grendel or die trying. The narrator emphasizes the fact that Wealhtheow's response matters by stating, "Ðam wife þa word wel licodon" [the woman liked those words very much, 639]. Yet although Wealhtheow figures prominently in this opening frame, she remains fully conventional, and her words and actions seem only to represent Hrothgar's desires. After listening to Beowulf's pledge, she returns to Hrothgar's side (641b).[22]

Wealhtheow's second appearance completes the narrative frame that encloses the story of Hildeburh, and she glosses or interprets that story. Although her actions and speech in this second scene suggest the possibility of subversion, of a woman's expression beyond her enclosure, the possibility is short-lived. Wealhtheow's ability to influence events beyond her enclosure is stopped short by the narrative intervention of Grendel's Mother. We shall see that any prospect of an unenclosed peace-weaver in the poem is forestalled with this monstrous reminder of the dangers of unconfined femininity.

In this second appearance, Wealhtheow weaves her way, gold-adorned, among the warriors, but here the similarities to her first appearance end:

Þa cwom Wealhþeo forð
gan under gyldnum beage   þær þa godan twegen
sæton suhtergefæderan;   þa gyt wæs hiera sib ætgædere,
æghwylc oðrum trywe.

. . . .

                Spræc ða ides Scyldinga:
(1162b–1164; 1168b, emphasis added)

[*Then* Wealhtheow came forward, walking under a golden
crown to where the two good men sat, nephew and uncle;
their peace was as yet unbroken, each true to the other. . . .
Then the woman of the Scyldings spoke.]

Wealhtheow's first speech follows the scop's tale of Finnsburg almost
immediately, and the temporal adverbs (1162b, 1168b) that bring
her forward and introduce her speech may signal a causal connection between her words and the story of Hildeburh. Wealhtheow
seems compelled to respond to the lay. She must, in particular, offer
up her interpretation to the two people most directly implicated by
it: Hrothgar and Hrothulf. Whereas in her first appearance, her
indirect discourse seemed a mere extension of Hrothgar's wishes,
the direct discourse of her two speeches marks a change. She resists
the unsatisfactory fate of Hildeburh by trying to ensure that events
in her own community unfold differently. Her speeches offer up her
interpretation of the Finnsburg episode as well as her attempts to
revise the ending.

    Wealhtheow's first speech, as Helen Damico has shown, is
controlled by imperative verbs, directed toward Hrothgar:[23]

Onfoh þissum fulle,   freodrihten min,
sinces brytta!   Þu on sælum wes,
goldwine gumena,   ond to Geatum spræc
mildum wordum,   swa sceal man don!
Beo wið Geatas glæd,   geofena gemyndig,
nean ond feorran   þu nu hafast.
Me man sægde,   þæt þu ðe for sunu wolde
hereri[n]c habban.   Heorot is gefælsod,
beahsele beorhta;   bruc þenden þu mote
manigra medo,   ond þinum magum læf

folc ond rice,   þonne ðu forð scyle,
metodsceaft seon.   (1169–1180a)

[Take this cup, my noble lord, giver of treasure. Be joyful,
gold-friend of men, and speak kind words to the Geats, so
should one do. Be gracious with the Geats, mindful of the
gifts near and far that you now have. Someone has told me
that you would have the warrior {Beowulf} for your son.
Heorot, the bright ring-hall, is cleansed; make use of your
many rewards while you can, and leave to your kinsmen
the people and kingdom when you shall go forth to see the
decree of fate.]

Through her strategic use of syntax, Wealhtheow's peace-weaving
words ("Onfoh þissum fulle" [1169a]; "Þu on sælum wes" [1170b]; etc.)
actually cushion her harsher intent: to tell Hrothgar that his pledge
to make Beowulf his adopted son and heir is not acceptable. She
will, instead, promote their nephew Hrothulf as heir to the throne,
thereby ensuring the eventual succession of her own sons.[24] Having
just witnessed the strife that can occur when the peace pledge fails,
she seems to be deliberately trying to avoid Hildeburh's fate. Thus
she creates a new version of the traditional peace-weaving text, a
new ending; rather than passively accepting events as they unfold
(as the men determine them), she wishes to shape the future herself.
Her commentary on Hildeburh's story is likewise seen in her opti-
mistic prediction that Hrothulf will treat her sons well; she is trying
to write a happier ending for her sons than that suffered by Hildeburh's son. By asserting that women can surmount the passive peace-
weaver role in order to influence political and dynastic decisions,
Wealhtheow actively rewrites the story of Hildeburh. Her commentary thus locates creative "textual" production at the site of female
enclosure. Even as her appearances encircle Hildeburh within the
narrative, her "reading" of Hildeburh grows outward from, and surrounds, that unsatisfactory peace-weaving narrative by offering a
new ending.

The short passage (1192–1214) that is textually framed between
Wealhtheow's two speeches also revises the peace-weaver's role. In
particular, it revises Wealhtheow's first appearance. Just as the Finn
episode opened up for Wealhtheow a space to speak within the

poem, after her first speech she has a new acting role, since she no longer appears to participate in the cupbearing ritual seen previously. Rather, beginning with line 1192, the actions of cupbearing are described with passive verbs.[25] The agent of these actions is invisible, written out of the picture syntactically:

> Him wæs ful boren,   ond freondlaþu
> wordum bewægned,   ond wunden gold
> estum geeawed,   earm[h]reade twa,
> hrægl ond hringas,   healsbeaga mæst
> þara þe ic on foldan   gefrægen hæbbe.   (1192–1196)

[The cup was carried to him and friendship offered with words, and twisted gold courteously presented {to him}. Two arm ornaments, a corselet, and rings, {and} the greatest of neck-rings I have ever heard about on earth.]

Whereas in the first cupbearing scene, Wealhtheow was the subject of the verbs ("Eode Wealhtheow forð," Weltheow went forth, 612b; "þa freolic wif ful gesealde," the noble woman gave the cup, 615; "grette Geata leod," she greeted the man of the Geats, 625; etc.), the agent of the passive verbs in this second passage is unspecified. If the agent were Wealhtheow, the poet would presumably have used syntax similar to that of the first cupbearing scene. Perhaps the cupbearer now is Freawaru, who we later learn also performed this activity during Beowulf's stay at Hrothgar's court. If Wealhtheow's main function is to initiate and perform the cupbearing ritual, as Michael Enright has recently argued, what happens when she stops serving?[26] Her transformation from a silent cupbearer to a commanding speaking presence is a rewriting of the peace-weaver's role and a disruption of it as well. By reprimanding Hrothgar and abandoning the ceremonial tasks of the peace-weaver, Wealhtheow unsettles (unweaves) the relationship he is attempting to build with Beowulf, even as she works to bind Hrothgar more closely to his own kin.

The narrative lingers only briefly on this cupbearing activity, but it keeps Wealhtheow firmly in mind as it describes the gifts bestowed on Beowulf and makes the first of several allusions to the death of Hygelac, Beowulf's king, in a fatal raid on the Frisians. John Leyerle has explained the structural operations of these allusions:

The poem interlaces these episodes to achieve juxtapositions impossible in a linear narrative. In the first episode the gift of a precious golden torque to Beowulf for killing Grendel is interrupted by an allusion to its loss years later when Hygelac is killed. Hygelac's death seeking Frisian treasure foreshadows Beowulf's death seeking the dragon's hoard. The transience of gold and its connection with violence are obvious.[27]

Perhaps not so obvious, but no less present, are the connections this scene establishes between Wealhtheow and Hygd, both of whom try to determine political and familial succession via the conduit of Beowulf. The narrator's allusion to Hygelac's fate is prompted by the neck-ring, an object that later in the poem links Wealhtheow to Hygd. Wealhtheow's two speeches frame this digression, and, as usual, the framing device both illuminates and is illuminated by the text it frames. Her first speech exposes the potential instability that could result from Hrothgar's rash promise of his kingdom to Beowulf and thereby anticipates the later predicament of Hygd, who likewise will try to determine political succession after Hygelac's death. The neck-ring symbolically links the two events. Stephanie Hollis has argued that Hygd's offer "endorses, *in principle*, the rectitude of Wealhtheow's involvement in determining the succession of the throne that she shares."[28] Yet however "right" we may see their actions to be, the poem does not permit Wealhtheow or Hygd to leave off being peace-weavers in order to become independent political thinkers. Peace-weaving, as an enclosed social role, does not allow them to operate outside of their frame of reference, to shape events independently from their husbands. In both cases, when Wealhtheow and Hygd try to shape political events, they are juxtaposed with a socially threatening female counterpart: Grendel's Mother and Modthryth, respectively, exemplars of the dangers of uncontrolled feminine power.

Following the neck-ring digression, Wealhtheow again becomes the agent of the active verbs as she begins her second speech. This speech too is governed by imperative verbs that signal her appropriation of an active political role. Paradoxically, although we might today read her actions as positive examples of feminine assertiveness, within the poem they represent the incipient disintegration of society.

By reprimanding Hrothgar, she undermines his authority.[29] Likewise, when she uses imperative verbs to address Beowulf, her act of commanding revises the passive peace-weaving role. Elaine Tuttle Hansen has shown that this type of "instructional" discourse, governed by imperative verbs, is typical of wisdom literature, which for Old English poetry often meant a father's instructions for his son, as in the Old English *Precepts*. The imperative mood, according to Hansen, "marks an utterance with the assumption of an authority that needs no justification for its right to command and expect obedience."[30] Thus only when Wealhtheow appropriates a specifically masculine form of syntax is she able to participate discursively. In her speeches she revises and transcends the conventionally silent, acquiescent peace-weaving role (as exemplified by Hildeburh) and assumes a masculine guise. We will see in the discussion of Grendel's mother below that the transgression of gender boundaries is one of the most threatening acts of the poem. When Wealhtheow adopts the language of a masculine genre for her own purposes, both her actions and her speech signal her desire to change the story, to revise the Hildeburh model, to write a new ending.

Yet in response to Hildeburh's firmly enclosed status, Wealhtheow offers only a partial possibility of release from the social and material bonds that confine the peace-weaver. Following her two speeches, Wealhtheow is silent, seen only once more as she (along with other members of Hrothgar's court) gazes silently at the head of Grendel that Beowulf has brought back from the mere. In this last image she is again subordinated to the more active males:

Þa wæs be feaxe   on flet boren
Grendles heafod,   þær guman druncon,
egeslic for eorlum   ond þære idese mid,
wliteseon wrætlic;   weras on sawon.   (1647–1650)

[Then Grendel's head was carried by its hair over the floor to where the men drank, terrible for the warriors, and the woman with them, a wondrous sight. The men looked at it.]

Here Wealhtheow is fully marginal, included almost as an afterthought among the group gazing on the monstrous head. Like

Hildeburh, she ends up nameless and inactive. This final "containment" of Wealhtheow is linked to our initial view of her, so that her active speaking role is framed by two scenes where she is passive and silent. The display of Grendel's head, of course, follows Beowulf's defeat of Grendel's Mother, who is paired with Wealhtheow in an instructive way. Grendel's Mother teaches us about the dangers of feminine power and authority and how to control them; thus it is no coincidence that Wealhtheow is framed between two mourning mothers, Hildeburh and Grendel's Mother, each—like Wealhtheow— seeking power in her own right, yet each powerless in the end.

WITHIN THE MERE: READING GRENDEL'S MOTHER

Grendel's Mother is undoubtedly the least enclosed woman in Old English literature. She and Hildeburh frame Wealhtheow in what appears to be a strictly regulated continuum moving from containment to release; Wealhtheow tries to move towards Grendel's Mother's end, but finally becomes more like Hildeburh. In the case of all three women, and in early English literature more generally, female escape from enclosure is undesirable. Within a system that deeply values female enclosure, it is precisely because Grendel's Mother is able to transgress boundaries that she is especially dangerous.

What makes Grendel's Mother so monstrous? She poses a real threat to Beowulf, of course, but the narrator diminishes her power early on by stating that she was less terrible than her son just as women are less powerful than men (1282b–1287). Thus her gender is foregrounded and linked to her actions. Although her species has been a matter of critical debate, it is legitimate to read her as a woman; not only are many of the epithets that describe her also used for other women in the poem, but descriptions of her thoughts and actions personify her.[31] She is, for example, "yrmþe gemunde," mindful of misery (1259b), her adventure is "sorhfulne," sorrowful (1277a), and her action vengeful (1278). I suggest that her position within (or more accurately, outside of) the society of the poem is so monstrous because she is a woman. Given that we will probably never come to a definitive understanding of such fundamental characteristics as her gender and species, we should consider instead the effect of not defining them. Nameless, indescribable, and illimitable, Grendel's Mother likewise stands outside of the institutional enclosure that governs the other women in the poem. Significantly, she is contained, named, and made known by the hero himself.

Grendel's nameless Mother occupies a substantial portion of the poem—roughly 400 lines. She is identified only by her biological function of having given birth to Grendel (a role that links her to nearly all the other women in the poem). Her namelessness defines her place in the poem's symbolic order: if naming one's enemies is a form of controlling them, this particular enemy is initially beyond control. According to Seth Lerer's recent analysis, one role of the act of naming in *Beowulf* is to diffuse anxiety.[32] Such naming becomes part of the larger project of story-telling, which instructs and entertains, and thus disempowers the named character or object by placing it within the familiar frame of language. Yet one fundamental threat goes unnamed: uncontrolled feminine power and sexuality in the form of the uncontained Grendel's Mother. She alone remains outside of the peace-weaving economy of exchange, and thus outside of any kind of physical or cultural enclosure.

The uncontainability of Grendel's Mother is mirrored neatly by the lexical ambiguities of her descriptions—neither male nor female, human nor animal. Yet the language used to describe her is centrally concerned with the thematics of enclosure we see informing all representations of women in *Beowulf*. In the case of Grendel's Mother, this means references to movement, space, boundaries, and borders—or the lack thereof. Both she and Grendel are "micle mearc-stapan," huge border-wanderers, 1348a, who keep to the moors ("moras healdan," 1348b); she goes on a sorrowful journey ("sorhfulne sið," 1278a) to avenge her son's death. Her attack on Æschere is marked by rapid movement: "Heo wæs on ofste,   wolde ut þanon, / . . . hraðe heo æþelinga   anne hæfde / fæste befangen,   þa heo to fenne gang" [she was in haste, wanted to get out of there. . . . Quickly she firmly grasped one of the noblemen, then she went to the fen, 1292a–95b].

When Hrothgar describes this event to Beowulf, he emphasizes her mysteriousness and her mobility by calling her "wælgæst wæfre" [wandering murderous spirit, 1331]. "Wæfre" (wandering) is a word associated with death in *Beowulf*; its two other occurrences (at 1150 and 2420) describe the events leading up to the final battle at Finnsburg, and Beowulf's fight with the dragon, respectively. In both of these cases, however, the adjective describes a wandering or fluctuating set of thoughts. Before Beowulf fights the dragon, his mind is sorrowful, restless, and ready for death: "Him wæs geomor sefa, / wæfre and wælfus" (2419–2420). Similarly, in recounting the Danes' final revenge on Finn, the narrator explains, "ne meahte wæfre mod / forhabban in hreþre" [The restless spirit could not remain in the breast, 1150–1151]. Both other occurrences describe a mental or emotional condition, but when "wæfre" describes Grendel's Mother it specifies her physical movement.[33]

Moreover, Hrothgar's account of the mere concerns its lack of limits: "No þæs frod leofað / gumena bearna, þæt þone grund wite" [There is no one of the sons of men wise {enough} who knows the bottom, 1366b–1367]. The rich descriptions mystify, rather than explain the mere:

> Hie dygel lond
> warigeað wulfhleoþu, windige næssas,
> frecne fengelad, ðær fyrgenstream
> under næssa genipu niþer gewiteð,
> flod under foldan. Nis þæt feor heonon
> milgemearces, þæt se mere standeð;
> ofer þæm hongiað hrinde bearwas,
> wudu wyrtum fæst wæter oferhelmað.
> Þær mæg nihta gehwæm niðwundor seon,
> fyr on flode. (1357b–1366a)

[They dwell in a secret land, the wolf-slopes, the windy headlands, the perilous fen-paths, where the mountain stream goes downwards under the headlands' mist, water under the earth. It is not far from here, in terms of miles, that the mere stands; frost-covered groves hang over it, the root-bound woods hang over the water. Each night one may see there a fearful wonder, fire on the water.]

Thus the space occupied by Grendel's Mother is really indescribable: it is secret, dangerous, under darkness, under the earth, a wonder. It can only be reached via a narrow and unknown path. As Hrothgar reminds Beowulf, "Eard git ne const, / frecne stowe, ðær þu findan miht / sinnigne secg; sec gif þu dyrre!" [You do not yet know the region, the terrible place, where you might find the sinful one; seek {her} if you dare].[34] Beowulf's response begins the process of confining Grendel's Mother:

> Ic hit þe gehate:　　　no he on helm losaþ,
> ne on foldan fæþm,　　ne on fyrgenholt,
> ne on gyfenes grund,　　ga þær he wille!　　(1392–1394)

> [I promise you this: {s}he will not escape into protection
> nor into the bosom of the earth, nor in the mountain woods,
> nor on the bottom of the sea; go where {s}he will.]

Beowulf limits the possibilities of her mobility. His own discourse begins to contain Grendel's Mother; his battle and eventual beheading of her will finish the task.

So far we have seen two ways that Grendel's Mother blurs conventional gender boundaries: at the level of language, she is described as both "wif" (woman) and "secg" (man); and at the level of plot, she is the only woman to wander outside her allotted space, the mere. Her third transgression of gender boundaries is social: she avenges the death of her son, a masculine action. As Jane Chance has argued, "it is monstrous for a mother to 'avenge' her son (2121) as if she were a retainer, he were her lord, and avenging more important than peace making" (*Woman as Hero*, 101). Grendel's Mother is physical, not verbal, and she uses violence rather than language to achieve her goals. She is thus unenclosed both literally and figuratively; after Grendel's death, no "imprisoning" male relatives govern her actions. Her environment is not a male-controlled enclosure, such as Heorot, but a fluid, bloody, feminized space that suggests as well the mysteries of the female body and the (perceived) dangers that lurk therein.[35]

In his battle with Grendel's Mother, Beowulf dominates and destroys the feminine threat.[36] The battle embodies both the disruption and the righting of *Beowulfian* gender boundaries. When Beowulf enters the mere, Grendel's Mother recognizes the violation (1497–1500) and seeks to reverse it by attempting to penetrate his armor with her fingers, but: "hring utan ymbbearh, / þæt heo þone fyrdhom　　ðurhfon ne mihte, / locene leoðosyrcan　la þan fingrum" [his ring-mail protected him from without, so that she could not penetrate that war-dress, the linked mailshirt, with her hateful fingers

(1504b–1505)]. His armor is impenetrable. The most dramatic moment in the action comes when the sword fails Beowulf, when it looks as though Grendel's Mother may overwhelm him. The ensuing struggle plays out anxieties about female sexuality: she again tries to penetrate his armor, this time with her blade, and she again fails (1545–1549). Her failure is mandated by the principles of female enclosure, which do not permit women to breach boundaries. Grendel's Mother, destined to exist on the borders of society, cannot cross the border of that society's most representative body. Beowulf's armor acts as both a literal and social barrier that she cannot cross.

Of course, at this moment, Beowulf spies the ancient sword and plunges it into Grendel's Mother's body (thereby reversing the rape imagery), killing her: "bil eal ðurhwod / fægne flæschoman" [the blade went through the doomed body (1567b–1568a)]. He then cuts off Grendel's head, bringing both it and the sword-hilt back to Hrothgar as his battle-spoils. Both of these prizes can be read as the "texts" of Grendel's Mother, subsuming her into the peace-weaving paradigm. The "texts" woven by the peace-weavers in *Beowulf* are their sons. In this respect, Grendel, as her product, is a failed attempt at perpetuating her lineage, a "giedd" (in the terms of "Wulf and Eadwacer") that "næfre gesomnad wæs." Like the speaker of the female elegy, and like Hildeburh, Grendel's Mother is contained by a system that leaves her alone to mourn the death of her son.

Lest this message of female containment be lost on the various audiences within and outside of the poem, Beowulf himself offers a re-telling of his fight with Grendel's Mother when he returns to Hygelac's court. Grendel's Mother, Beowulf tells Hygelac, carried Æschere's body away to a spot "(un)der firgenstream" [under a mountain stream, 2128b], here the sole descriptor of a place that previously took several lines to describe. He similarly downplays his entry into the mere:

> Ic ða ðæs wælmes,   þe is wide cuð,
> grimne gryrelicne   grundhyrde fond.
> Þær unc hwile wæs   hand gemæne;
> holm heolfre weoll,   ond ic heafde becearf
> in ðam [guð]sele   Grendeles modor
> eacnum ecgum;   unsofte þonan
> feorh oðferede;   (2135–2141a)

[I then found the guardian of the deep water, the grim terror,
as is now widely known. For a while we shared hands {in
battle}; the sea welled with blood, and with a powerful
sword-edge, I cut off the head of Grendel's Mother in the
battle-hall; with difficulty I went from there with my life.]

Thus the bloody and bottomless pit has become simply "the deep
water," and the horror of Grendel's Mother is reduced to a single
half-line, "grimne gryrelicne" (2136a). The dangerous battle is made
to seem roughly equitable until Beowulf prevails. Most importantly,
the horror of Grendel's Mother "þe is wide cuð" [is now widely
known, 2135b], contained and unfrightening.

(EN)CLOSING THE LOOP:
READING HYGD, MODTHRYTH, AND FREAWARU

Following the intervention of Grendel's Mother, three final stories
about women in *Beowulf*—Hygd, Modthryth, and Freawaru—serve
to interpret and supplement those stories already told.[37] Structurally, these stories conform to a tightly regulated pattern. The stories
of Hygd and Modthryth, intertwined in the manuscript, present
interpretations of the two paradigms of women seen thus far in the
story. Just as Beowulf was responsible for both destroying Grendel's
Mother and reducing the anxiety she provoked by telling a greatly
diminished version of her story, so too the narrative accounts of
both Hygd and Modthryth offer diminished and contained versions
of the poem's two models of femininity (passive and active). Beowulf's
predictions about the future of Freawaru—a text which itself is deeply
embedded within other women's texts—effectively ends the story-
cycle by normalizing her story, asserting the peace-weaver's failure
as the inevitable order of things.

The stories of Hygd, Modthryth, and Freawaru are significant
both structurally and thematically. Structurally, these stories form a
ring composition or multiple framework of the sort that has often
been identified as a governing structural principle within the poem,
and that we have seen operating with some regularity in the stories
of *Beowulf's* women. Like the frames discussed earlier, ring structures invite readers' attention and participate in the construction of
meaning. John Niles has usefully defined ring composition as:

a chiastic design in which the last element in a series in some way echoes the first, the next to the last the second, and so on. Often the series centers on a single kernel, which may serve as the key element. . . . The poet uses ring composition as a means of traveling from the immediate reality . . . to an 'other' legendary reality that is used as a point of comparison . . . then back again to the present reality.[38]

This is precisely the design of the three final women's stories in *Beowulf*. A brief summary of how this pattern governs these three stories will be helpful before going into a more detailed analysis of how each revises prior "texts" and how the passage overall establishes the peace-weaving paradigm as one of firm and stable enclosure.

The initial description of Hygd, linked to the later passage in which she receives Wealhtheow's gift of a neck-ring, opens the frame for these final stories. This frame encompasses, within only 150 lines, five stories about women. Structurally, the stories are precisely balanced:

A. initial description of **Hygd** (1926–1931a, ca. 5 lines)
  B. description of **Modthryth** (1931b–1962, ca. 30 lines)
    C. Beowulf's prediction of **Freawaru's** future (2016b–2069a, ca. 50 lines)
  B[1]. Beowulf's description of **Grendel's Mother** (2115–2144, ca. 30 lines)
A[1]. Beowulf gives **Hygd** the neck-ring (2172–2176, ca. 5 lines)

The opening and closing descriptions of Hygd firmly identify her as a conventional peace-weaver, and the final passage links her to Wealhtheow through the exchange of the neck-ring. Likewise, the story of the evil Modthryth is symmetrically balanced with Beowulf's narration of his fight with Grendel's Mother. Embedded deep within frames A and B, A[1] and B[1], is Beowulf's prediction (C) about the inevitable failure of Freawaru's peace-weaving alliance, the lengthiest of the stories at roughly fifty lines. Thus the accounts of Hygd enclose the two stories of tamed feminine aggression and transgression; these in turn enclose the doomed peace-weaver of the future, Freawaru.

The narrator's first mention of Hygd explicitly recalls that of Wealhtheow—both passages catalogue queenly behavior. Though young, Hygd is "wis welþungen," wise and accomplished (1927). She is generous and kind, "næs hio hnah swa þeah / ne to gneað gifa" (1929b–1930a), and like Wealhtheow she distributes treasures, "maþmgestreona" (1931a). Like the other peace-weavers, Hygd is married and thus confined symbolically. The descriptive language encloses her as well: she is "under burhlocan" [under or within the castle-enclosure, 1928], so that her world, like Wealhtheow's, does not extend beyond the walls of her husband's court. Later the narrator makes the connection between the two women explicit:

> Hyrde ic þæt he ðone healsbeah   Hygde gesealde,
> wrætlicne wundurmaððum,   ðone þe him Wealhðeo geaf,
> ðeod(nes) dohtor,   þrio wicg somod
> swancor ond sadolbeorht;   hyre syððan wæs
> æfter beahðege   br[e]ost geweorðod.   (2172–2176)

> [Then I heard that he {Beowulf} gave the neck-ring to Hygd, the splendid, wondrous jewel that Wealhtheow gave him; {gave it} to the king's daughter, {and} three horses also, supple and saddle-bright; afterwards, her breast was adorned on account of receiving the neck-ring.]

This five-line passage, which closes the frame around the women's stories, is itself a brief ring composition, with the neck-ring literally encircling the passage ("healsbeah," 2172, and "beahðege," 2176) and encircling also Hygd herself, embedded in the passage as "ðeod(nes) dohtor," surrounded by descriptions of bright treasure. The circular image of the neck-ring is perfectly appropriate for joining and circumscribing (both literally and figuratively) these two idealized women. Thus Hygd's story is a solid link in the intratextual chain, and lest we miss its significance, the narrator evokes the image of Hygd's breast, adorned with the neck-ring. The grammatical construction of the passage is curiously passive; the neck-ring itself seems to be the true agent of the action, or rather, perhaps, the vehicle through which Beowulf transacts the exchange between women.

The account of Modthryth, as has often been noted, marks a surprising intervention into Hygd's story.[39] Modthryth is notable in part because her story is one of the few in Old English poetry that actually uses the term "peace-weaver," "freoðuwebbe" (1942a)—here used to define what Modthryth is not. The possibly faulty manuscript does not permit us to know whether the relationship between Hygd and Modthryth is deliberate, or even if such a relationship existed, but the contrast between the behavior of the two women is explicit.[40]

In telling Modthryth's story, the narrator rewrites the text of Grendel's Mother by filtering it through the lenses of Hildeburh, Wealhtheow, and Hygd. Through this interpretive act, the anti-peace-weaver is tamed and reconfigured to fit the poem's own social values. Modthryth initially resembles Grendel's Mother: violent, unviewable in daylight, fatal for men to encounter. Overing writes:

> Modthryth causes a temporary shudder of discomfort, fol-
> lowed by a generalized sigh of relief that the disorder she
> threatens has been contained and that things are once more
> under the control of the masculine economy.   (103)

The "shudder of discomfort" must certainly stem from Modthryth's evocation of Grendel's Mother and Beowulf's close call with her. Like Grendel's Mother, Modthryth seizes with "deadly bonds," "wælbende" (1936a), any man who dares to penetrate her personal domain. For Grendel's Mother, that domain was a physical space, the mere. For Modthryth, the domain is more ephemeral, but no less personal: she demands that any man who dares to look at her be killed (1932–1940a). Death in both scenes is determined by sword, and it seems likely that the shudder Modthryth evokes is the glimpse into what could have been Beowulf's fate. The Modthryth passage leaves ambiguous just what exactly (that is, whose death) is settled by sword—presumably the death of those men who stare at her. Yet we have already seen the outcome of one such sexual battle, when feminine aggression was tamed through the death of Grendel's Mother. The symmetry of these two stories links and compares the two "texts." Modthryth's story revises that of Grendel's Mother and proposes an alternate ending, as Modthryth is transformed into a model queen.

Like Grendel's Mother, Modthryth temporarily subverts norma-tive gender paradigms in the poem, even as her story illustrates the process by which a woman moves from outside to inside; that is, it narrates the process of her enclosure or domestication.[41] We can see this as a kind of "reading process" in which the poem reads the stories of earlier women into its account of Modthryth's behavior. The audience evaluates that behavior based on what they (and we) know about the roles open to women in the poem. To diffuse the disruptive feminine threat, Modthryth is tamed, confined within a marriage, after which, we are told, she becomes a good queen, conforming to the models we have already seen of Wealhtheow and Hygd.[42]

Regardless of the extent, however, to which Modthryth is able to subvert normative gender, the lesson of her story is that enclosure within the social structure of marriage is essential for conventional femininity. A woman outside the system must be contained. Her unconventional (unpeace-weaver-like) behavior clearly meets with the narrator's disapproval: "Ne bið swylc cwenlic þeaw / idese to efnanne,   þeah ðe hio ænlicu sy, / þætte freoðuwebbe   feores onsæce / after ligetorne   leofne mannan" [That was not a queenly custom for a woman to perform, though she be beautiful, that a peace-weaver should deprive a dear man of life after a pretended injury, 1940b–1943]. Once she is contained by marriage, Modthryth's threat is diffused as her story is appropriated and retold by ale-drinking men: "ealodrincende oðer sædan" [ale-drinkers told another story, 1945]. Once married, they say, Modthryth became famous for her goodness: "ðær hio syððan well / in gumstole,   gode mære, / lifgesceafta lifigende breac" [There on the throne she was afterwards famous for generosity, while living made use of her life, 1951b–1953].[43] The words contain her both spatially (on her throne) and narratively, rejecting her violent behavior. Female characters in *Beowulf* are most threatening when they produce death; peace-weaving can only signify as a creative act. When women cannot be identified as mothers, or when mothers produce death, the social order perceives its greatest threat. The threat is controlled through the poem's readings and revisions of both of these dangerous women, as their stories are framed by the normative accounts of peace-weavers.[44]

The final woman's story in *Beowulf* is that of Freawaru, Hrothgar and Wealhtheow's daughter. Beowulf himself tells this story, as a revised version of the stories he has heard (or seen) so far. In short, he predicts that the marriage Hrothgar has arranged for his daughter with Ingeld is doomed to failure, because the presence of Freawaru and her retainers at her husband's court will painfully remind the Heathobards of their long-standing feud with the Danes (2024b–2069a). Such a situation is ripe for violence, Beowulf asserts, "þeah seo bryd duge" [though the bride be good, 2031b]. Beowulf's story interprets texts he knows already: the story of Hildeburh, the resulting political negotiations at Heorot, the facts he has evidently learned there about Freawaru's impending marriage. He turns the story into an explicit commentary on the shortcomings of tribal warfare and the resultant impossibility of weaving a permanent peace between hostile factions—which leads, ironically, to the impossibility of permanent female enclosure. The transient settlements achieved through peace-weaving alliances can ensure female enclosure only temporarily, and thus the threat of unenclosed women can never be fully eradicated.

Beowulf's commentary on peace-weaving establishes, finally, textual production in the poem as a masculine act. Put in a somewhat complicated way: Freawaru's story is Beowulf's reading of Wealhtheow's reading of the scop's reading of Hildeburh. Freawaru's story is Hildeburh's, at several removes, filtered through every other woman's story, including those of Grendel's Mother, Hygd, and Modthryth. In Beowulf's prediction, the old Heathobard will incite the young warrior to break the peace with the Danes, because in Hildeburh's story, men's language created violence and death. Likewise, the old Heathobard's speech will destroy Freawaru's peace-weaving. The containment of feminine textuality in the poem is thus realized when Beowulf interprets known texts to "write" Freawaru's future.

The story of women in *Beowulf* effectively ends when the narrator interprets Beowulf's reading of Freawaru in a passage that essentially sums up the hero's lesson about the hopelessness of the heroic ideal:

> Swa sceal mæg don
> nealles inwitnet   oðrum bregdon
> dyrnum cræfte,   deað ren(ian)
> hondgesteallan.   (2166b–2169a)

[So should kinsmen do, not weave nets of malice for each other through secret skill, {nor} prepare death for their companions.]

The narrator's weaving imagery recalls the distinction made earlier by Beowulf between women's and men's acts. One ought not to use weaving to create violence, because weaving is a feminine craft through which women attempt to ensure peace. Once again, the poem foregrounds the dangers of transgressing gender boundaries.

The structural embeddedness of Freawaru's story is significant, but its greater message, I would argue, lies in the fact that Beowulf himself tells the story. We have seen a wide variety of female transgressions, both corporeal and textual, in the poem, ranging from Wealhtheow's appropriation of masculinist discourse to the death-producing acts of Grendel's Mother and Modthryth. Beowulf's final act of narrative containment limits the multiplying textual links between women in the poem and ensures that no further interpretations are possible (a point confirmed by the fleeting descriptions of Grendel's Mother and Hygd that close the frame). Beowulf's narrative achieves closure: except for a brief mention of Hygd (2369–2372, in a passage reminiscent of Wealhtheow), no other named women appear in the poem.

In effect, *Beowulf* produces its category of "the feminine" through its ever-expanding repetition and interpretation of the enclosed peace-weaver motif. The hero himself sets the limits for this expansion. In this way, Beowulf illustrates Judith Butler's concept of gender performativity:

> Gender is . . . *a set of repeated acts within a highly rigid regulatory frame* that congeal over time to produce the appearance of substance, of a natural sort of being. A political genealogy of gender ontologies, if it is successful, will deconstruct the substantive appearance of gender into its constitutive acts and locate and account for those acts *within the compulsory frames set by the various forces that police the social appearance of gender.* (*Gender Trouble*, 33; emphasis added)

Examining the women's stories in *Beowulf* as discrete yet interdependent strands of the same fabric permits us to analyze the poem's gender operations in the way Butler proposes. A rhetoric of enclosure "frames" women in the poem (and in Old English literature more generally) so that the condition of being framed or enclosed produces femininity. When enclosure (seen in a variety of social and textual structures) begins to be seen as normative or "natural" for the women of *Beowulf*, any divergence from that norm—that is, any escape or release from enclosure such as we see to varying degrees in nearly all the women in the poem—is necessarily unnatural, unfeminine. The condition of enclosed femininity is, in this formulation, one of the forces that determines "the social appearance of gender."

The textual and rhetorical enclosure of women in Beowulf illustrates the broad sociocultural conventions of female enclosure at work in early medieval England. *Beowulf*, a text that, regardless of its site of production, is hardly likely to be directly concerned with issues of female monasticism, nevertheless displays the cultural thematic of enclosure as an identifying mark of the feminine. Structurally, framing devices and ring patterns can be found throughout the poem, of course; they are not exclusive to its treatment of women. But when women are treated by the poem, framing devices are ubiquitous—all women in *Beowulf* frame and are framed by each other, and both the frames and the framed texts (the enclosures and the enclosed) are mutually interpretive entities. By separating the monolithic figure of the peace-weaver into its individual acts, or stories, and by examining how each appearance interprets and develops each prior and each subsequent woman's story, we can better understand how *Beowulf* normalizes and regulates femininity. In the following chapters we shall see that this structural duality of enclosure and enclosed continues to work both literally and figuratively. The bodies of women in *Juliana* and Ælfric's *Lives of Saints* themselves act as enclosures, even as the texts, like *Beowulf*, find multiple ways of enclosing those bodies.

NOTES

1. Paull F. Baum, "The *Beowulf* Poet," *Philological Quarterly* 39 (1960): 389–399; rpt. in *An Anthology of* Beowulf *Criticism*, ed. Lewis E. Nicholson (Notre Dame and London: University of Notre Dame Press, 1963): 353–365. References to the 1963 version will be provided parenthetically in my text.

2. I use the term "written" rather than "composed" or "originated" because I am primarily interested in the late Anglo-Saxon Christian culture that preserved the poem in the manuscript form that we have today. The debate surrounding the date of the poem continues, and I will not engage that debate here. For my purposes, I will consider the date of the poem to be the date of the manuscript. For a recent and cogent overview of the dating controversy, see Roy Michael Liuzza, "On the Dating of *Beowulf*," in Beowulf: *Basic Readings*, ed. Peter S. Baker (New York: Garland, 1995): 281–302.

3. The relationship between *Beowulf* and Christianity has, of course, long been a matter of critical debate; scholars now largely agree that the poem as it is preserved in the manuscript has been shaped by the cultural manifestations of Christianity in Anglo-Saxon England, and thus represents a fusion of pre-Christian Germanic and Christian Latinate cultures. For a general overview of the relationship, see Fred C. Robinson, *"Beowulf,"* in *The Cambridge Companion to Old English Literature,* ed. Malcolm Godden and Michael Lapidge (Cambridge: Cambridge UP, 1991), 142–159. In *Beowulf and the Appositive Style,* Fred C. Robinson discusses the poem's deliberate ambiguity as an attempt to reconcile its own Christian present with the pre-Christian past of its characters (42–43). As Dorothy Whitelock explains, "if a heathen poem on this subject once existed, it must have been very different from the work that has come down to us. As has often been pointed out, the Christian element is not merely superimposed; it permeates the poem . . . an acceptance of the Christian order of things is implicit throughout the poem. It pervades the very imagery" ("The Audience of *Beowulf,"* reprinted in Whitelock, *From Bede to Alfred* [London: Variorum Reprints, 1980]: 1–111; quote from 3–4).

4. The "passive" Anglo-Saxon woman has long been a critical commonplace. For representative views, see Alain Renoir, "A Reading Context for 'The Wife's Lament,'" in *Anglo-Saxon Poetry: Essays in Appreciation,* ed. Lewis E. Nicholson and Dolores Warwick Frese (Notre Dame: Notre Dame University Press, 1975), 224–241; and Richard Schrader, *God's Handiwork: Images of Women in Early Germanic Literature* (Westport, CT: Greenwood Press, 1983). For useful critiques of this view of passive femininity, see Helen Bennett, "The Female Mourner at Beowulf's Funeral: Filling in the Blanks/ Hearing the Spaces," *Exemplaria* 4.1 (1992), 35–50; and Gillian Overing, *Language, Sign, and Gender in* Beowulf (Carbondale: Southern Illinois University Press, 1990), 76–81. Helen Damico rejects the passive model altogether, seeing Wealhtheow, especially, as an active, war-minded valkyrie figure. See Beowulf's *Wealhtheow and the Valkyrie Tradition* (Madison: University of Wisconsin Press, 1984).

5. Among the recent studies investigating the "textuality" of Old English poetry are Allen Frantzen, *Desire for Origins: New Language, Old English, and Teaching the Tradition* (New Brunswick: Rutgers UP, 1990); Overing, *Language, Sign, and Gender in* Beowulf; Katherine O'Brien O'Keeffe, *Visible Song: Transitional Literacy in Old English Verse* (Cambridge: Cambridge UP, 1990); Seth Lerer, *Literacy and Power in Anglo-Saxon England* (Lincoln: University of Nebraska Press, 1991); and Martin Irvine, *The Making of Textual Culture: "Grammatica" and Literary Theory 350–1100* (Cambridge: Cambridge UP, 1994), especially Chapter 9, "The implications of grammatical culture in Anglo-Saxon England." Several of these studies discuss at length the long-

standing scholarly debates surrounding *Beowulf*, including its oral origins, its composition, and its date—issues I will not engage here. My reading of the poem is based not on its oral foundations but rather on its preservation in the manuscript, that is, as a textual artifact, governed by what Walter Ong has called the "restructured consciousness" of literacy: see Ong, *Orality and Literacy: The Technologizing of the Word* (London: Routledge, 1982), especially Chapter 4, "Writing Restructures Consciousness." For a good recent overview of the orality-literacy debate, see Carol Braun Pasternack, *The Textuality of Old English Poetry* (Cambridge: Cambridge UP, 1995), especially Chapter 1. On the relationship of *Beowulf* to literate Latinity, see also (*inter alia*) Eric John, "*Beowulf* and the Margins of Literacy," *Bulletin of the John Rylands University Library of Manchester* 56 (1973–4), 388–422; rpt. in Peter Baker, ed., *Beowulf: Basic Readings* (New York: Garland, 1995), 51–77; and John Niles, *Beowulf: The Poem and its Tradition* (Cambridge, MA: Harvard UP, 1983), 66–95.

6. John Niles, "Locating *Beowulf* in Literary History," *Exemplaria* 5.1 (1993), 81–82.

7. Beowulf *and the Appositive Style*, 25.

8. Because the model is by now well-known, I will not include a lengthy definition or explanation here. See Jane Chance, *Woman as Hero in Old English Literature* (Syracuse: Syracuse University Press, 1986), 1–11, for a good cultural analysis of the peace-weaver in Old English literature and Anglo-Saxon culture; for a detailed lexical analysis, see L. John Sklute, "*Freoðuwebbe* in Old English Poetry," in *New Readings on Women in Old English Literature*, ed. Helen Damico and Alexandra Hennessey Olsen (Bloomington: University of Indiana Press, 1990), 204–210. While Chance sees peace-weaving as a passive and tragic role (10), Sklute argues that peace-weavers are diplomats, actively working to reduce hostilities and promote peace. Although the role of the peace-weaver is now familiar to Anglo-Saxonists, the term appears only three times in Old English poetry, once in reference to a male angel, once for comparative purposes to describe why a woman's behavior is not appropriate (this is Modthryth, in *Beowulf*, discussed below), and only once (in *Widsith*) to describe a woman who has been given in marriage as a token of peace between hostile tribes— the standard definition. The social structure represented by this practice is, however, quite common.

"Peace-weaving" as an anthropological system transacts women as commodities within a homosocial economy. As we will see in subsequent chapters, the homosocial bond between male reader and "masculine" spiritual meaning is enabled through the feminine letter of the text. Similarly, the female peace-weaver joins (weaves) a variety of male social groups. See Gayle Rubin, "The Traffic in Women," in *Toward an Anthropology of*

Women, ed. Rayna B. Reiter (New York and London: Monthly Review Press, 1975), 157–210, for the now-classic feminist anthropological reading of this phenomenon. On women as objects of exchange in *Beowulf*, see Christopher Fee, "Beag & Beaghroden: Women, Treasure, and the Language of Social Structure in *Beowulf*" *Neuphilologische Mitteilungen* 97 (1996): 285–294.

9. See Overing xxiv; Chance 3, 106, and *passim*.

10. Irvine, "Medieval Textuality and the Archaeology of Textual Culture," in *Speaking Two Languages: Traditional Disciplines and Contemporary Theory in Medieval Studies*, ed. Allen J. Frantzen (Albany: SUNY Press, 1991), 181–210, quote from 192.

11. Clanchy, *From Memory to Written Record: England 1066–1307*, 2nd ed. (Oxford: Blackwell, 1993). Clanchy is referring here to twelfth-century manuscripts, but the practice and principle are the same for earlier texts. For a general discussion of the functions of the marginal gloss in Anglo-Saxon texts, see Michael Lapidge, "The Study of Latin Texts in late Anglo-Saxon England I: The Evidence of Latin Glosses," and R.I. Page, "The Study of Latin Texts in late Anglo-Saxon England II: The Evidence of English Glosses," both in *Latin and the Vernacular Languages in Early Medieval Britain*, ed. Nicholas Brooks (Leicester: Leicester University Press, 1982), 99–140 and 141–165, respectively.

12. See John Leyerle, "The Interlace Structure of *Beowulf*," *University of Toronto Quarterly* 37 (1967), 1–17; see also Chance, who links peace-weaving to the material practices of weaving in Anglo-Saxon England (*Woman as Hero*, 4–5 and *passim*).

13. Carruthers, *The Book of Memory: A Study of Memory in Medieval Culture* (Cambridge: Cambridge University Press, 1990), 12.

14. Throughout this chapter, all references to *Beowulf* are to Fr. Klaeber, ed., *Beowulf and the Fight at Finnsburg*, 3rd ed. (Lexington MA: D.C. Heath, 1950). Internal citations will refer to line numbers. Unless otherwise noted, translations are my own.

15. In addition to Pauline Head's recent book, cited in note 16 below, there is a substantial body of scholarship showing the structural and aesthetic functions of framing devices, envelope patterns, and ring structures in Old English poetry. See (*inter alia*) Adrien Bonjour, *The Digressions in* Beowulf (Oxford: Blackwell, 1950); Adeline Courtney Bartlett, *The Larger Rhetorical Patterns in Anglo-Saxon Poetry* (New York: Columbia University Press, 1935); John Niles, Beowulf: *The Poem and Its Tradition* (Cambridge: Harvard University Press, 1983); Constance B. Hieatt, "Envelope Patterns and the Structure of *Beowulf*" *English Studies in Canada* 1 (1975): 249–265; Ward Parks, "Ring Structure and Narrative Embedding in Homer and *Beowulf*" *Neuphilologische Mitteilungen* 89 (1988): 237–251; H. Ward Tonsfeldt, "Ring Structure in *Beowulf*" *Neophilologus* 61 (1977): 443–452. In general, these studies have

shown the various ways that such narrative techniques intensify or illuminate poetic themes by drawing attention to relationships between the framed text (often called a "digression") and the "main" text. In addition, the framing device itself may help to show the relationship between texts within and outside of the frame. For example, the appearances of Wealhtheow that frame the Finn episode prompt the audience to consider the similarities between her situation and Hildeburh's.

16. Head, *Representation and Design: Tracing a Hermeneutics of Old English Poetry* (Albany: SUNY Press, 1997), 66.

17. See Overing xxiv; 81.

18. It is interesting to note that the moment when Hildeburh mourns beside the funeral pyre is the most fully embedded moment in the episode. In "Ring Structure in *Beowulf*," H. Ward Tonsfeldt has shown that the Finn episode is a tightly structured ring pattern, with five levels of events leading into and out of this precise moment (especially pp. 448–452).

19. The connections between Hildeburh and Wealhtheow, either as parallel figures or as diametrically opposed, have often been noted; see Chance, 99–101; Damico, 19–20; Robinson, 26.

20. "Ring Structure in *Beowulf*," 449–451.

21. The peace-weaver's duties have been discussed at length in recent scholarship. See Chance, 1–11; Damico, 8–9; and Michael J. Enright, *Lady With a Mead-Cup: Ritual, Prophecy, and Lordship in the European Warband from La Tène to the Viking Age* (Dublin: Four Courts Press, 1996), 1–37.

22. Damico shows that structurally Wealhtheow's first appearance is governed by an envelope pattern, in which the sounds of celebration that immediately precede her appearance are matched by nearly identical descriptions following it. Thus this first Wealhtheow episode, the first structural component in the narrative frame surrounding Hildeburh's story, is itself textually enclosed. See Damico, 9–11.

23. Damico, 8. See also Overing, 95–97.

24. See Damico, 127–132, for a lengthy discussion of Wealhtheow's support of Hrothulf. See also Irving, *Rereading* Beowulf, for a discussion of Wealhtheow's inability to transcend the boundaries of her role, in spite of the potential this scene would seem to offer for just such a transcendence (74).

25. Like other Germanic languages, Old English has no synthetic passive, but forms passive voice (for the most part) through the use of "to be" verbs, as in this passage. See Bruce Mitchell and Fred C. Robinson, *A Guide to Old English*, 5th ed. (Oxford: Blackwell, 1992), 111.

26. See Enright, *Lady With a Mead Cup*, 5–8.

27. Leyerle, "The Interlace Structure of *Beowulf*," rpt. Fulk, *Interpretations*, 152.

28. Hollis, *Anglo-Saxon Women and the Church* (Woodbridge, Suffolk: The Boydell Press, 1992), 154, Hollis's emphasis.

29. See Irving, 61; Damico, 127–132.

30. Elaine Tuttle Hansen, *The Solomon Complex: Reading Wisdom in Old English Poetry* (Toronto: University of Toronto Press, 1988), 47.

31. See Chance, 38. A recent article by Melinda Menzer deals convincingly with the issue of Grendel's Mother's humanity by showing that the latter element in the compound *aglæcwif* consistently refers in Old English to a female human; that is, *wif* is not simply a gender marker, but more specifically is a marker of gendered personhood. See Melinda J. Menzer, "*Aglæcwif* (*Beowulf* 1259A): Implications for *-Wif* Compounds, Grendel's Mother, and Other *Aglæcan*" *English Language Notes* 34 (September 1996): 1–6. In addition, several scholars have attempted through lexical means to re-evaluate the "inherent nobility" of Grendel's Mother; see Keith P. Taylor, "*Beowulf* 1259a: The Inherent Nobility of Grendel's Mother" *ELN* 31 (1994): 13–25; Kevin Kiernan, "Grendel's Heroic Mother," *In Geardagum* 6 (1984): 25–27; and Christine Alfano, "The Issue of Feminine Monstrosity: A Reevaluation of Grendel's Mother," *Comitatus* 23 (1993): 1–16.

32. *Literacy and Power in Anglo-Saxon Literature*, 192.

33. It may contain a pun. *Wæfre* is not etymologically linked to the Old English verb *wefan*, to weave, but several of the verb forms have homophonic correspondences. The OE word for spider, *gangelwæfre*, or sometimes *wæfregange* (Bosworth-Toller defines this as a "ganging weaver, spider") suggests a close correlation between Grendel's Mother and the poem's other "weavers." There may also be an echo here of that other non-peace-weaver, Modthryth, who is likewise described in the language of weaving.

34. On the "topographical uncertainty" of the mere, see John Niles, Beowulf: *The Poem and Its Tradition* (Cambridge: Harvard University Press, 1983), 16–19. Later in his study, Niles asks, "Why does the poet emphasize that the path to Grendel's mere was 'unknown' (1410b) when just the day before, men from far and near had traced Grendel's track to the same pool (841–856a)? . . . .It is one thing to fight a known enemy in known surroundings, as the hero had done with Grendel, and quite another to risk one's life in an unknown territory that is equated with the very source of evil. Each landscape fits its scene like the same vista seen first by day and then by night, when even familiar surroundings seem strange" (170–171).

35. See Chance 103–104.

36. See Jane Chance's cogent analysis of this scene, which she reads as a pseudo-rape scene (*Woman as Hero*, 102–4).

37. A fourth possible woman, the "geatisc meowle" (line 3150b), may or may not appear briefly at Beowulf's funeral to mourn his death with her songs. The manuscript is faulty at this point and has been the subject of

numerous speculative reconstructions. Currently most scholars consider the "geatisc meowle" emendation to be the most plausible. For a feminist interpretation of the problematic nature of this reconstruction, see Bennett, "The Female Mourner at Beowulf's Funeral."

38. Beowulf: *The Poem and Its Tradition*, 152–153.

39. My understanding of Modthryth has been greatly enhanced by the recent analyses of Gillian Overing, in *Language, Sign, and Gender*, and Mary Dockray-Miller, "The Masculine Queen of *Beowulf*," *Women and Language* 21 (1998): 31–38. I am grateful to Mary Dockray-Miller for allowing me to see an earlier version of her article.

40. Donaldson suggests that "a transitional passage introducing the contrast between Hygd's good behavior and Modthryth's bad behavior as young women of royal blood seems to have been lost." *Beowulf*, trans. E. Talbot Donaldson. Ed. Joseph Tuso (New York: Norton, 1975), 34 n.2. See also Klaeber's notes on Modthryth for a thorough discussion of the "Thryth-Offa" digression (195–200) and Paul E. Szarmach, "The recovery of texts," in *Reading Old English Texts*, ed. Katherine O'Brien O'Keeffe (Cambridge: Cambridge University Press, 1997), 124–145, especially pp. 134–137.

41. Overing constructs this model somewhat differently:

> Modthryth offers a variation on Hildeburh's silent declaration of paradox; she reveals the trace of something that we know cannot exist in the world of the poem: the trace of a woman signifying in her own right. Her initial gesture is strikingly alien, incomprehensible, until translated into the binary language of the masculine economy (*Language, Sign, and Gender*, 106).

Until the translation occurs, however, Overing shows that Modthryth "escapes, however briefly, the trap of binary definition" (106). In other words, she escapes the demands of female enclosure, but not for long; the poem's project is to contain her.

42. However, Mary Dockray-Miller argues persuasively that rather than conforming, Modthryth is unconventional precisely because she succeeds at marriage where all other women in the poem fail or are expected to: "The cornerstone of Modþryðo's unconventionality is her success in the role in which the others fail . . . . Unlike the other marriages described in the poem, Modþryðo's succeeds both emotionally and politically . . . . Modþryðo's supposed acquiescence to the status quo actually undermines it; her success as a queen (not a peace-pledge) defies the system that devalues yet necessitates the woman as peaceweaver" ("The Masculine Queen of *Beowulf*," 36). Socially and politically, however, as Offa's queen (or as peace-pledge), Modthryth has been metaphorically contained by a system outside of which she once stood.

43. Trans. Donaldson, 34.

44. This is not to say that peace-weaving leads to peace; just the opposite, as Overing has shown. But the normalizing functions of the role cannot be underestimated; even Beowulf knows the limitations of this compulsory system.

CHAPTER 3

Textual/Sexual Violence:
The Old English *Juliana* and
the Anglo-Saxon Female Reader

In the opening lines of his address to the nuns at Barking, *de Virginitate*, written in the late seventh or early eighth century, Aldhelm outlines the cultural structures that defined much of women's monastic literacy in Anglo-Saxon England:

> Reverentissimis christi virginibus omnique devotae germanitatis affectu venerandis et non solum corporalis pudicitiae praeconio celebrandis, quod plurimorum est, verum etiam spiritalis castimoniae gratia glorificandis, quod paucorum est. . . .

> [To the most reverend virgins of Christ, (who are) to be venerated with every affection of devoted brotherhood, and to be celebrated not only for the distinction of (their) corporeal chastity, which is (the achievement) of many, but also to be glorified on account of (their) spiritual purity, which is (the achievement) of few . . . .][1]

Above all, Aldhelm praises the sophistication of the nuns' literacy skills and textual practices, admiring the "extremely subtle sequence of [their] discourse" ("sagacissima sermonum serie").[2] He shows no surprise at finding this sophistication in women's writing; rather, he displays his own rhetorical skill for the nuns' pleasure and edification. For the history of women's literacy in early medieval England, Aldhelm's work is important for what it reveals about the reading and writing practices of Anglo-Saxon nuns. He wrote in response to

101

the nuns' letters, which do not survive, but in which they apparently described the nature and extent of their scriptural studies and
requested his response to their work. The complexity of Aldhelm's
Latin points both to the nuns' highly advanced literacy, and to his
desire to gain the respect of readers he obviously admires.[3]

Aldhelm's opening words describe the constant paradox facing
the medieval female religious: in the struggle between the body and
the spirit, the nun must maintain not only corporeal chastity but also
spiritual purity. Both body and spirit must be kept intact, protected
from hostile invaders of any kind. The *exempla* Aldhelm provides to
illustrate the supreme importance of monastic celibacy are, as we
might expect, full of instances in which the intact virginal body is
threatened—either physically tortured or mutilated, or subject to
spiritual temptation. *De Virginitate* is the primary example of an
early medieval text that assumes nuns' literacy skills, and which uses
those skills to promote the ideology of chastity. By focusing on the
nuns' great wisdom and extensive learning, Aldhelm subordinates
the practices of the body to those of the mind. Just as the nuns'
literacy becomes their means to chastity, textual—and thus spiritual,
rational—practices regulate the corporeal. The nuns know the value
of proper Scriptural interpretation; that is, they know how to read
beyond the literal meaning of a (scriptural) text to its spiritual truth.
Comparing the nuns' textual practices to the athleticism of Olympic
wrestlers, Aldhelm writes:

> Et quidem universa haec . . . apud vestri discipulatus indus-
> triam non exterioris hominis motibus aguntur, sed interioris
> gestibus geruntur, siquidem microcosmum id est minorem
> mundum ex duplici et gemina materiae substantia constare
> vestrae sagacitatis solertiam non arbitror latere, quin potius,
> sicut exterioris hominis natura, qui in propatulo formatus
> visibiliter conspicitur, haud difficillime deprehendi potest,
> ita interioris qualitatem . . . a vestra prudentia membratim
> et particulatim subtiliter investigatam reor.

> [And truly all these things {the skills of textual interpreta-
> tion} . . . are not, according to the industry of your disci-
> pline, performed with the motions of the outer man, but
> with the actions of the inner man, given that I do not

think it concealed from your wisdom that the microcosm—
that is, the 'smaller world'—consists in a two-fold and twin
substance of material; but rather, just as the nature of the
outer man—having been formed in open view is seen
clearly—can be perceived with no difficulty, so the quality
of the inner man . . . has, I think, been subtly investigated
bit by bit and stage by stage by your intelligence.[4]

In other words, Aldhelm seems to be saying, the nature of the outer
and inner selves, of particular importance for early Christianity, has
been thoroughly studied by the nuns at Barking. These women readers
were fully conversant with the Augustinian practice of reading beyond
the letter of the text to the spiritual truth it contains.[5] Aldhelm's
accounts of virgin saints and martyrs inscribe the Augustinian model
by focusing readers' attention on the horrors inflicted upon the saint's
physical body, and by simultaneously reminding readers of the body's
insignificance, directing their readerly focus instead to the spirit both
of the saint and of the narrative.

In early medieval saints' lives, the saint embodies the narrative.
The saint's body emblematizes Christian reading practices, by functioning as a text containing both literal and figurative meaning.
Christian readers are meant to identify with the saint, who is Christ's
representative on earth. For the female saint—as for the female
reader—this conflict between the body and the spirit is to be resolved
through the patristic insistence that women must reject not only
their earthly bodies, but even—especially—their gender. They must
progress, as St. Ambrose says, "to complete manhood."[6]

It is not surprising, then, that accounts of early medieval female
saints often interrogate the Aristotelian binarism that associated man
with reason and woman with the body. A number of early virgin martyrs sought to reject (or transcend) their female natures and "become
male"[7] in order to gain access to heaven, a concept precisely articulated by certain patristic writers. In St. Jerome's definition, "As long
as woman is for birth and children, she is different from man as
body is from soul. But if she wishes to serve Christ more than the
world, then she will cease to be a woman and will be called man."[8]
Yet paradoxically, though a female saint may desire to "be called
man," her female body frequently occupies our attention through
much of her story.

This chapter will consider how the Old English *Juliana*—a ninth-century vernacular poetic version of a Latin prose *vita*—uses textual allegory to explore the slippery ground of gender construction and identity.[9] The close relationship in medieval literary theory between literalism and the female body will permit us to see how the feminine corporeal text, the body of Juliana, functions as a sign to be interpreted both literally and figuratively by readers within the narrative and outside of it. The monastic ideal of virginal incorruptibility masculinizes the body of the female virgin, enabling her to penetrate (to read an obscure or veiled text) but not to be penetrated. Even as Juliana herself performs the masculine act of reading spiritually, her body is always read as feminine (and in a feminine way) by the "pagans." In its insistence on the closed female body, *Juliana* negotiates the possibilities posed by threats of violation and penetration into the enclosures of cloister and body: it attempts to map out gender roles and rules in a culture that simultaneously threatens and seeks to protect consecrated women.[10] This poem may well have had serious implications for Anglo-Saxon female audiences desirous of chastity but facing the real and immediate threat of violence and rape at the hands of Danish invaders.

To what extent were cloistered Anglo-Saxon women threatened or endangered? While specific historical events may be impossible to recover, various extant historical records allow us to understand more precisely the nature of these threats. The Anglo-Saxon Chronicle, for the year 835, records only a single event: "Her heþne men oferhergedon Sceapige" ["In this year heathen men ravaged Sheppey"].[11] In 865, the historical record is slightly expanded: "Her sæt heþen here on Tenet 7 genamon friþ wiþ Cantwarum, 7 Cantware him feoh geheton wiþ þam friþe, 7 under þam friþe 7 þam feohgehate se here hiene on niht up bestel, 7 oferhergeade all Cent eastewearde" ["In this year the heathen army encamped on Thanet and made peace with the people of Kent. And the people of Kent promised them money for that peace. And under cover of that peace and promise of money the army stole away inland by night and ravaged all eastern Kent"].[12] The devastating effects of the Scandinavian invasions of England from the late eighth through the eleventh centuries are, of course, well known. But what the Chronicle leaves unsaid is perhaps more horrifying that what it records: Sheppey and Thanet were home to flourishing Anglo-Saxon female religious houses, communities of seventy or more women who had taken various religious vows. According to Jane Schulenburg, "at least forty-one houses for women (including double foundations) were destroyed by the Danes. Very few of the English women's communities survived these repeated onslaughts by the Vikings; in fact, by the time of the Norman Conquest, only nine houses for women in Britain remained."[13]

This is the historical context in which we must read *Juliana*, a poem that may have been written for and received with great interest by Anglo-Saxon female readers. Like most hagiography, Anglo-Saxon female saints' lives are profoundly concerned with the manipulation of the virginal body and the protection of that body when it is threatened (as it invariably is) with exposure, torture, mutilation, or rape. In its intense focus on the body of the saint, *Juliana* explores for female religious readers the threats of—and desirable responses to—such violations of the dual enclosures of cloister and body.

The story of Juliana, a fourth-century virgin martyr, follows the pattern of most such accounts. Although she has already committed herself (and her virginity) to Christ, Juliana's father has promised her in marriage to a wealthy pagan ruler. The men are so enraged when she refuses to marry that they have her tortured repeatedly and imprisoned, before beheading her. Juliana survives the torture unharmed, but ultimately chooses death over the loss of virginity. While it is impossible to determine whether Anglo-Saxon nuns ever read or owned copies of *Juliana*, the example of Aldhelm's work shows that similar works were written specifically for Anglo-Saxon female readers.[14] The Old English version of the legend of Juliana is generally assumed today to have been written in similar circumstances, meant to inspire an Anglo-Saxon female religious audience who presumably would enjoy learning about the adventures of the powerful Christian virgin.[15] Regarding *Juliana*'s audience, Rosemary Woolf has commented:

> While no Anglo-Saxon nun need expect to endure such persecutions [as Juliana does], there was a model for them in Juliana's rejection of a prosperous lover and committal of her virginity to God. . . . Above all, for a feminine audience there is the pleasure in seeing the principle of heroic magnification applied to a woman.[16]

Yet in fact a number of Anglo-Saxon nuns did endure physical persecution and torture, and if none could have withstood the tortures
imposed upon Juliana, we should perhaps attribute the difference in
degree to hagiographical hyperbole. It is worth asking why such
works would be pleasurable for female religious readers, since in
spite of their "happy" endings, the female characters are repeatedly
tortured and threatened with rape.

The historical circumstances of Anglo-Saxon female readers, facing the threat of the Danish invasions, can help answer this question.
When nuns read of (perhaps even wrote of) female heroics in texts
such as *Juliana*, they witnessed both an affirmation of the value of
female chastity, and the ideological negotiations at work in the monastic discourse of enclosure dictating that the female religious must
remain inviolate, impermeable to either spiritual or physical invaders;
she must "become male." In a text like *Juliana*—a hagiographical and
thus idealized portrait, likely read by female readers—the discourse of
enclosure functions both on a physical, spatial level and a spiritual
one: the woman is closed *and* enclosed: she must maintain her body
as an impenetrable fortress (a favorite metaphor in female saints'
lives) against evil intrusions. She must guard herself, as Leoba wrote to
Boniface, "contra hostis occulti venenata iacula" ["against the poison
darts of the hidden enemy"] (see above, pages 50–51).

Juliana explores for female monastic readers the various defenses
of chastity. As Kathryn Gravdal has written in a different context,
the poem "allowed women listeners, as well as male poets and audiences, to examine attitudes about sexual violence and the relation
of gender to power in their society."[17] The torture scenes in *Juliana*
place particular emphasis on the integrity of the virginal female body,
an ideal that was threatened in very real ways for early medieval religious women. The "heroics of virginity" practiced by early medieval
nuns in defense of their bodily integrity included self-mutilation,
suicide, or murder, since the loss of virginity meant that "they were
still perceived as somehow at fault; and as disgraced persons, the
onus of the burden was on them."[18] According to Margaret Miles,
"In most Christian literature . . . rape was represented as a fate worse
than death for Christian virgins. More to be feared than martyrdom,
which was, if necessary, to be welcomed, the loss of bodily integrity
threatened to nullify the virgin's primary identity."[19] Thus for the
early medieval religious woman, as for the virgin martyr, subjectivity

was wholly dependent on the intact female body. Ironically, the only option for the virgin subject was typically violent death. In Aldhelm's description of St. Lucia in *De Virginitate*, written specifically for female readers, the saint first endured repeated torture and then, "salvo pudoris signaculo et consummato vitae curriculo gloriosum martirii triumphum meruit, dum mucrone confossa maluit purpureum sanguinem fundere quam pretiosam pudicitiam perdere" ["having preserved the seal of her chastity and having finished the course of her life, was found worthy of the glorious triumph of a martyr, since she preferred to spill out her crimson blood, having been pierced by the sword, rather than to lose her precious virginity"].[20]

Thus it is through martyrdom that Juliana and female saints like her define their primary identity and acquire not only status but subjecthood. Throughout the *de Virginitate*, Aldhelm describes female saints whose virginity was violently and horribly threatened, but who maintained their bodies like strong walls, fortresses, even rocks, rather than sacrifice their virginity. Occasionally, their bodies assume masculine attributes in order to counteract this threat. Thus, even while they are clearly sexualized—it is common for the martyrs to be stripped or thrown into brothels, and we are frequently reminded of the lascivious-mindedness of their (male) enemies—they are simultaneously de-feminized, and they must of necessity assume masculinizing traits in order to preserve virginity and therefore identity.

Rather than being defined as either male or female, masculine or feminine, the female saint may take on the cultural accretions of gender; she is at once feminine and masculine. In Aldhelm's story of St. Eugenia, perhaps the clearest example of this phenomenon, the saint converts to Christianity, joining a monastery:

> non muliebriter quaesitura rasis cincinnorum criniculis sub tonsura masculini sexus contra iura naturae sanctorum coetibus aggregatur et militonum Christi catervis sine castitatis cicatrice salvo pudoris signaculo adsciscitur.
>
> [. . . not like a woman, but, against the laws of nature, with her curling locks shaved off, in the short crop of the masculine sex—and she was joined with the assembly of saints and was recruited to the troops of Christ's army with the

seal of her purity unbroken, and with no blemish on her chastity.][21]

But the true transgression in this story comes when another woman tries to force herself sexually on Eugenia, believing the cross-dressed saint to be an attractive young man. We are reminded forcefully of Eugenia's essentially (i.e., biologically) female nature, even as her masculinity is her defense against sexual dangers. In response to the woman's advances, "velut ferrato apologiticae defensionis clipeo retundens strofosae accusationis catapultas de falsitatis faretra prolatas in ipsos, a quibus diriguntur, retorsit" ["Eugenia hurled back the missiles of deceitful accusation (taken) from the quiver of falsehood against those who had launched them, blunting (them) with the manifesto of her self-defence as if with an iron-clad shield"].[22] Her militaristic response stems from her masculine identity at this point. Paradoxically, it is the masculine that protects the feminine—or rather, it protects the female. For St. Eugenia, identity is gained through the sublimation of the essential or biological and emerges instead through culturally defined masculinizing actions.[23]

The threat to female chastity is common in a wide range of medieval literatures, serving a variety of functions. Gravdal has shown that the representation of rape in the Old French romances deflects the audience's attention away from "a consideration of the consequences of sexual violence and from a reflection on the physical suffering of women."[24] Saints' lives, in contradistinction, fix the attention of the audience firmly on the horrific consequences of sexual violence done to the consecrated female virgin. *Juliana* follows the pattern of female saints' lives outlined elsewhere by Gravdal: it "creates and offers the female audience a discourse that glorifies the sublimation of female sexuality."[25] The Old English poem offers a mixed message: as it forces its readers' attention on acts of sexual violence, foregrounding the image of the sexualized female heroine, it sublimates her sexuality by insisting on her virginity, thereby reinforcing the monastic ideology that requires the closed, intact female body. Thus the hagiographical scenes of sexual violence against women elide signs of femininity. But more than simply putting aside their virginity and "becoming" male, saints such as Juliana or Eugenia assume a layer of masculinity—that is, an external manifestation of the masculine (whether in actions or in clothing) that encloses and protects the culturally feminine saint and her biologically female body. The saints' lives both display and deny that body: the display is the work of the virgin's pagan torturers; the denial of female sexuality is the result of monastic ideology.

We return, then, to Woolf's statement: "for a feminine audience there is the pleasure in seeing the principle of heroic magnification applied to a woman." Why is this pleasurable? Why would women readers "like" to read about heroic virgins—about the brutal torture of Juliana, or Holofernes' lecherous designs on Judith? I would like to approach this problem from a different direction, by suggesting that the basis of the poem's readerly pleasure lies in the fact that it constructs a masculine reader, one who reads allegorically and thus derives pleasure from the (feminine) text. As we shall see, medieval literary theory correlates "good" reading, that is, spiritual reading of an allegorical text, with masculinity. Texts themselves are figured female; the masculine reader must penetrate the literal text to access its spiritual truth. To represent and to narrate heroic virginity, *Juliana* develops similarly gendered models of textual allegory, of spiritually healthy Christianity, emphasizing the need to fortify and protect the vulnerable female body. The poem writes masculinity onto its own female readership, constructing a doubly (or multiply) gendered reader. To derive spiritual meaning from the text, women readers, too—especially—must read beyond its literal level, must read "like men," must "master" the text.

Christian allegory is, of course, a common feature of saints' lives. A figure such as Juliana functions as a type of Christ, undergoing ritualized scenes of persecution; a symbol of the Church (*ecclesia*); the soul battling the body; and the virtuous obedient Christian.[26] Yet the poem also demonstrates the complex relationship in medieval literary theory between textual allegory and the female body. As Carolyn Dinshaw has shown, the models of textual analysis developed by Jerome and Augustine (derived from St. Paul) associate the literal text with female corporeality:

> Taking pleasure of the text is analogous to taking carnal pleasure of a woman. . . . Woman, in this Pauline model of reading, is not the 'hidden truth' but is dangerous cupidity: she is what must be passed through, gone beyond, left, discarded, to get to the truth, the spirit of the text.[27]

The letter of the text, its "female" body, is a useless shell, a container for the spirit, which, embedded within its (feminized) enclosure for the skillful reader to uncover, is male.

Jerome's version of this model of reading suggests that the truths within texts are both "feminine and fertile" (Dinshaw, 23) and trans-formable; their literal meanings can (and should) be converted to spiritual use. He defends his own use of pagan literature through reference to the pagan woman of Deuteronomy 21:10–13:

> quid ergo mirum, si ego sapientiam saecularem propter elo-quii uenustatem et membrorum pulchritudinem de ancilla atque captiua Israhelitin facere cupio, si, quidquid in ea mortuum est idolatriae, uoluptatis, erroris, libidinum, uel praecido uel rado et mixtus purissimo corpori uernaculos ex ea genero . . . ?

> [Is it surprising that I too, admiring the fairness of her form and the grace of her eloquence, desire to make that secular wisdom which is my captive and my handmaid, a matron of the true Israel? Or that shaving off and cutting away all in her that is dead whether this be idolatry, pleasure, error, or lust, I take her to myself clean and pure . . . ?][28]

In Jerome's analysis, the pagan text becomes a diplomatic func-tionary between opposing groups of men; to use the language of Old English poetry, the pagan text assumes the role of the peace-weaver, "shuttling" diplomatically between two hostile forces. For an appro-priate, "healthy" Christian reading, the allegorical female body of the text must be unveiled, stripped and transformed, in order for the reader to make use of the spiritual truth within the literal text. The relationship between (male) reader and (masculine) spirit is thus a homosocial one, with the feminized text as the medium of exchange.[29] As Gayle Rubin has suggested, "If it is women who are being transacted, then it is the men who give and take them who are linked, the woman being a conduit of a relationship rather than a partner to it. . . . If women are the gifts, then it is men who are the exchange partners."[30] For women readers to participate in this economy, they must "progress to the manhood of Christ," "be called male," to complete the homosocial bond, since the economy dictates that only a masculine reader can penetrate a feminine text.[31]

Like Jerome, Augustine perceives pleasure in the interpretive act, in deciphering an obscure or ambiguous text: "Nunc tamen nemo ambigit et per similitudines libentius quaeque cognosci et cum aliqua difficultate quaesita multo gratius inueniri" ["no one doubts that things are perceived more readily through similitudes and that what is sought with difficulty is discovered with more pleasure"] (2.6.8).[32] He compares "good" and "bad" interpretation, favoring strenuous, spiritually rigorous interpretation of Scriptural ambiguity over lazy, prideful, or misguided reading of Scriptures, and emphasizing the dangers inherent in the latter (2.6.7–8; 3.5.9). Desiring only literal meaning in what one reads represents a dangerous "indifference" to the act of reading: "Qui enim prorsus non inueniunt, quod quaerunt, fame laborant; qui autem non quaerunt, quia in promptu habent, fastidio saepe marcescunt; in utroque autem languor cauendus est" ["Those who do not find what they seek directly stated labor in hunger; those who do not seek because they have what they wish at once frequently become indolent in disdain. In either of these situations indifference is an evil"] (2.6.8). Augustine perceives the greatest danger in the act of literal interpretation: "Cum enim figurate dictum sic accipitur, tamquam proprie dictum sit, carnaliter sapitur" ["That is, when that which is said figuratively is taken as though it were literal, it is understood carnally"] (3.5.9). The bad reader reads only the literal text; "mors animae," the "death of the soul" results when the reader subjects his or her understanding "to the flesh in pursuit of the letter" ("intelligentia carni subicitur sequendo litteram"): "Ea demum est miserabilis animi seruitus, signa pro rebus accipere; et supra creaturam corpoream, oculum mentis ad hauriendum aeternum lumen leuare non posse" ["There is a miserable servitude of the spirit in this habit of taking signs for things, so that one is not able to raise the eye of the mind above things that are corporal and created to drink in eternal light"] (3.5.9).

Yet reading spiritually can carry its own dangers, and this is the paradox facing the female religious: spiritual truths must also be protected, veiled against the gaze of the insufficiently trained or irreverent reader. At the beginning of his *Commentary on the Dream of Scipio*, Macrobius argues in favor of veiling sacred truths, so that they will not be "prostituted" by uninitiated readers. His exemplum shows what can happen when truths are unveiled; he depicts the exposed Eleusinian truths, or "goddesses," as whores:

> [v]iso sibi ipsas Eleusinias deas habitu meretricio ante aper-
> tum lupanar videre prostantes, admirantique et causas non
> convenientis numinibus turpitudinis consulenti respondisse
> iratas ab ipso se de adyto pudicitiae suae vi abstractas et pas-
> sim adeuntibus prostitutas.

> [The Eleusinian goddesses themselves, dressed in the gar-
> ments of courtesans, appeared to [Numenius] standing before
> an open brothel, and when in his astonishment he asked the
> reason for this shocking conduct, they angrily replied that he
> had driven them from their sanctuary of modesty and had
> prostituted them to every passer-by.][33]

Juliana embodies the tension between the Pauline model of reading—as developed by Jerome and Augustine, in which the feminine textual body contains (masculine) truth but must be passed through or transformed to be of use—and the Macrobian model seen here, in which the truth itself is female and must be guarded from public exposure. The body of the female virgin saint is both an enclosure, a vessel that must be discarded, passed through, or transformed in order to reach the spirit within, and a spiritual text of truth that must itself be enclosed, veiled against exposure to the pagan/vulgar gaze, which is analogous to rape.

Juliana's body is the text read by readers within and outside of the poem. The torture she undergoes at the hands of the pagans Affricanus and Eleusius demonstrates the evil inherent in "pagan reading"—in taking pleasure only in literal interpretation, in preferring the signifier to the signified. Even as the action of the poem centers on Juliana's body, her body itself becomes the site of interpretation, the central text. The pagans strip and torment her textualized body, yet are unable to read beneath the physical surface. The spirit within her body will never yield to them because of their "indifference" to reading beyond the literal level. The reader of *Juliana*, in contrast, if she or he is reading beyond the literal level of the text, will read the poem and its heroine allegorically (i.e., spiritually, like men). Juliana herself represents a good reader, when, about halfway through the poem, she debates with a devil. Because she correctly perceives him to be a devil beneath his angelic disguise, Juliana demonstrates that the disguise, the literal appearance, is the veil that must be stripped from a text to uncover its spiritual "truth." The two interpretive sites of battle—the torture of Juliana, and Juliana's own debate with the devil—exemplify the gendered processes of Christian reading and of pagan misreading.[34]

Almost as soon as the poem opens, we see scenes of misreading. Both Eleusius (Juliana's suitor) and Affricanus (her father) reject Christian wisdom, even though it is available to them. Eleusius often goes "ofer word godes" [against the word of God, 23a] to visit heathen idols. His lust for Juliana, in fact, seems causally related to his idol-worship; after one visit, "*Ða* his mod ongon / fæmnan lufian   (hine fyrwet bræc)" [*then* his heart began to love the woman, desire tormented him, 26b–27, emphasis mine]. Affricanus, too, is presented initially as someone who misunderstands the truth; he pledges his daughter in marriage to Eleusius, but:

Ða wæs sio fæmne   mid hyre fæder willan
welegum biweddad;   wyrd ne ful cuþe,
freondrædenne   hu heo from hogde,
geong on gæste.   (32–35a)

[Then at her father's will the woman was pledged to the rich man; he did not fully know how the young woman, in her soul, hated that fate, (conjugal) affection.]

A number of oppositions emerge early in the poem. Most obviously, the Christian Juliana is juxtaposed with the pagan men. Within this dichotomy are others: the use of private oaths (Juliana has pledged herself to Christ in her heart) vs. public declarations—Eleusius is particularly outraged because she rejects him in public, "on wera mengu" [before many people, 45b]; the material vs. the spiritual—Juliana specifically rejects Eleusius' wealth in favor of God's love; physical violence vs. spiritual calm—when Eleusius hears Juliana's rejection, he is "yrre gebolgen" [swollen with anger, 58b], "firendæ-dum fah" [stained with sins, 59a], and he is "hreoh ond hygeblind" [wild and mind-blinded, 61a], when he summons her father. This particularly physical imagery culminates when the men meet: their voices rose up, "[r]eord up astag," as they leaned their spears together, ". . . hy togædre   garas hlændon" (62b–63). The obvious phallic imagery, the celebration of the masculine body, operates on a superficial, literal level. Yet at the same time, the very carnality of the opening scenes in fact marks a gender reversal: the men are strongly identified with their earthbound bodies (i.e., feminized), while Juliana is aligned with the spirit.

Eleusius's anger stems primarily from his wounded pride at having suffered a public rejection. Affricanus is semantically linked to him, since upon learning of his daughter's behavior, he too is "yrre gebolgen" [swollen with anger, 90b]. Both men fail to understand the true spiritual meaning of Juliana; they misread her Christian virtue as stubborn willfulness. Thus when Juliana rejects Eleusius's marriage offer, the men are unable to interpret her action in terms of their own experience. Affricanus can only locate signification in economic terms: Eleusius is wealthier than she, "æhtspedigra" (101b), and "therefore it is worth it" to her, "Forþon is þæs wyrþe" (103a), to marry him. In allegorical terms, neither of the men (her readers) can see past her literal body, that is, they simply cannot comprehend her indifference to either material wealth or the threat of physical pain. Their inability to see Juliana's spiritual side and their persistent misreadings of her true meaning—that is to say, their literalism— feminize these pagan readers. In Ambrose's terms, Juliana, as a true believer, will progress to "manhood" but Affricanus and Eleusius remain feminized non-believers. Because they cannot "penetrate" this text, and because Juliana prefers death to marriage, she is protected from pagan assault.

Juliana's body, on display in the public square, becomes the focus for most of the rest of the poem: "Duguð wafade / on þære fæmnan wlite,   folc eal geador" [The assembly gazed with fascination at the woman's beauty, all the people together, 162b–163]. As Kathryn Gravdal has written, such scenes "[open] a licit space that permits the audience to enjoy sexual language and contemplate the naked female body. . . . Hagiography affords a sanctioned space in which eroticism can flourish and in which male voyeurism becomes licit, if not advocated."[35] In a vividly erotic scene, Eleusius orders Juliana's torture:

Ða for þam folce   frecne mode
beotwordum spræc,   bealg hine swiþe
folcagende,   ond þa fæmnan het
þurh niðwræce   nacode þennan,
ond mid sweopum swingan   synna lease.   (184–188)

[Then in front of the people, with a fierce mind, the people's leader became violently enraged, spoke threats; he commanded the woman, (who was) without sin, through torture, to be stretched out naked and beaten with rods].

The insistent focus on Juliana's body demonstrates Affricanus's literal misreading of her spirit. Readers outside of the poem, looking in, view Juliana from two perspectives. First, she is repeatedly described in terms that emphasize her inner virtue: she is blessed ["seo eadge," 105a, 130a], noble of spirit ["æþele mod," 209a], wise ["gleaw," 131a], holy ["halig," 237b]. In contrast, we also assume the gaze of the pagan "reader." Juliana's naked body is presented in extremely physical terms: after being whipped, Juliana is hung by the hair for six hours, where her "sunsciene" [sun-bright, 229a] body is again beaten, before being thrown in prison. By directing our gaze to Juliana's body, the poem aligns the reader with the (male) viewpoint of Affricanus and Eleusius, while simultaneously reminding us of the spiritual truth enclosed within that body; the Christian reader can identify with both the sinners and the saint.[36]

Juliana's concerns, once she is in jail, turn wholly inward: "Hyre wæs Cristes lof / in ferðlocan fæste biwunden" [The praise of Christ was firmly enclosed in her heart, 233b–234]. The spatial dimensions of Christ within her heart, her heart within her body, and her body within its cell evoke a striking image of Christian female piety; she is like the female anchorite, both enclosure and enclosed one. Like the anchorite's cell, the female body (and allegorically the church, *ecclesia*) is designed for practical, physical purposes of containment. More important is the thing contained, the spirit within the letter, the truth behind the veil. Without the spirit, the letter (Juliana's body) is meaningless, an empty sign. This finally is the lesson of the torture scene for readers of the poem; it is a lesson that Affricanus and Eleusius cannot and will not learn. As Jerome explains: "non norunt animae pulchritudinem considerare, sed corporum" ["They fail to appreciate the beauty of the soul and only value that of the body"].[37]

The poem is poised between two sites of interpretation: the pagan "misreadings" of Juliana's words and of her body, and Juliana's own encounter with a potentially tricky "text"—the devil in angel's clothing who appears in her cell. This encounter demonstrates how a reader might confront and grapple with—unclothe—an ambiguous, difficult, or obscure text. Here again, Augustine can clarify Juliana's interpretive practice. In Book Three of *On Christian Doctrine*, Augustine explains how to avoid the dangers of interpreting literally Scriptures which may at first appear to condone "cupiditas": "Et iste omnino modus est, ut quicquid in sermone diuino neque ad morum honestatem neque ad fidei ueritatem proprie referri potest, figuratem esse cognoscas" ["Whatever appears in the divine Word that does not literally pertain to virtuous behavior or to the truth of faith you must take to be figurative"] (3.10.14). Historical context will help guide readers' interpretations, for, as Augustine explains, although a thing may seem "shameful" ("flagitium") to modern readers, those readers must consider both the figurative meaning of the thing and "quid igitur locis et tempori et personis conueniat" ["what is proper to places, times, and persons"] (3.12.19) historically: "Ita quod in aliis personis plerumque flagitium est, in diuina uel prophetica persona magnae cuiusdam rei signum est" ["In this way what is frequently shameful in other persons is in a divine or prophetic person the sign of some great truth"] (3.12.18). A clear example of Augustine's point can be seen in the torture of Juliana: readers must understand that there is no shame in her nakedness, because of the multiple ways in which her body figures Christ and the church.

The devil who appears in Juliana's cell represents the opposite: something evil disguised as something good; a thing that appears to represent charity but in fact embodies cupidity. The process of reading the devil, enacted by Juliana, remains the same. The Old English version presents a crucial revision of the Latin source, which reads: "Putabat autem S. Juliana quod angelus Dei esset, et dicit illi: Tu quis es?" [Saint Juliana supposed he was an angel of God and she said to him, 'Who are you?'].[38] Yet the Old English Juliana does not immediately believe what she sees, but rather she is unafraid ["seo þe forht ne wæs," 258b] and asks him at once where he came from: "hwonan his cyme wære," (259b). She wants to know his source, to go beneath his literal surface—she reads, in other words, like a man, stripping and penetrating the veiled text. Her interpretive act feminizes the devil, but his body proves to be an empty shell when penetrated by this spiritually healthy, masculinized reader.

When the devil appears in "engles hiw" [angel's form, 244b], he wrongly appeals to Juliana on solely physical and material grounds. When he urges her to make an offering to the pagan gods, he believes she can be convinced with an argument used by both men: she ought to make her oblation quickly to avoid being killed "fore duguðe" [in front of all the people, 256]. Fear of public humiliation and exposure in this poem are the province of the pagans. To these men the material body is the (empty) center of their belief; they are concerned with material wealth, with the exchange of female bodies, and the exposure of this empty materialism would ruin them. Thus when the devil threatens Juliana with public exposure, she can immediately classify him. She knows not to believe the literal body she sees in her cell—the angel—but, distrusting the letter of the text (as knowledge of Augustine would have taught her), she seeks an allegorical meaning when her own belief system doubts the literal text.

To identify and interpret accurately this ambiguous "text," Juliana first calls on God to reveal the truth of the "færspelle" [the sudden news, 267b]. The beautiful voice that answers her from heaven directs her to an action that may at first seem surprising (it has discomfited many modern readers of the poem); when the poem is considered as an allegory of reading, however, when we understand Juliana to be applying the principles of interpretation to this ambiguous (though evil) text, her actions make sense. The heavenly voice tells her:

Forfoh þone frætgan   ond fæste geheald.
oþþæt he his siðfæt   secge mid ryhte,
ealne from orde,   hwæt his æþelu syn.   (284–286)

[Seize the demon and hold him fast until he tells truthfully about his errands, from the beginning, what his origins are].[39]

When Juliana follows these instructions, the devil provides a lengthy confession in which he reveals his methods. Thus her physical (masculine) action is critical for her interpretive success—literally seizing the devil forces him to give up his "truths." In other words, the devil's body, too, must be tormented before it reveals the "spirit" and thus (like Jerome) Cynewulf provides a lesson in reading not just holy Scripture, but pagan texts and bodies.

The devil's confession, which describes how he makes men and women into sinners, can be read as a text revealing its truth, exposing the mechanisms of how it means. What has not often been remarked on, however, is that the battle metaphors used by the devil to tempt Christians into sin are also metaphors of rape:

> Ic þæs wealles geat
> ontyne þurh teonan;   bið se torr þyrel,
> ingong geopenad,   þonne ic ærest him
> þurh eargfare   in onsende
> in breostsefan   bitre geþoncas
> þurh mislice   modes willan,
> þæt him sylfum   selle þynceð
> leahtras to fremman   ofer lof godes,
> lices lustas.   (401b–409a)

> [I open the gate of the wall through injuries; when the tower is penetrated, the entrance opened, then I first send into [the Christian] through a flight of arrows, bitter thoughts into his mind, through various desires of his heart, so that he thinks it better for himself to perform vices, lusts of the body, over the praise of God].

The devil admits that such assaults can only work on weaker Christians; he will not be able to penetrate—to violate—those who hold their bodies more tightly closed, as Juliana does.[40] The weak Christian is open, exposed, vulnerable to such an assault, whereas the model of virginity is impenetrable. According to John Bugge:

> [T]he prevailing imagery [of the devil's speech] is that of assault, penetration, intrusion. It is in service of the theme of the baleful wound of sin, and placed in a context wherein virginity is strongly emphasized. For Cynewulf, therefore, not only does the unbreached castle represent the physical

integrity of the body, but that integrity, in turn, stands for a profound spiritual reality, the ontological impermeability and, so to speak, indiscerptibility [i.e. indivisibility] of the virgin soul, totally insulated from the corruptive impingement of matter upon spirit.[41]

Juliana's "ontological impermeability" is a fundamental component of the discourse of enclosure that determines the poem's representation of her, and the representation of all powerful women in Old English poetry. Paradoxically, the female body can only be a site of power when it remains closed, impermeable, when it is contained— when, in other words, it is not feminine. Thus, the closed, virginal, female body is masculinized—Juliana, through this rejection of femininity (permeability), is able to read beneath and beyond the literal text, to penetrate the text for its spiritual meaning, to "become male." The impermeability prevents the female heroine of Old English Christian poetry from any taint of female (carnal) sexuality. Throughout the poem, the fear of publicity and exposure are identified with Affricanus, Eleusius, and the devil, whereas steadfastness, *stabilitas*, "buttressing" are Juliana's qualities (as well as those of the strong Christian described by the devil in his confession).[42]

The rape metaphors used by the devil must have had immediate implications for Cynewulf's female readers. Alexandra Hennessey Olsen has argued, in a study of the Old English *Judith*, that the scene in which Judith decapitates Holofernes functions as an inverted rape scene: Judith is, she believes, "a woman realistically worried about what might happen to her" in Holofernes's tent, and thus the scene "presents an ironic inversion of that realistic situation in which men reduce women to objects to be abused."[43] Olsen suggests that the scene "seems designed to shock its audience and keep the subject of rape in their conscious minds."[44] I would like to shift this argument slightly to suggest that in fact literate Anglo-Saxon women did not need to be reminded of the physical dangers facing them; rather, because physical assault (including rape) was already in their conscious minds, the subject emerges in literary representations. The histories of Anglo-Saxon female religious houses offer a grim confirmation of this suggestion: foundations at Sheppey, Barking, Shaftesbury, and Thanet were frequent landing sites for Danish invaders. The abbey at Minster-in-Thanet, for example, was first raided in the mid-eighth century; like foundations at Barking, Ely, and elsewhere, it was burnt to the ground (with the nuns inside) by the Danes in the ninth century.[45] After being rebuilt, Minster-in-Thanet was destroyed yet again in 980, and in 1011 the abbess was taken captive by the Danes.[46] A ninth-century charter grants the nearby convent of Lyminge "a small piece of land in the city of Canterbury as a refuge in necessity,"[47] apparently in recognition of the geographical vulnerability of this coastal convent. Significantly, the houses most frequently destroyed were important centers of literary activity, as again the example of Aldhelm and his female readers at Barking illustrates. When we consider the high levels of literacy among Anglo-Saxon nuns, it is not hard to imagine these convents as places where literature exploring the threats of violence and rape may have been produced or received with profound interest.

Perhaps the most shocking and explicit story is that of the abbess Ebba and her nuns at Coldingham, who knew in advance of the approaching invaders "who roam[ed] through every place . . . ravishing holy women."[48] These nuns, to defend their virginity, cut off their noses and lips with razors, preferring self-mutilation to rape—thereby both anticipating and appropriating male action. The Danes, repelled by the sight, burned down the convent with the nuns inside it. Even if legendary, such histories offer a compelling picture of both the dangers facing Anglo-Saxon nuns, and the powerful ideology of enclosure that guided their actions. Thus, while *Juliana* confronts the threats of violence facing Anglo-Saxon nuns, it points as well to a problematic paradox inherent in monastic enclosure: the protective cloister may become a tomb. When nuns resist violation and rape, protecting their bodily enclosures, the (preferred) result is often death within the architectural enclosure of the convent walls. The ideology of monastic enclosure cannot permit the kind of penetration the devil describes to Juliana, when he explains how he wins away weak Christians. Stories of virgin martyrdom, then, both confirm Christian ideology and create a context in which the nuns have responsibility for their own spiritual safety. The power of the virgin martyr always stems from her denial of female sexuality, through her appropriation—her accumulation—of masculinizing actions and behaviors.

Reading the rape metaphors in the poem, and the histories of the real rapes of Anglo-Saxon women, suggests multiple ways in which Anglo-Saxon female religious readers might interpret *Juliana*. The recourse a nun might have against the threat of physical violation is precisely developed in the discourse of enclosure: because she cannot hope to win a physical battle against pagan invaders (in spite of the model of Judith) she can only fight the spiritual battle to keep her body enclosed and inviolate, impenetrable by any sort of pagan forces. The poem's model of the Christian body withstanding penetration from the devil's arrows takes on immense significance in this context: women do after all become responsible for their own protection (and, by analogy, their own salvation), even if—or because—they are bound up in the discourse of enclosure circumscribing the female body. Enclosure (theoretically) provides protection from both physical and spiritual assault; as we have seen, literal use of the flesh—the opening of the consecrated female body—is the sign of the pagan, the prostitution and rape of truth by uninitiated readers.[49]

Following Juliana's imprisonment and verbal battle with the devil, Eleusius attempts one final time to torture her into marrying him: he tries to burn her and then boil her in molten lead. Again, as in the previous torture scenes, we see an ironic inversion of the male/female, spirit/body binarisms typical of early medieval thought. Juliana's body remains untouched by the tortures. As a Christian virgin she has distanced herself so far from her own flesh that it cannot signify, it cannot be corrupted. As Peter Brown has written about the passion of St. Eulalia, "the body itself has become symbolic of the triumph of the martyr over disintegration."[50] The integrity of Juliana's body symbolizes her pure spirituality. Eleusius, in contrast, becomes pure animal, "wilde deor" (597b) in his rage at Juliana's incorruptibility (it means, of course, that he will not be able to experience her flesh for himself). Finally Juliana erases completely any femininity she may have had, when she reverses the male gaze that has been directed at her body, turning her gaze upon the devil:

> Þa seo eadge biseah
> ongean gramum,   Iuliana,
> gehyrde heo hearm galan   helle deofol.
> Feond moncynnes   ongon þa on fleam sceacan,
> wita neosan . . .   (627b–631a)

[Then the blessed Juliana looked towards the fierce one, heard the hell-devil sing miseries. Then the enemy of mankind began to take flight, to seek torments].

This is her final appropriation of male power, as well as a decentering for us, as readers, from her body to her spirit.

Juliana's final speech confirms the model of enclosure as the ideal mode for the female religious. The Old English poet significantly changes his Latin source in this speech; in the Latin, Juliana instructs her listeners to "build your houses on firm rock, so you will not be shattered by the coming fierce winds," before instructing them in many other religious matters.[51] The Old English Juliana develops the theme of foundational firmness at greater length, instructing her listeners in language informed by her conversation with the devil:

> Weal sceal þy trumra
> strong wiþstondan   storma scurum,
> leahtra gehygdum.   Ge mid lufan sibbe,
> leohte geleafan,   to þam lifgendan
> stane stiðhydge   staþol fæstniað,
> soðe treowe   ond sibbe mid eow
> healdað æt heortan,   halge rune
> þurh modes myne. . . .
> . . .
> Wærlic me þinceð   þæt ge wæccende
> wið hettendra   hildewoman
> wearde healden,   þy læs eow wiþerfeohtend
> weges forwyrnen   to wuldres byrig.   (650b–657a;
>   662–664)

[A strong wall will more firmly withstand the beating of storms, the thoughts of sins. With the peace of love, clear faith, and resolution, make fast a foundation to the living rock and hold peace in your hearts and true faith, the holy mysteries through your mind's desire. . . . I think it prudent that you be vigilant against the enemies, the hostile violence; keep watch lest enemies deny you the way to the city of heaven].[52]

Her speech encompasses the dual vision of Christian virginity, of enclosure and enclosed one: she exhorts the people to maintain their own bodies as firm enclosures so that they may hold true faith within, and it is only by maintaining this *stabilitas* that they can enter the greater foundation of heaven. Her message must seem striking to both her Nicodemian audience who presumably have watched throughout the day as Affricanus and Eleusius have attempted to shatter her bodily foundation through physical torture; and to an Anglo-Saxon monastic readership themselves facing "hostile violence" and the potential loss of bodily integrity.

Traditionally scholars group *Juliana* with the Old English poems *Elene* and *Judith*, because these are the only three extant Old English narratives to feature a female protagonist, and all three exemplify the heroic values of Christian sainthood. While the three characters share a number of physical and mental characteristics, it is often remarked that Juliana is "different" somehow from the other two; in particular, she lacks the physical aggressiveness and military bearing and actions of Elene and Judith. It is usually assumed, therefore, that the poem *Juliana* is less concerned with Juliana's physicality, and more concerned with her spirituality. The physical body of Juliana, however, is of primary importance in the Old English poem; and the battle that she fights is acted out within—and on—her own body. Her body is the site of pagan desires, the battleground between the pagan use of the body, of carnality, and the truth to be found within that body, or beyond it, in the Christian spirit.

The assumption of masculine attributes served, theoretically, to protect the vulnerable female religious; gender "progression" was the beginning of the journey to salvation. The power and authority of the female subject of *Juliana* (both the saint herself and her female reader) lay in her ability to use those masculine attributes to her own spiritual—if not physical—advantage. Above all, "becoming male" meant maintaining a closed, impenetrable body, impervious to any kind of hostile attack; to do so meant acquiring or "layering on" those masculine attributes (whether spiritual or literal) that would serve to protect the female saint. This resultant *integritas* permitted agency and identity; by maintaining their bodies as enclosures, Juliana, Eugenia, and others circulated with relative freedom in a world of men. In my next chapter, I turn to a more detailed analysis of the female saint's body in a group of virgin martyr narratives collected in Ælfric's *Lives of Saints*. In these Lives, the female body is typically subjected to graphic torture and public display—a surprising phenomenon for a culture that deeply values the enclosure and containment of women's bodies. We shall see that this paradox can be resolved by studying the complex relationship between the female saint's body and the textuality that informs Ælfric's own hermeneutics.

NOTES

1. Rudolph Ehwald, ed. *Aldhelmi Opera*. Monumenta Germaniae Historica Auctorum Antiquissimorum Vol. XV (Berlin: Weidmann, 1961), 228. Translation from Michael Lapidge and Michael Herren, eds. and trans., *Aldhelm: The Prose Works* (Cambridge and Totowa: Brewer/Rowman and Littlefield, 1979), 59.

2. Ehwald, 229; trans. Lapidge and Herren, 59.

3. Surprisingly, Aldhelm's work has received scant attention from feminist literary critics. See, however, the excellent recent analysis by Stephanie Hollis, in her *Anglo-Saxon Women and the Church* (Woodbridge, Suffolk: The Boydell Press, 1992), 75–112; and Jane Chance, *Woman as Hero in Old English Literature* (Syracuse: Syracuse University Press, 1986), 33–52.

4. Ehwald, 230–231; trans. Lapidge and Herren, 60–61.

5. For patristic and medieval theories of reading spiritually, see G.R. Evans, *The Language and Logic of the Bible* (Cambridge: Cambridge University Press, 1984), 72–100; and Beryl Smalley, *The Study of the Bible in the Middle Ages* (Notre Dame: Notre Dame University Press, 1964), 1–26.

6. See below, note 8.

7. Several recent studies have discussed this phenomenon. See, for example, Elizabeth Castelli, "'I Will Make Mary Male': Pieties of the Body and Gender Transformation of Christian women in Late Antiquity," in *Body Guards: The Cultural Politics of Gender Ambiguity*, ed. Julia Epstein and Kristina Straub (New York: Routledge, 1991), 29–49; John Anson, "The Female Transvestite in Early Monasticism: The Origin and Development of a Motif," *Viator* 5 (1974): 1–32; Margaret Miles, *Carnal Knowing: Female Nakedness and Religious Meaning in the Christian West* (Boston: Beacon Press, 1989). On the philosophical bases of the Aristotelian binarism, see Elizabeth V. Spelman, "Woman as Body: Ancient and Contemporary Views," *Feminist Studies* 8 (1982): 109–131. The phrase "becoming male" is borrowed from Miles, 53ff.

8. "Quamdiu mulier partui servitet liberis, hanc habet ad virum differentiam, quam corpus ad animam. Sin autem Christo magis voluerit servire quam saeculo, mulier esse cessabit, et dicetur vir." *Commentariorum in*

Epistolam ad Ephesios libri 3, Patrologia latina 26: 533. Ambrose, too, asserts this gendered opposition: "Quae non credit, mulier est, et adhuc corporei sexus appellatione signatur; nam quae credit, occurrit in virum perfectum, in mensuram aetatis plenitudinis Christi." ["She who does not believe is a woman and should be designated by the name of her bodily sex, whereas she who believes progresses to complete manhood, to the measure of the adulthood of Christ."] *Expositio evangelis secundum Lucam, Patrologia latina* 15: 1844. Both passages quoted in Dinshaw, *Chaucer's Sexual Poetics*, 204–205 n. 64. Castelli, "I Will Make Mary Male," lists numerous similar patristic references.

9. The Old English text of *Juliana* is found in *The Anglo-Saxon Poetic Records* vol. III, ed. George Philip Krapp and Elliot Van Kirk Dobbie (New York: Columbia University Press, 1936), 113–133. References to this text will be cited parenthetically. Unless otherwise indicated, translations are my own. On Cynewulf's source for *Juliana*, see the edition by Rosemary Woolf, *Juliana* (London: Methuen, 1955); and Daniel Calder, *Cynewulf* (Boston: Twayne, 1981), 75–82.

10. Feminist scholars have only recently begun to consider the possible responses of medieval women readers to graphic scenes of violence in Middle English virgin martyr narratives. See especially Jocelyn Wogan-Browne, "Saints' Lives and the Female Reader," *Forum for Modern Language Studies* 27.4 (1991): 314–322; and Catherine Innes–Parker, "Sexual Violence and the Female Reader: Symbolic 'Rape' in the Saints' Lives of the Katherine Group," *Women's Studies* 24 (1995): 205–217.

11. A.H. Smith, ed., *The Parker Chronicle* (London: Methuen, 1935), 17.

12. Smith, *The Parker Chronicle*, 23. Both Chronicle translations are from Dorothy Whitelock, *English Historical Documents*, 172, 176.

13. Jane Tibbetts Schulenburg, "Women's Monastic Communities, 500–1100: Patterns of Expansion and Decline," in *Sisters and Workers in the Middle Ages*, ed. Judith M. Bennett, Elizabeth A. Clark, Jean F. O'Barr, B. Anne Vilen, and Sarah Westphal–Wihl (Chicago: University of Chicago Press, 1989), 208–239; and David Knowles and R. Neville Hadcock, *Medieval Religious Houses: England and Wales*, 2nd ed. (London: Longman, 1971). Both provide accounts of individual Anglo-Saxon female foundations.

14. Ælfric, too, addressed a statement in favor of virginity to a female reader; see below Chapter 4, p. 163 and n. 44.

15. As my discussion of Aldhelm's readers indicates, in pre-Conquest England, levels of (Latin) literacy were high among noble and/or religious women. Anglo-Saxon nuns wrote (and read) letters and biographies, copied scriptures, and composed Latin verses, many of which exist today but remain inaccessible or untranslated (see Christine Fell, "Some Implications of the

Boniface Correspondence," in *New Readings on Women in Old English Poetry*, ed. Helen Damico and Alexandra Hennessey Olsen [Bloomington: Indiana University Press, 1990], 29–42; and Peter Dronke, *Women Writers of the Middle Ages* [Cambridge: Cambridge University Press, 1984]). Although no Old English vernacular poetry is known to have been written by a woman, nearly all Old English poetry is anonymous. We must not rule out the possibility of female authorship for a period in which nuns often wrote prolifically; several nuns are known to have authored saints' lives, and we have seen that two Old English lyrics have a first-person female persona.

16. Rosemary Woolf, "Saints' Lives," in *Art and Doctrine: Essays on Medieval Literature*, ed. Heather O'Donoghue (London: Hambledon, 1986), 226–227.

17. Kathryn Gravdal, *Ravishing Maidens: Writing Rape in Medieval French Literature and Law* (Philadelphia: University of Pennsylvania Press, 1991), 18.

18. Jane Tibbetts Schulenburg, "The Heroics of Virginity," 59.

19. Margaret Miles, *Carnal Knowing*, 74; Schulenburg, "The Heroics of Virginity," passim. Augustine, however, advises that sexual assault may harm the body but cannot touch the pure Christian soul:

. . . the consecrated body is the instrument of the consecrated will; and if that will continues unshaken and steadfast, whatever anyone else does with the body or to the body, provided that it cannot be avoided without committing sin, involves no blame to the sufferer.

See Augustine, *City of God*, trans. Henry Bettenson (London: Penguin, 1972; rpt. 1984), 284. Yet as Schulenburg has demonstrated in "The Heroics of Virginity," the burden of lost virginity, even if lost involuntarily, was profound.

20. Ehwald, 294; trans. Lapidge and Herren, 109.

21. Ehwald, 297; trans. Lapidge and Herren, 110.

22. Ehwald, 297–298; trans. Lapidge and Herren, 111.

23. See chapter 4 below for a more thorough discussion of Ælfric's version of the Life of St. Eugenia.

24. Kathryn Gravdal, "Chrétien de Troyes, Gratian, and the Medieval Romance of Sexual Violence" *Signs* 17 (1992), 584–585.

25. *Ravishing Maidens*, 24.

26. For an excellent analysis of the ways that Juliana figures Christ and the church, see Joseph Wittig, "Figural Narrative in Cynewulf's *Juliana*," *Anglo-Saxon England* 4 (1975): 37–55.

27. Carolyn Dinshaw, *Chaucer's Sexual Poetics*, (Madison: University of Wisconsin Press, 1989), 21–22. My discussion of literalism and the female

body in medieval textuality is indebted to Dinshaw's careful and convincing analysis of Jerome, Augustine, and Macrobius.

28. Jerome, Epistula LXX (Ad Magnum, Oratorem Urbis Romae). In *Epistulae*, edited by I. Hilberg. Corpus Scriptorum Ecclesiasticorum Latinorum. Vol. 54. (Vienna: Verlag der Österreichischen Akademie der Wissenschaften, 1996), 702. Trans. W.H. Fremantle, *The Principle Works of St. Jerome. A Select Library of the Nicene and Post-Nicene Fathers of the Christian Church*, second series 6 (Grand Rapids: Eerdmans, 1954), 149.

29. Although this act of stripping or unveiling the text might seem to "un-enclose" it, I would argue that the opposite effect occurs: the spiritual truth remains firmly embedded within the literal text and is likewise enclosed figuratively in the transaction that takes place when a reader interprets that text. Like the literal bodies of female saints, the literal text may be beautiful to look at but is finally dispensable.

30. Gayle Rubin, "The Traffic in Women: Notes on the 'Political Economy' of Sex," in *Toward an Anthropology of Women* ed. Rayna R. Reiter (New York and London: Monthly Review Press, 1975), 174. See also Luce Irigaray: "*The virginal woman . . . is pure exchange value*. She is nothing but the possibility, the place, the sign of relations among men." *This Sex Which is Not One*, trans. Catherine Porter (Ithaca: Cornell University Press, 1985), 186; emphasis in original. Similarly, Eve Kosofsky Sedgwick writes, "in any erotic rivalry, the bond that links the two rivals is as intense and potent as the bond that links either of the rivals to the beloved" (21); "in any male-dominated society there is a special relationship between male homosocial (*including* homosexual) desire and the structures for maintaining and transmitting patri-archal power." *Between Men: English Literature and Male Homosocial Desire* (New York: Columbia University Press, 1985), 25; emphasis in original.

31. In addition to Dinshaw, my analysis here is indebted to Rita Cope-land, "Why Women Can't Read: Medieval Hermeneutics, Statutory Law, and the Lollard Heresy Trials," in *Representing Women: Law, Literature, and Feminism*, ed. Susan Sage Heinzelman and Zipporah Batshaw Wiseman (Durham: Duke University Press, 1994), 253–286. Copeland skillfully dissects the complicated "metaphysic" that results when a female reader confronts a feminized (literal) text (see pp. 256–259).

32. Augustine, *De Doctrina Christiana*, in Opera IV.i. Ed. Joseph Martin. Corpus Christianorum Series Latina XXXII (Turnhout: Brepols, 1962), 36. Translation from *On Christian Doctrine*, trans. D.W. Robertson (Indianapolis: Bobbs–Merrill, 1958). All subsequent citations and translations will be to these two texts and will refer to book, chapter, and paragraph number.

33. Macrobius, *Commentarii in Somnium Scipionis* 1.2.19, ed. J. Willis (Leipzig: Teubner, 1963). Text and translation cited in Dinshaw, 203, n. 55. See Dinshaw's discussion, pp. 20–21.

34. Claude Schneider suggests that when Cynewulf juxtaposes Juliana's passive yet determined spirituality to the pagans' aggressive militarism, the poet deliberately devalues the latter. See "Cynewulf's Devaluation of Heroic Tradition," *Anglo-Saxon England* 7 (1978): 107–118.

35. *Ravishing Maidens*, 24.

36. Laura Mulvey's influential article, "Visual Pleasure and Narrative Cinema," *Visual and Other Pleasures* (Bloomington: Indiana University Press, 1989), articulates the theory behind the male gaze:

> The determining male gaze projects its fantasy onto the female figure. . . . In their traditional exhibitionist role women are simultaneously looked at and displayed, with their appearance coded for strong visual and erotic impact so that they can be said to connote *to-be-looked-at-ness*. . . . A woman performs within the narrative; the gaze of the spectator and that of the male characters . . . are neatly combined without breaking narrative verisimilitude" (Mulvey, 19; emphasis in original).

Compare this to Jerome's comments on gazing on female virgins:

> Therefore I conjure you before God and Jesus Christ and his elect angels to guard that which you have received, not readily exposing to the public gaze the vessels of the Lord's temple (which only the priests are by right allowed to see), that no profane person may look upon God's sanctuary. . . . And assuredly no gold or silver vessel was ever so dear to God as is the temple of the virgin's body. . . . [U]nchaste eyes see nothing aright. They fail to appreciate the beauty of the soul, and only value that of the body (Letter XXII, 31).

In a certain sense, Mulvey and Jerome make the same point: that the female body can be viewed only from a male viewpoint. The distinction that Jerome makes between the acceptability of the priests' gaze over the pagans' is the same point I have been discussing: spiritually healthy readers are by definition male-identified, and thus the audience, in identifying with the male gaze when viewing the naked female body, assumes a masculine perspective. Readers thus gaze on Juliana's nakedness in both a spiritually licit sense and a materially illicit sense; they occupy the position of both the spiritually initiated reader and the "unchaste" pagan, both the saints and the sinners.

37. Jerome, Epistula XXII (Ad Eustochium), 176; trans. Fremantle, 31.

38. *Acta S. Julianae*, ed. William J. Strunk, rpt. in *The Juliana of Cynewulf* (Boston: D.C. Heath, 1904), 38. Translation mine.

39. For the translation of *æþelu* as "origins," see *The Dictionary of Old English, s.v.*

40. As Claude Schneider remarks, the devil "display[s] a brute-force mentality which prompts him to recommend a more elaborate torture, a bath of molten lead (573b–577a), when simpler diabolics such as scourging and burning have failed. Such tactics are suited to stone fortresses, not to spiritual ones" ("Cynewulf's Devaluation," 114). See also John P. Hermann, who situates this scene within a broader realm of spiritual warfare. Hermann offers a valuable analysis of Juliana's *stabilitas* against the devil, but he does not discuss the gendered implications of this passage. *Allegories of War: Language and Violence in Old English Poetry* (Ann Arbor: University of Michigan Press, 1989), 156ff.

41. Virginitas: *An Essay in the History of a Medieval Ideal* (The Hague: Martinus Nijhoff, 1975), 55–56.

42. See also Hermann, 154–157.

43. "Inversion and Political Purpose in the Old English *Judith*," *English Studies* 63 (1982), 291.

44. Olsen, "Inversion and Political Purpose," 292.

45. See Schulenburg, "Women's Monastic Communities," 222–223. See also *The Victoria History of the Counties of England*, ed. William Page et al. Vol. 12:2 (London: St Catherine Press, 1926), 16; also vol. 18.2, 151.

46. Dorothy Whitelock, ed. *English Historical Documents c. 500–1042* (New York: Oxford University Press, 1955), 222; see also *The Victoria History of the Counties of England*, vol. 18:2, 151.

47. Whitelock, 474.

48. Schulenburg, "The Heroics of Virginity," 47, relates this and several other similar accounts.

49. Ironically, at the end of the poem Eleusius is trapped at sea on a ship that eventually is destroyed in a storm. Along with his men, he is consigned to the worst kind of enclosure:

Þær XXX wæs
ond feowere eac   feores onsohte
þurh wæges wylm   wigena cynnes,
heane mid hlaford,   hroþra bidæled,
hyhta lease   helle sohton.
Ne þorftan þa þegnas   in þam þystran ham,
seo geneatscolu   in þam neolan scræfe,
to þam frumgare   feohgestealda
witedra wenan,   þæt hy in winsele
ofer beorsetle   beagas þegon,
æpplede gold.   (678b–688a)

[There the life of thirty plus another four of the warrior class, as despised as their lord, was sought by the surge of the waves;

deprived of comforts, lacking hope, they sought hell. In that
gloomy home, that deep cave, the thanes, the band of retainers,
did not need to expect their allotted treasures from their leader,
[or] that they in the hall, on the hall–bench, would receive rings
and bright gold.]

On this ironic use of heroic conventions, see Schneider, "Cynewulf's
Devaluation of Heroic Tradition."
　　50. *The Cult of the Saints* (Chicago: University of Chicago Press, 1981),
83.
　　51. Translation from Michael J. Allen and Daniel Calder, *Sources and
Analogues of Old English Poetry* (Cambridge: D.S. Brewer, 1976), 32.
　　52. Hermann likewise considers that the poem's probably female readership would have made the link between Juliana's "firmness" and their own
monastic vows. See *Allegories of War*, 169–170.

CHAPTER 4

Bodies and Borders: The Hermeneutics of Enclosure in Ælfric's Lives of Female Saints

The *Lives of Saints*, written by the homilist Ælfric of Eynsham in the last decade of the tenth century, problematize the relationship between gendered bodies and their borders in ways profoundly reminiscent of the monastic ideology of enclosure discussed in the preceding chapters. This collection of saints' lives and homilies, translated by Ælfric at the request of two Anglo-Saxon noblemen, presents vernacular accounts of "the martyrdom and lives of the Saints whom monks celebrate amongst themselves, with their services" ["þæra halgena ðrowungum and life . . . þe mynster-menn mid heora þenungum betwux him wurðiað"].[1] Thus the *Lives of Saints* represent a popular vernacular dissemination of texts that had previously been read only within monastic communities. The interest of Ælfric's *Lives* lies not so much in their originality as in the circumstances of their production: because the *Lives of Saints* are themselves the products of an author who was profoundly interested in issues of textual interpretation, the *Lives of Saints* offer a rare opportunity to apply theory to practice, that is, to analyze these narratives within the critical discourse of the author who produced them.[2]

Ælfric's *Lives* of female virgin martyrs conform to hagiographic conventions: they present stories of young Christian women whose virginity is violently threatened, but who maintain their bodily integrity in the face of grave danger. The inevitable emphasis on the saint's body and her potential sexuality points to the key paradox in medieval hagiography that I described in the previous chapter: the bodies of female virgin martyrs are of primary importance in texts that purport not to be about the body at all. This chapter will account for that paradox through an analysis of Ælfric's own hermeneutics. In

Ælfric's *Lives* of female virgin martyrs, as in *Juliana*, I will suggest,
the saints' bodies function as texts that display the tensions between
the practices of reading literally—as the pagan torturers do—and
spiritually—as the saint herself does, along with (ideally) all Christian
readers who identify with these texts. While Ælfric's female saints
display many of the characteristics of heroic virginity so prominent
in earlier Old English poetry, it is a virginity constantly under assault,
at risk of penetration, or punished by confinement. At the same time,
the *Lives* anticipate the *sponsa christi* imagery so prevalent in women's
devotional literature of the later Middle Ages. Ælfric's *Lives*, I will suggest, confront and negotiate issues of gender and sexuality through
textuality. In ways profoundly reminiscent of the female elegies,
Beowulf, and *Juliana*, the *Lives of Saints* relate bodies to borders, and
gender to interiority, in order to normalize and prescribe femininity.[3]

Like all saints' lives, Ælfric's narratives are meant to teach, to
"refresh by their exhortations," as Ælfric says, those who "are sloth-
ful in the faith, since the Passions of the Martyrs greatly revive a
failing faith" ["sed magis fide torpentes recreare hortationibus, quia
martyrum passiones nimium fidem erigant languentem"] (Skeat, 2–3).
One of the principal ways that saints' lives achieve their didactic
purpose is through multiple levels of audience identification: Christian
readers identify with the saint, and thus, by extension with Christ;
but hagiography also permits audience identification through another
device—the crowd scene, the public spectacle of torture. Scenes of
watching are a common feature of the genre.

Ælfric's narratives, like so many medieval saints' lives, revolve
around what Kathryn Gravdal has called a "sexual plot," in which
the saint is sexualized through the threat of rape, forced prostitution, the eroticized display of the saint's naked body, and so forth.[4]
Within such plots, Gravdal argues, representations of sexual violence
can serve three ideological purposes. First, such scenes "glorif[y] virginity": "[u]nder physical assault, the female saint becomes a soldier
of Christ. . . . The threat of rape thus opens a space for female heroism"
as the female saint becomes a type of *miles christi*. Second, the female
saint can become a type of Christ, through "a specifically female form
of *imitatio christi*" in which the attempted seduction of the saint imi-
tates the temptation of Christ. Finally, in hagiographic scenes of
sexual violence, because "no rape is ever completed," the narratives
emphasize God's power and justice (23–24). Gravdal's groundbreaking

study of rape in medieval French literature and law, moreover, demonstrates that behind these narrative functions of sexual violence, medieval literary texts normalize the textual representation of violence against women's bodies which is rationalized, made "licit" in medieval culture (24). Such cultural legitimation, in fact, becomes the business of saints' lives, so that such violence becomes all but invisible to many readers of these texts, because it is so common.

How can we interpret images of extreme and gruesome corporeality in texts that are meant to offer spiritual "refreshment"? How, in other words, can we read the bodies of female virgin martyrs, and in particular, how can we learn from Ælfric the reading lessons that will enable our own interpretations? Are these narratives about the body in spite of their apparent rejection of it? In the pages that follow, I will argue that the *Lives* of Saints Agatha, Agnes, Lucy, and Eugenia demonstrate that the saint's body is the key to each text's spiritual message. In each *Life*, the saint's body acts as a text that displays the tensions between the practices of reading literally (like the pagans) and spiritually (like the saint herself and all Christian readers). The saint's body functions as the hermeneutic tool that enables spiritual signification, to the extent that it is precisely through the display of literal violence that spiritual meaning is achieved.[5] The bodies of female virgin martyrs are of primary importance in texts that repeatedly deny that the body matters at all; Ælfric's hermeneutics rewrites sexual violence as spiritual exegesis.

In Ælfric's *Lives*, the thematics of female enclosure can thus be found at the level of the texts—specifically, the bodies of the saints themselves. Like sacred or scriptural texts, saints' bodies are beautiful on the outside, but contain important spiritual mysteries deep within their surfaces. Through the use of corporeal metaphors, Ælfric identifies two ways of reading sacred texts: readers may read *lichamlice*, (carnally, in terms of the body), or *gastlice*, (spiritually, allegorically). Reading *lichamlice* is, for Ælfric, akin to the literal sense and refers to both the literal understanding we might have upon first viewing (or reading) an object, and to bodily behaviors.[6] Ælfric's corporeal hermeneutics also encompasses another body metaphor: *ða nacodon word*, the naked word. Again the metaphor is based upon the notion of a corporeal text, a text-as-body; like the saint herself, the naked words of scripture must be "clothed" by the homilist with the veil of spiritual meaning. Acting as both text and reader, the female saint interprets the spiritual message contained within, and yet enveloping, her own flesh.

The key to understanding Ælfric's hermeneutics occurs in a homily for Midlent Sunday (*Dominica in Media Quadragessima*), which explicates Christ's miracle of the loaves and fishes. Following a general explanation of the various symbols in the biblical account, Ælfric precisely describes the act of interpretation:

> Ðis wundor is swiðe micel 7 deop on getacnungum;   oft gehwa gesihð fægere stafas awritene. þonne herað he ðone writere 7 þa stafas 7 nat hwæt hi mænað;   Se ðe cann þæra stafa gescead. he herað heora fægernysse. 7 ræt þa stafas. 7 understent hwæt hi gemænað; on oðre wisan we scawiað metinge. 7 on oðre wisan stafas. ne gæð na mare to metinge buton þ[æt] ðu hit geseo. 7 herige; Nis na genoh þ[æt] ðu stafas scawie. buton þu hi eac ræde. 7 þ[æt] andgit understande;   swa is eac on ðam wundre þe god worhte mid þam fif hlafum. ne bið na genoh þ[æt] we ðæs tacnes wundrian. oþþe þurh þ[æt] god herian buton we eac þ[æt] gastlice andgit understandon;[7]

> [This miracle is very great and deep in meanings. Often someone sees beautiful letters written, then praises the writer and the letters, but does not know what they mean. He who understands the art of the letters praises their beauty, and reads the letters, and understands their meaning. In one way we observe a painting, and in another way letters. Nothing more is needed for a painting than that you see and praise it; but it is not enough to look at the letters unless you also read them and understand their meaning. So it is also with the miracle which God worked with the five loaves; it is not enough that we admire the symbol or praise God for it, unless we also understand its spiritual meaning.]

Ælfric distinguishes between those who simply admire and praise beautiful letters written on a page, and those who know how to understand the spiritual meaning found "deop" within those written characters. It is important to note his rather lenient attitude towards those who simply look and admire. As Paul Szarmach has suggested, the distinction Ælfric makes here is really between "no understanding at all and its antinomy, understanding. . . . The human element, praise—which both learned and unlearned may give to fair writing, to illustration, or to God—appears to be part of the process of understanding." Further, Szarmach notes that "praise is insufficient by itself without true understanding to complete it. . . . By implication those who praise and do not understand are not on the wrong path so much as not far enough along the way."[8] Thus Ælfric establishes the process of exegesis as a continuum, thereby implicitly acknowledging the inevitability of the literal sense: all readers first see, admire, and praise beautifully written characters, while skilled readers will proceed to interpret their spiritual signification.[9]

Ælfric's source for this passage is Augustine, who, in the *Tractates on the Gospel of John*, likewise distinguishes between "looking" and "understanding," in a similar hermeneutic continuum. The miracle of the five loaves, Augustine writes, is "exhibitum oculis ubi exerceretur intellectus, ut inuisibilem Deum per uisibilia opera miraremur" ["displayed to the eyes, that the understanding might be put to work upon it so that we might revere the invisible God through visible works"].[10] Thus, the visual evidence of a miracle signifies its spiritual meaning. However, simply viewing and praising miracles is insufficient without asking "quid nobis loquantur de Christo" ["what they say to us about Christ"].[11] Ælfric's statement, "Þis wundor is swiðe micel, and deop on getacnungum," considerably condenses Augustine's more fully developed explanation:

> Hoc ergo miraculum, sicut audiuimus quam magnum sit, quaeramus etiam quam profundum sit; non tantum eius superficie delectemur, sed etiam altitudinem perscrutemur. Habet enim aliquid intus, hoc quod miramur foris. Vidimus, spectauimus magnum quiddam, praeclarum quiddam, et omnino diuinem, quod fieri nisi a Deo non possit;

> [Therefore, as to this miracle, as we have heard how great it is, let us seek also how profound it is; let us delight not only in its surface, but let us also search out its depth. For it has something interior; this at which we wonder on the outside. We have seen, we have watched something great,

something magnificent, and completely divine, which cannot be done except by God.][12]

Full understanding of miracles must come through both witnessing
the literal event and also understanding the deep spiritual meaning
contained within that event. For both Augustine and Ælfric, skilled
readers—those able to interpret the spiritual sense—start at the same
place as unskilled viewers; that is, they admire the letters' beauty,
praise them, and then proceed to the interpretation. This material
function of the letters themselves will, I believe, be central to our
understanding of Ælfric's saints, and in particular to the material
and spiritual ways of reading the carefully crafted texts of the saints'
bodies.[13]

When Ælfric distinguishes between *lichamlic* and *gastlic* reading,
typically he is explaining some aspect of the Old Testament in terms
of the New.[14] While *gastlic(e)* translates straightforwardly into Modern
English as "spiritual(ly)," *lichamlic(e)* is a somewhat more flexible term.
Derived from the Old English *lichama*, body, it carries a sense of
mortality; *lichama* can also be translated "corpse." Thus *lichamlic(e)*
bears the reminder of the mortality of the flesh, as well as the sense
of "that which is done with or through the body" or "carnally, cor-
poreally," as opposed to the immortal essence of *gast*. (Cf. St. Paul's
admonition to the Corinthians: "For the letter killeth, but the spirit
quickeneth" 2 Corinthians 3.6). Ælfric uses *lichamlic(e)* to refer not
just to bodily practices, but also to a kind of literal understanding—
that is, a bodily behavior or action based on a literal reading of an
Old Testament text. Thus for Ælfric understanding a text *lichamlice*
means understanding it both by means of the body, and in the
literal sense.

Ælfric's method of scriptural interpretation thus can be viewed
as a corporeal hermeneutics, in which sacred texts are interpreted
either literally (through the body) or spiritually, that is, understood
for the hidden messages they contain. The juxtaposition of *lichamlic*
and *gastlic* is found throughout the First and Second Series of Catholic
Homilies; it occurs frequently in Second Series Homily XV, *Sermo De
Sacrificio in Die Pascae* [Sermon on the Sacrifice on Easter Day]. In
explaining the mysteries ["gerynu"] of the Holy Eucharist, Ælfric
explicitly contrasts the spiritual and the bodily or carnal at least

seven times[15]—not surprising, of course, in a homily explaining that Christ's body becomes the spirit. The following example is typical:

> Sume ðas race we habbað getrahtnod on oðre stowe. sume we willað nu geopenian. þæt þe belimpð to ðam halgan husle; Cristene men ne moton healdan nu ða ealdan .æ. lichamlice. ac him gedafenað þæt hi cunnon hwæt heo gastlice getacnige . . . æfter gastlicum andgite. . . .[16]

> [Some of this narrative we have interpreted in another place. Some {of it} we will now open, that which concerns the holy eucharist: Christian men may not now hold the old law bodily but it is appropriate that they know what it symbolizes spiritually . . . according to the spiritual sense. . . .]

Ælfric's move here between carnal and spiritual understanding is a slippery one, conflating literal behavior with spiritual understanding: men are not allowed to follow the old law *lichamlice* (with their bodies) but it is appropriate that they know what it signifies *gastlice*. The distinction between bodily and spiritual readings of Old Testament laws is similarly found in In *Natale Sanctarum Uirginum* [the Homily on the Nativity of Holy Virgins]:

> Eal seo gelaðung ðe stent on mædenum. and on cnapum. on ceorlum and on wifum. eal heo is genamod to anum mædene. swa swa se apostol Paulus cwæð. to geleaffullum folce; Disponsaui uos uni uiro virginem castam. exhibere christo; Þæt is on englisc. Ic beweddode eow anum were. þæt ge gearcian an clæne mæden criste; Nis ðis na to understandenne lichamlice. ac gastlice; Crist is se clæna brydguma. and eal seo cristene gelaðung is his bryd. . . . (Godden, 329–330)

> [The whole church, which consists of virgins and of young men, of husbands and of wives, is all called one virgin, as the apostle Paul said to the faithful: Disponsaui uos uni uiro virginem castem exhibere christo; that is, in English: I have betrothed you to one man so that you may prepare a

pure virgin for Christ. This is not to be understood bodily
but spiritually. Christ is the pure bridegroom and the whole
Christian church is his bride.]

To "understand bodily" in the sense that Ælfric uses it here, is to
understand literally, which of course is prohibited. This distinction
becomes particularly urgent in *Octabas et Circumcisio Domini* [the
Homily on the Octave and Circumcision of Our Lord], where Ælfric
reminds his listeners:

> Nis nu alyfed cristenum mannum þæt hi ðas ymbsnidenysse
> lichamlice healdon: ac þeahhwæðere nan mann ne bið.
> soðlice cristen buton he þa ymbsnidenysse on gastlicum
> þeawum gehealde;　(Clemoes, 226)

> [It is not now permitted for Christian men to practice cir-
> cumcision bodily, but nevertheless, no man is truly a
> Christian, unless he practices circumcision in his spiritual
> behavior.]

At the least, *lichamlic(e)* carries a double meaning: "literally," and
"with, through, or by means of the body" (*corporaliter*). Yet to understand "bodily" is insufficient, even "illicit"; such understanding has
not yet progressed beyond carnal literalism to spiritual truth.[17]

Finally, to return to the Homily on the Sacrifice of Easter Day,
we see what is perhaps Ælfric's most frequently cited discussion of
the literal vs. the spiritual sense, in which he distinguishes between
the body in which Christ suffered, and that which is found in the
Eucharist:

> Micel is betwux þam lichaman þe crist on ðrowade. and ðam
> lichaman þe to husle bið gehalgod; Se lichama soðlice ðe
> crist on ðrowode wæs geboren of Marian flæsce. mid blode.
> and mid banum. mid felle. and mid sinum. on menniscum
> limum. mid gesceadwisre sawle geliffæst. and his gastlica
> lichama ðe we husel hata ð is of manegum cornum gegaderod
> buton blode. and bane. limleas. and sawulleas. and nis for
> ði nan ðing þæron to understandenne lichamlice. ac is eall
> gastlice to understandenne. (Godden, 154)

[There is much difference between the body in which Christ suffered and the body which is consecrated for the Eucharist; truly the body in which Christ suffered was born of the flesh of Mary, with blood and with bones, with skin and with sinews in human limbs, brought to life with a rational soul, and his spiritual body which we call the Eucharist is gathered from many grains, without blood or bones, limbless and soulless, and therefore there is nothing in it to be understood bodily but all is to be understood spiritually.]

Again, *lichamlice* carries a dual meaning: "of or pertaining to [Christ's] body" and "literally." Ælfric insists on naming parts of Christ's material body—blood, bones, skin, sinews, limbs—as well as on the literal composition of the communion loaf (it is made of grain) thereby delineating the differences between the literal composition of physical objects and their spiritual symbolism. As with beautiful letters on a manuscript page, both Christ's literal body and the communion loaf become the visible tokens of a greater (deeper, to use Ælfric's term) spiritual message.

With another body metaphor, *ða nacodon word*, the naked word, Ælfric bridges the gap between literal and spiritual interpretation:

We habbað nu gesæd sceortlice on Englisc
þis halige godspell, swa swa ge gehyrdon nu,
þa nacedan word ana; ac we nu wyllað
mid fægerum andgite hi gefrætewian eow,
þæt hi licweorðe beon to lare eow eallum,
gif ge þæt gastlice andgit mid godum willan underfoð.[18]

[We have now said briefly in English this holy gospel, as you have just heard, the naked words alone; but now we will adorn them for you with fair meaning, so that they may be acceptable to you all as teaching, if you receive that spiritual meaning with good will.]

Here Ælfric refers simply to bare, unexplicated words as they are found on the manuscript page. The homilist "clothes" the words' nakedness, "adorns" them with spiritual meaning, in order to make that meaning accessible to an unskilled audience. The metaphor recurs in the Letter to Sigeweard, where Ælfric again distinguishes between the words on the page and the meaning the homilist endows them with: "Nu miht þu wel witan þæt weorc sprecað swiþor þonne þa nacodan word, þe nabbað nane fremminge" [Now you may well know that the work speaks much more than the naked word, which has no purpose].[19] A third and related use of the metaphor is found in the Preface to Genesis, in a passage in which Ælfric warns against the dangers of unlearned priests, unskilled in Latin, who may fail to interpret properly (that is, *gastlice*) the lessons of the Old Testament:

> We secgað eac foran to þæt seo boc is swiþe deop gastlice to understandenne, 7 we ne writaþ na mare buton þa nacedan gerecednisse.   Þonne þincþ þam ungelæredum þæt eall þæt andgit beo belocen on þære anfealdan gerecednisse, ac hit ys swiþe feor þam.   (Crawford, 77)

> [We also say beforehand that the book is very deep to understand spiritually, and we write no more than the naked narrative. Then the unlearned think that all the meaning is locked in the one-fold narrative, but that is very far from {the case}.]

The danger inherent in the "naked" narrative ("naceden gerecednisse"), then, is that it may be perceived by unskilled readers as a one-fold (i.e., singular or unique) narrative ("anfealdan gerecednisse"). "Naked words" are analogous to the "fair characters" with which this discussion began, and it takes a skilled interpreter to "unlock" the spiritual meaning contained deep within the literal surface. There is a material depth to Ælfric's understanding of literal and spiritual meanings in texts. Spatial metaphors such as "deop" and "belocen" suggest that meaning is contained within textual layering. Spiritual truth is found only by looking into—that is, interpreting—literal surfaces.

Ælfric's corporeal hermeneutics can inform our understanding of how the bodies of virgin saints and martyrs function as texts that embody literal and spiritual meanings. As we have seen, corporeal metaphors take on powerful hermeneutic values in Ælfric's system of sacred exegesis. Through metaphors of body, spirit, materiality, and space, Ælfric conflates texts and bodies, such that reading the text of a saint's life means interpreting the hermeneutic truths contained within her body, on public display throughout each *vita*. Most important, this hermeneutics exposes the dangers inherent in focusing solely on the "naceden gerecednisse," the "naked" or "literal" text of each saint, even as it depends upon those "naked texts" to convey a deeper spiritual message.

For modern readers reading medieval virgin martyr narratives can be a somewhat alienating experience, not least because of the extended descriptions of torture and attempted mutilation performed on the saint's body. How are we to understand such descriptions, concerned as they are with the display, exposure, and attempted rupture of female bodies? Perhaps more importantly, how can they help us to read medieval constructions of gender and femininity? What do they say about how medieval readers perceived and were conditioned by these representations of women, Christianity, and (sexual) violence? Elaine Scarry's discussion of pain and torture in her important study, *The Body in Pain*, can help illuminate the "cultural logic" of torture, that is, the discursive structures and power relations that develop within scenes of torture.[20] Scarry's work investigates pain and torture in circumstances far removed from medieval saints' lives, but provides a useful interpretive framework for reading these narratives. The "grammar" of torture that Scarry describes has important implications for the representations of torture in the saints' lives.

Pain, Scarry argues, because it is internal, invisible, "resists verbal objectification" (12). Thus the expression of pain may only be achieved through an external agent, whereby a weapon of torture "convey[s] something of the felt-experience of pain to someone outside the sufferer's body." Because the agent of pain "either exists . . . or can be pictured as existing . . . at the external boundary of the body, it begins to externalize, objectify, and make sharable what is originally an interior and unsharable experience" (15–16). Conveying the felt experience of pain to another is only possible through the perceptions of "inside" and "outside" the body; that is, only when the pain can be imagined at the body's "border," so to speak, can it begin to be felt by another.

Making visible the (potential) pain inflicted on bodies is a central function of saints' lives. Of course that potential is never realized;

but nonetheless the agents of pain—torturers, racks, rods, whips, burning coals—are explicitly described. Saints' lives narrate the potentiality of pain that might result from the breakdown of the Christian will. The audiences of these texts can begin to share in these narratives of pain when the pain is made explicit through the vehicle of the saint's body—which itself becomes an agent for expressing that potentiality. The audience can readily identify with the saint's human body, and thus representations of violence "convey something of the felt-experience of pain to someone outside the sufferer's body."

Scarry shows that in torture, human pain is translated into a "fiction of power" closely resembling the intentions of the torturers in virgin martyr narratives:

> In the very processes [torture] uses to produce pain within the body of the prisoner, it bestows visibility on the structure and enormity of what is usually private and incommunicable, contained within the boundaries of the sufferer's body. It then goes on to deny, to falsify, the reality of the very thing it has itself objectified by a perceptual shift which converts the vision of suffering into the wholly illusory but, to the torturers and the regime they represent, wholly convincing spectacle of power. . . . It is, of course, precisely because the reality of that power is so highly contestable, the regime so unstable, that torture is being used. (27)

The pagan torturers in the *Lives* of virgin martyrs, members or leaders of what the Christian reader knows to be a highly unstable regime, strive to expose or rupture the saint's body; they believe that torturing her (what Ælfric might call reading her *lichamlice*) will yield the "truth" of her body and deny her Christian spirit. They wrongly assume their own power, an irony which can take on richly comic tones in some saints' lives, because the Christian audience knows that the power is indeed a fiction. The tension between pagan and Christian in these narratives is worked out through "an obsessive, self-conscious display of agency" (Scarry, 27) as the pagan torturers construct their own fiction of power.

Hagiography is imaginative literature, generic, stylized, and above all didactic. The Christian reader of saints' lives ought, by definition, to locate herself or himself within the body of the saint; the process of identification with the saintly protagonist is crucial to the narrative success of the text. The process of imaginative identification for the Christian reader was considered to be the most appropriate method for scriptural reading (*lectio divina*). Together with "ruminatio," the "spiritual nutrition" gained from the physical pronouncing and oral experience of divine words, and "reminiscence," the stimulation of the memory through verbal echoes, the active imagination of the monastic reader permitted an intense degree of identification with the text being read.[21] As Jean Leclercq describes it, the imagination allowed medieval readers to:

> picture, to 'make present,' to see beings with all the details provided by the texts: the colors and dimensions of things, the clothing, bearing, and actions of the people, the complex environment in which they move. They liked to describe them and, so to speak, re-create them, giving very sharp relief to images and feelings. The words of the sacred text never failed to produce a strong impression on the mind.[22]

This is also the activity the twelfth-century writer Aelred of Rivaulx recommends in his *De Institutione Inclusarum* ("Rule for a Recluse"). While not specifically a prescription of reading practices, Aelred's suggestions to his female reader are instructive for us because they show the extent to which the medieval recluse is expected to situate herself "bodily" in the biblical events on which she meditates. To cite one example:

> Hinc euntem in Bethleem cum omni deuotione prosequere, et in hospitium diuertens cum illa, assiste et obsequere parienti, locatoque in praesepi paruulo, erumpe in uocem exultationis, clamans cum Isaia: *Paruulus natus est nobis, filius datus est nobis.* Amplectere dulce illud praesepium, uincat uerecundiam amor, timorem depellat affectus, ut sacratissimis pedibus figas labia, et oscula gemines.

> [Next with all your devotion, accompany the Mother as she makes her way to Bethlehem. Take shelter in the inn with her, be present and help her as she gives birth, and when the infant is laid in the manger break out into words of

exultant joy together with Isaiah and cry: "A child has been born to us, a son is given to us." Embrace that sweet crib, let love overcome your reluctance, affection drive out fear. Put your lips to those most sacred feet, kiss them again and again.[23]

Thus Aelred instructs his reader not merely to envision the events of Christ's life, but to "live" them simultaneously, by inserting herself into the biblical stories, making bodily contact with the biblical characters.

The identification with suffering described variously by Scarry, Leclercq, and Aelred is precisely what Ælfric suggests in the Homily on the Nativity of Holy Martyrs. While the martyrs obviously suffered intensely, their suffering pales in comparison to what may lie ahead for non-believers. And although his audience may not be able to prove their belief through the kinds of suffering the martyrs faced, Ælfric asserts that his fellow Christians are no less martyrs:

> Twa cynn sind martirdomes. An dearnunge. oðer eawunge; Se ðe on ehtnysse for cristes geleafan his lif alæt. se bið openlice martir; Eft se ðe forberð ðurh geðyld hosp. and teonan. and ðone lufað þe hine hatað. and his agene unlustas. and þæs ungesewenlican deofles tihtinge forsihð. se bið untwylice martyr on digelre dæde. . . . And we magon beon martiras ðeah ðe we mid isene acwealde ne beon. gif we þæt geðyld on urum mode unleaslice healdað. (Godden, 314–315)

> [There are two kinds of martyrdoms. One is secret, the other public. He who loses his life through persecution for belief in Christ is openly a martyr; but he who, in patience, suffers insult and injury, and loves the one who hates him, and rejects his own lusts and the accusations of the unseen devil, he is certainly a martyr in secret deed. And we may be martyrs, although we are not killed with iron, if we truthfully hold that patience in our minds.]

Reading or listening to the lives of Christian martyrs means, for Ælfric, that readers actively imagine and identify with suffering. Readers are not permitted to look away, to ignore or objectify the pain, but rather they become subjectively engaged with it. The experience of imagining felt pain is inherent in the reading lessons taught by the *Lives* of virgin martyrs. Scenes of torture create in readers the desire to suffer (to be a secret martyr) on behalf of—and alongside—Christ. Yet at the same time, because the saint herself does not experience (and may even welcome) pain, saints' lives dismantle the fictional power of the pagan regime. Saints' lives deconstruct the cultural logic of real torture that Scarry describes, by not allowing the fiction of power to develop, by not allowing real pain to be felt by the victim of torture. Nonetheless, the torture scenes create within readers the active identification of felt-pain. Thus the tortured bodies of the martyrs are essential for the operations of the narrative; representations of the literal enable spiritual signification.

The *Lives* of Saints Agatha, Lucy, Agnes, and Eugenia exemplify this process. Structurally, their plots follow that of *Juliana*. In each case, a young Christian woman is the object of a pagan ruler's desire. When she refuses to submit to him, she is tortured and eventually killed for her faith. In the process, the bodies of the virgins are consistently misread by the torturers (and by other non-Christians), who focus single-mindedly on the saint's literal flesh. As Ælfric's hermeneutics suggests, however, meaning is not to be found at the level of the "naked" text, and skilled Christian readers will read beyond its literal surface—the object of so much narrative attention—to reach its spiritual meaning.

In the Life of St. Agatha, the virgin is set against two pagan opponents early in the text. Quintianus, the "murderous persecutor" ["se cwealm-bære ehtere"] (194) and suitor wishes to corrupt the virgin; to do so, he sends her to a prostitute, Aphrodosia, so "þæt heo (Agatha) . . . hire (Aphrodosia's) þeawas leornode ./ and hire (Agatha's) mod awende þurh þæra myltestrena forspennincgæ" [so that she {Agatha} . . . might learn her {Aphrodosia's} habits, and her mind {might be} changed through the seductions of the prostitutes] (196).[24]

Aphrodosia's attempts to corrupt Agatha focus on the desire to bend her will, "hire mod awende" (196). Skeat translates the verb, "awendan," as "pervert" but the verb also carries textual connotations: "awendan" is the verb most commonly used by Ælfric to mean "translate," as in "on englisc to awendan" [to translate into English].[25]

In the scene with Aphrodosia, the verb refers to the attempts to change Agatha's mind. The verb thus carries not only the sense of "pervert" or "corrupt" as it has commonly been rendered (the context requires this sense), but also the sense of "translation," of material transformation. To change, "awendan," Agatha's mind in this sense suggests changing her nature, using the mental transformation to effect the bodily corruption. Several lines later, Ælfric uses the verb "gebigan," to bend: "Þa seah affrodosia . þæt heo þære femnan mod / gebigan ne mihte" [Then Aphrodosia saw that she could not bend the woman's mind] (trans. Skeat, 196–197). The verb carries material connotations of "bending," "turning," even "crushing" (see *DOE, s.v. gebigan*), in addition to the sense of shaping someone's thoughts. This semantic context suggests that Aphrodosia wants to change Agatha's mind in order to corrupt her body; Quintianus would corrupt her body in order to change her mind. For both, however, body and spirit are inseparable, mutually determinant aspects of Agatha's self.

When Quintianus learns that, despite her best attempts, Aphrodosia has been unable to corrupt the virgin, he orders Agatha brought to him and a lengthy debate ensues. Agatha deflects his questions, skillfully turning his words back against him. Quintianus' reaction to the saint's rhetorical skill perfectly illustrates his literalism. He is so angry at her verbal ability that he commands his men to strike her "mid handum . . . / gelome on þæt hleor . þæt heo hlydan ne sceolde" [continually on her face with their hands so that she could not make a sound] (198).[26] He recognizes the power of Agatha's rhetoric, but "reads" her literally, believing that Agatha's mouth is the source of her words, and he seeks to counteract that power through physical violence.

When, after being thrown in a dark prison, Agatha still refuses to submit to Quintianus' desires, he orders her stretched and twisted on a rack, sure that the torture will persuade her:

Agathes andwyrde on ðære hencgene þus .
Swa ic lust-fullige on þisum laðum witum .
swa swa se ðe gesihð . þone þe he gewilnode .
oððe se þe fint fela gold-hordas .
Ne mæg min sawl beon gebroht mid blysse to heofonum .
butan min lichama beo on þinum bendum genyrwod .
and fram ðinum cwellerum on þinum copsum agrapod . (202)

[Agatha answered from the rack thus: 'I take such pleasure from these hateful tortures, just like someone who sees that which he has desired, or someone who finds many gold-hoards. My soul may not be brought blissfully to heaven unless my body is bound by your fetters and grasped in your bonds by your torturers.]

Here Agatha articulates how the virgin martyr lives work: the martyrs welcome torture precisely because the torture of the body is the vehicle for the soul's salvation. She makes the cause and effect relationship explicit. Thus, the saint gains salvation through imprisoning, enclosing structures. Only through being tightly bound can the saint gain spiritual release from those earthly bonds: confining the body frees the soul.

The most compelling event in Life of St. Agatha follows immediately on the speech just cited. Quintianus, enraged at her resolve, orders her breast to be cut off:

Þa gebealh hine se wælhreowa and het hi gewriðan
on ðam breoste mid þære hencgene and het siððan
    ofaceorfan .
Agathes him cwæð to . Eala ðu arleasosta
ne sceamode þe to ceorfanne þæt þæt ðu sylf suce .
ac ic habbe mine breost on minre sawle . ańsunde .
mid þam ðe Ic min andgit eallunga afede . (202)

[Then the cruel man bellowed, and commanded (his men) to torture her on the breast on the rack, and after that ordered it cut off. Agatha said to him, 'Oh, you most cruel man. Aren't you ashamed to cut off that which you have sucked on yourself? But I have my breast completely whole in my soul, and I shall nourish my understanding entirely with it.']

The spatial metaphor in Agatha's speech, which identifies her body as container for true spiritual understanding, exemplifies Ælfric's hermeneutics: a literal text may transmit one kind of literal surface meaning, but it contains the spiritual truth, the "gastlic andgit," within.[27] Likewise, Agatha's own interpretive act transforms the violent mutilation of her literal breast into a spiritual triumph. Her distinction between the literal and the spiritual breast confirms that cutting off the exterior flesh will not affect the interior spirit. Like a text, Agatha's literal surface symbolically contains meaning; inability to interpret the sign system correctly denies signification to uninitiated readers. Quintianus, like all pagan torturers, mistakenly believes that literally opening up the saint will give him access to her. But as we know, only an initiated reader can open up that body to reveal its meaning.

Yet what about Agatha's breast? Allen Frantzen has argued that the disfigurement "masculinizes" the saint. When her breast is cut off, he suggests, she is "manlike," and when it is restored, she is "restored to womanhood." Agatha's sexual identity, in his view, is "central to the story, for she has transcended the female body and become, however briefly, like a man."[28] I would argue, however, that rather than enabling her to "transcend" her gender, the text insists upon Agatha's female body, does not permit us to forget that body as the object of physical violence. Agatha's breast, even as lack, draws attention to itself, and thus although she may be "breastless," Agatha can never be fully masculinized. She is always associated with the female breast (this is likewise true in the iconography) even when—especially when—hers is missing. Her own references to suckling in the speech cited above emphasize the lactative and nutritive—that is, the biologically female—functions of the breast.[29]

In fact, these images of suckling and nurturing, which at first seem unexpected in the narrative of a virgin saint, may anticipate the rich tradition of maternal imagery found in religious literature from the twelfth century onward. While we are not to assume that Quintianus has literally sucked from Agatha's breast, her statement aligns her generally with all women, and specifically with both the Virgin Mary and Christ. As the representative of Mary, Agatha's body can nourish souls; as Caroline Walker Bynum has shown, Christ's body was similarly represented in medieval culture as able to nourish bodies through suckling.[30] Further, the medieval identification of breast milk with transmuted blood meant "an association of Christ's wounds with woman's body" (Bynum, 271), while late medieval artists depicted the "breast [of the Virgin] as food, parallel to the bleeding (i.e., nurturing) wound [of Christ]" (Bynum, 271–272). Thus just as the blood of Christ's wound will provide nourishment for Christians, the wounding of Agatha's breast signals its similarly nutritive capabilities. Agatha herself is nourished through the breast (i.e., Christ) within her own soul. Yet in a richly ironic twist, as soon as she makes this point, Quintianus orders her to be deprived of food and drink; clearly he has not yet learned the difference between literal and spiritual that Agatha has continually tried to teach him.

Agatha's identity lies in both the essential materiality of her female body, and in the spiritual truth enclosed by that body. Quintianus believes that the outer breast matters; Agatha asserts that it does not, drawing attention away from the literal body to the spiritual breast. This image was anticipated by Aphrodosia, who reported to Quintianus: "'Stanas magon hnexian . and þæt starce isen / on leades gelicnysse . ærðan þe se geleafa mæge / of agathes breoste . beon æfre adwæsced'" [Stones may get soft, and hard iron may become like lead, before the faith in Agatha's breast can ever be destroyed] (196). Quintianus evidently took Aphrodosia's words literally when he ordered the mutilation. Agatha reconfirms the idea that the breast to which both she and Aphrodosia refer is spiritual, not corporeal. The breast emblematizes the hermeneutic function of the virgin martyr narratives: its violent mutilation stirs our horror and pity, yet the saint's denial of the significance of her own flesh reminds us that the truth of this text is not found at the literal level, but deep within its (her) beautiful surface. Agatha's spiritual reading of her own body depends upon its literal sense, while the torturer's repeated assaults on her flesh demonstrate his inability to read beyond the literal level.

Agatha is spared further tortures (specifically, being rolled naked on burning coals and broken tiles) when a sudden earthquake kills Quintianus's main counselors.[31] Following the earthquake, Agatha is returned to her cell:

Hwæt ða Agathes inwerdlice clypode .
mid astrehtum handum to þam hælende þus . . . .   (206)

[Indeed then Agatha spoke inwardly with her hands outstretched to the Savior thus . . . .]

The juxtaposition of "inwardly" ["inwerdlice"] and "outstretched" ["astrehtum"] points again to the spatial relations of body and soul found throughout this *Life*: she prays inwardly, symbolically stretching her hands towards Christ, who, like her breast, is wholly contained within her soul. The images of interiority (Agatha within her cell, stretching inwardly towards God) suggest the "true" enclosure of the saint's body, enfolding Christ within her soul—and the soul within the covering of the body (much like Juliana who encloses the love of Christ within her heart). The saint simultaneously moves away from, yet into, the body towards Christ. The spatial dimensions of the saint within the cell, moving ever inward, ever enclosing, evoke a striking image of female piety: the saint is both enclosure and enclosed one; the letter of the flesh encloses the spiritual truth within.

Ælfric's Life of St. Lucy follows directly on the life of Agatha in the manuscript, and like Agatha, Lucy herself provides a lesson in reading bodies as texts. The spatial dimensions of the virginal female body are again of concern in this life, which opens with an image of female rupture: Lucy's mother, Eutychia, has suffered from "a flux of blood" ["arn blod"], hemorrhaging for four years before Lucy convinces her to touch the tomb of St. Agatha and be healed: "þu bist sona hal" [you will soon be whole] (210). In a dream vision at the tomb, St. Agatha confirms that Eutychia has been healed:

þinre meder geheolp þin halga geleafa .
and efne heo is gehæled . halwendlice ðurh crist .
and swa swa þeos burh is gemærsod þurh me . fram crist .
swa bið siracusa burh . þurh þe gewlitegod .
forðan þe þu gearcodest criste . on þinum clænan
   mægð-hade .
wynsume wununge .   (212)

[Your holy faith helped your mother, and she is fully, wholesomely healed by Christ, and just as this town is honored through me from Christ, so the town of Syracuse will be made glorious through you because you prepared yourself for Christ in your pure virginity, a joyful dwelling.]

Agatha's speech to Lucy contains two important images of bodies-as-boundaries: first, through Agatha's intercession, Eutychia's body is healed, made whole.[32] Second, Agatha describes Lucy's virginity (her bodily boundaries) as a "wynsume wununge," a joyful dwelling in which she resides. Virginity is a protective enclosure in which the virgin dwells with Christ.

The image of the virgin as dwelling-place resurfaces in Lucy's argument with her pagan suitor Paschasius:

> . . . pascasius orgellice befran .
> wunað se halga gast on þe eornostlice .
> Lucia andwyrde þam arleasan and cwæð .
> Se apostol behet þam ðe healdað clænnysse .
> þæt hi sind godes templ . and þæs halgan gastes wunung .
>   (214)

[Paschasius scornfully asked, 'Does the holy ghost really dwell in you?' Lucy answered the wicked one and said, 'The apostle promised those who maintain chastity that they will be God's temple and the dwelling-place of the holy ghost.']

The verbal repetition of "wununge," habitation or dwelling-place, confirms the virgin's body as a protected site, an enclosed and sacred space ["templ"]. The saint's body encloses and protects the spiritual self, the soul.

The tension between literal and spiritual interpretation structures the debate between Lucy and Paschasius. Lucy's explanations function as lessons in which she interprets the violence done to her body in terms of hermeneutic truth. In describing her body as the "Holy Ghost's habitation," Lucy has spoken metaphorically, of course, but Paschasius understands her literally:

> Þa cwæð se arleasa . Ic hate þe ardlice lædan .
> to þæra myltestrena huse . þæt ðu þinne mægð-had forleose .
> þæt se . halga gast þe fram fleo . ðonne þu fullice byst
>   gescynd .   (214)

[Then the wicked one said, 'I order you to be led at once to the prostitutes' house, so that you will lose your virginity and so that the holy ghost will fly out of you when you are foully corrupted.]

The sacred space of Lucy's virginal body is juxtaposed to the "prostitutes' house" (a space which by its nature implies a penetration of the female body). Paschasius here reads the "text" of Lucy's body literally, believing that rupturing that body will open up the dwelling place and release the Holy Ghost. In a response that seems meant to reassure a Christian audience who might find themselves in a similar danger, Lucy asserts that a substantive difference separates body and will:

> Lucia andwyrde þus . ne bið ænig gewemmed .
> lichama to plihte . gif hit ne licað þam mode . .
> . . . .
> gif þu me unwilles gewemman nu dest .
> me bið twifeald clænnysse . geteald to wuldre .
> Ne miht þu gebigan minne willan to þe .
> swa hwæt swa πu minum lichaman dest . ne mæg πæt
>   belimpan to me.   (214)

> [Lucy answered thus: 'No one's body is dangerously corrupted if it does not please the mind. . . . If you force me to be corrupted against my will now, a twofold purity will be gloriously assigned to me. You cannot bend my will to yours; whatever you may do to my body, that cannot happen to me.']

Ælfric's Life of St. Lucy thus echoes the statement found in Aldhelm's *de Virginitate*, a work known to have been written specifically for female monastic readers, which asserts that spiritual corruption need not result from forced loss of bodily integrity.[33]

The subsequent events illustrate Lucy's statement. As Paschasius attempts to drag her towards the brothel, her body becomes rooted to the spot; although he tries pulling her with ropes and even harnessing a team of oxen to her body, she cannot be moved. When Paschasius covers her body in oil, and lights a fire around her, she remains unburnt. Her body has become an immutable force, solid and impenetrable. Lucy herself, in a passage which again seems specifically geared towards her "audience(s)", explains how to understand the torture of a martyr:

Ic abæd æt criste þæt ðis cwealmbæra fyr
me ne gewylde . þæt þu wurðe gescynd .
and hit þam geleaffullum afyrsige þære ðrowunge
   forhtunge .
and þam unge-leaffullum þa yfelan blysse of-teo .   (216)

[I have prayed to Christ that this deadly fire will not over-
power me, (and) that you will be humiliated and that it
(the fire) will remove the fear of torture from the faithful
and will take away the evil joy from unbelievers.]

Lucy's words explicate Ælfric's hermeneutics. Witnessing the torture done to the saint's body is fundamental to understanding her
spiritual truth; seeing Lucy unburnt in the fire (and unharmed by
all the various tortures) dispels the fear of torture from believers
and frustrates non-believers. Lucy's words recall as well the two kinds
of readers imagined by Ælfric in the Homily on Midlent Sunday:
those literal readers who admire only beautiful appearances without
understanding, and those spiritual readers who look deep within
the letters to comprehend allegorical truths. Most importantly,
Lucy's words point to the paradox inherent in the representation of
virgin martyrs: in a text that asserts the body's insignificance, we
see that in fact Lucy's body—and, in particular, the violence done
to that body—is the key to providing both textual and spiritual
meaning.

Lucy's imperviousness to torture finally results in the infuriated
Paschasius ordering her stabbed with a sword, "so that her insides
fell out [lit. unwound]" ["þæt hire wand se innoð ut"] (216). Death
by sword is common in virgin martyr narratives (with obvious
phallic implications),[34] as is the ability of the saint to live for several
days after receiving a mortal wound. This final wounding is a literal
rupture, confirming the paradox that the saint's body both does and
does not matter. The literal rupture of Lucy's body proves that her
body is finally of no significance, but the representation of violence
done to that body is of central importance to prove that point.

Ælfric's Life of St. Agnes—not unexpectedly—tells of a young
Christian virgin who is tortured and finally killed when she refuses
to agree to marry her pagan suitor and to worship his gods. Following
tradition, Ælfric associates St. Agnes with the Song of Songs, giving

her a lengthy (38-line) speech in which she identifies Christ as her
true bride-groom, and herself as a *sponsa Christi*.[35] Like St. Agatha,
Agnes displays rhetorical skill in rejecting her suitor. When he offers
marriage, beautiful clothing, jewelry, and other riches, she responds:

> . . . Ic hæbbe oðerne lufiend .
> þinne ungelican . on æðelborennysse
> seðe me bead bæteran frætegunga .
> and his geleafan hring me let to wedde .
> and me gefrætewode . mid un-asmeagendlicra
>   wurðfulnysse .
> He befeng minne swiðran . and eac minne swuran .
> mid deorwurðum stanum . and mid scinendum
>   gimmum .   (170–172)

> [I have another lover, different from you in noble lineage,
> who has given me better ornaments and for his faith, left
> me a ring as a pledge, and he adorned me with unbeliev-
> able honor. He enclosed my right hand and also my neck
> with valuable stones and with shining gems.]

The metaphor of the virgin martyr as *sponsa Christi*, used explicitly
by Ælfric only in this *Life*, clearly illustrates the conflict of the literal
and the spiritual, by pitting the literal suitor (Sempronius) against
the spiritual one (Christ). Agnes's speech details the mysteries of a
spiritual marriage to Christ, employing frankly sexual metaphors to
describe the relationship:

> his bryd-bedd me is gearo . nu iu mid dreamum .
> . . . .
> Of his muðe ic under-feng meoluc . and hunig .
> nu iu ic eom beclypt . mid his clænum earmum .
> his fægera lichama is minum geferlæht .
> . . . .
> Þam anum ic healde minne truwan æfre .
> þam ic me befæste mid ealre estfulnysse .
> Þonne ic hine lufige . ic beo eallunga clæne .
> þonne Ic hine hreppe . ic beo unwemme .
> ðonne Ic hine under-fo . ic beo mæden forð .

and þær bærn ne ateoriað . on ðam bryd-lace .
þær is eacnung buton sare . and singallic wæstmbærnyss .
(172)

[Now his bridal bed is already prepared for me with pleasure.
. . . From his mouth I have received milk and honey. Already
now I am clasped in his pure arms, his fair body is joined
with mine. . . . To him alone, I will hold my pledge forever;
to him I entrust myself, complete with all devotion. When
I love him, I am entirely pure; when I touch him, I am
unpolluted; when I receive him, I am still a virgin; and a
child will not be lacking in that marriage. There is conception without sorrow and continual fertility.]

Agnes's words underscore the mystery by which her literal body
provides access to spiritual truth. The metaphor of spiritual marriage
to Christ, read through the body of the virgin—"clæne" (pure),
"unwemme" (unpolluted), "mæden forð" (still a virgin), "eacnung"
(conception), "wæstmbærnyss" (fertility)—sits in sharp juxtaposition to the literal violence in the torture scenes that follow.[36]

When Agnes refuses Sempronius's command to worship the
pagan goddesses, he orders her to be stripped, led naked through
the streets, and forced into a brothel. Miraculously, if not unexpectedly, God subverts this attempted literal reading in three ways: first,
as soon as her clothing is torn off, Agnes's body is instantly covered
by her hair; second, God sends a bright light to blind anyone who
tries to look at her nakedness; third, he clothes her in a beautiful,
perfectly-fitting garment. Thus Agnes's body is simultaneously sexualized and de-sexualized, at once the public spectacle of the male
gaze and the spiritual mystery that is hidden from view. The image
of Agnes naked dominates this section, not least because of the
judge's command that the news of her nakedness be announced
throughout the streets. Yet the illicit spectacle of the naked virgin
body is immediately subverted by the various layers—hair, light,
clothing—which enclose and protect it. Moreover, the corrupt enclosure that threatens the virgin becomes instead a means to her salvation; in this case, "Þa wearð þæra myltestrena hus mannum to
gebæd-huse" [Then that prostitutes' house became a prayer-house
for men] (178). Interestingly, the shining light protects Agnes not

only from being seen, but also from being touched; when her suitor tries to rush at her, intending to assault her sexually, he is struck down as if dead ["swa dæd"], and only Agnes's intervention with God can bring him back to life.

Finally, the torture and martyrdom of Agnes can be seen to conform to previous examples of the genre. The virgin is forced into a great fire, which leaves the saint unharmed but turns outward and burns up the surrounding crowd before it is miraculously extinguished. Her actual death by sword is typically anti-climactic, followed by a miracle subsequent to death usually seen in these *Lives*. The Life of St. Agnes overall provides fewer detailed descriptions of torture than the others we have seen, but it emphasizes instead both the material aspects of a spiritual relationship between the virgin and Christ, and the need to conceal the saint's naked body from a pagan gaze, by clothing it with spiritual adornment.

The Life of St. Eugenia offers a fascinating variation on the theme of the virgin martyr plot, which, as several scholars have recently noted, presents a valuable opportunity to examine how late Anglo-Saxon hagiography dealt with issues of sexuality and gender. In the Life of St. Eugenia, long before the scenes of torture and martyrdom take place, the saint cross-dresses as a man in order to join a Christian monastery against her parents' will.[37] The male disguise protects the virgin, both from her family who want to remove her from the monastery, and from the male monks themselves. The construction of a material male self—through clothing, hairstyle, and behavior—provides a layer of protection, a kind of enclosure, into which the virgin withdraws to practice Christianity. The dramatic tensions produced by this disguise once again exemplify the tensions between literal and spiritual reading practices, as the *Life* acts out the struggle between interiority and exteriority which is the hallmark of Ælfric's corporeal hermeneutics.

Early female saints have numerous reasons for assuming masculine disguises.[38] Initially, the family of the virgin may have refused to allow her to practice Christianity, and thus the disguise offers freedom from these familial constraints. Second, the male disguise theoretically offers protection from sexual assault, a threat even within the monastery. Third, the assumption of masculine attributes may have permitted the saint to approximate male spirituality, and thus to achieve a higher level of spiritual life than a female body would permit. This third reason has typically been cited by scholars as the rationale behind the cross-dressing saint; citing Jerome and Ambrose, these scholars have demonstrated a patristic belief in male superiority and female inferiority which on the surface informs the Lives of transvestite saints.[39] Vern L. Bullough, citing Philo, Jerome, and Ambrose (among others) outlines the late antique and early medieval belief that by literally cross-dressing, the female saint could achieve a spiritual transformation as well:

> [F]or [Philo] progress meant giving up the female gender, the material, passive, corporeal, and sense-perceptive world, and taking the active, rational male world of mind and thought. The easiest way for women to approach the male level of rationality was for them to deny their sexuality, to remain virgins. . . . It would seem logical then to argue that the female who wore male clothes and adopted the role of the male would be trying to imitate the superior sex. . . .[40]

This line of reasoning has proved attractive to scholars trying to come to grips with scenes of cross-dressing and unconventional sexuality, and indeed, there is merit in it. Yet it tells only half the story. Like Agatha's breast, the bodies of female cross-dressed saints are never completely invisible; they never vanish entirely from the reader's gaze or the narrative focus. The dramatic narrative tension found in the Life of St. Eugenia depends directly on the threat of exposure of the female body within the male disguise.

In fact, this threat of exposure is Eugenia's main impetus for cross-dressing; she apparently adopts the disguise because it will allow her to enter the monastery without her parents' knowledge, and also because it will conceal her womanhood from the monks:

> wolde ðam cristenan genealecan
> on wærlicum hiwe . þæt heo ne wurde ameldod.   (28)

> [She wanted to approach the Christians in a man's clothing, so that she would not be found out.]

The masculine disguise, however, is merely a socially gendered layer that conceals the essential female body within (a literal body that, in the terms of Ælfric's hermeneutics, itself functions as a protective layer). The layering of gender identities onto Eugenia offers multiple opportunities for reading the saint literally or spiritually, *lichamlice* or *gastlice.*

The first "reading" of Eugenia, by the bishop, goes beneath her masculine surface to the essential female body within (thus it is a *gastlic* reading of the body, made possible in this case by a vision). The bishop offers a spiritual reading of this body-as-text, going beyond (beneath) its surface appearance to the truth it contains:

> He genam hi þa onsundron . and sæde hyre gewislice .
> hwæt heo man ne wæs . and hwylcere mægþe .
> and þæt heo þurh mægð-had mycclum gelicode .
> þam heofon-lican cyninge . þe heo gecoren hæfde .
> and cwæð þæt heo sceolde swiðlice æht-nyssa .
> for mægð-hade ðrowian . and þeah beon gescyld
> þurh þone soðan drihten . þe ge-scylt his
>   gecorenan.   (28–30)

> [Then he took her aside, and told her wisely that she was not a man, and who {her} people were, and that through the virginity that she had chosen, she had greatly pleased the heavenly king, and said that she would, on account of her virginity, violently suffer tortures, and yet she would be shielded through the true Lord who shields his chosen ones.]

The bishop's true understanding of Eugenia is sharply contrasted to the reactions of her (as yet unconverted) family when they learn of her disappearance. Believing her to be dead, Eugenia's father:

> . . . het asmiðigen . of smætum golde
> hyre anlycnysse . and þa wurðode
> swa swa halige gydenan . ac hit wæs gold swa
>   þeah.   (30–32)

> [ordered her image constructed out of pure gold and then worshipped it, just like a holy goddess; but it was still just gold.]

Whereas the bishop (her spiritual father) accepts the masculine disguise and offers her protection, Eugenia's literal father, Philip, thinks only of her body. Her family worships the replica of her body as a graven image, believing her true identity to exist there in the literal sense. Ælfric dryly reminds us, however, that the statue "was still just gold."

In the most famous episode of the Life of St. Eugenia, she is elected abbot by the unsuspecting monks, and in this role she gains power in both medicine and exorcism. She heals a wicked woman, Melantia, and becomes the object of Melantia's lust. When Eugenia rejects Melantia's seduction attempt and instead tries to convince her to reject her evil ways, Melantia, embarrassed, tries to turn tables by claiming that Eugenia (still disguised as abbot) had been the lustful one. There is, however, very little narrative tension in this scene. Ælfric makes Melantia's wickedness clear, and we have no reason to believe that Eugenia will succumb. Moreover, the drama that might arise from Eugenia's disguise is repeatedly denied; Ælfric consistently refers to Eugenia in gender-specific terms, so that even if Melantia may be unaware of the saint's true identity, the audience is not allowed to forget. Ælfric's emphasis on Eugenia's biological sex ("halige mæden," 139, "wlytegan mædene," 146, "soðfæste fæmne," 148, etc.) throws Melantia's insistence on surface appearances into sharp relief.

Dramatic tension increases when the judge who is to assess Melantia's accusations against Eugenia turns out to be Philip, Eugenia's father. Recent critics have identified this scene as a kind of crisis of gender, a pivotal moment which reveals a great deal about Anglo-Saxon attitudes towards gender and (female) sexuality. The typical analysis of this scene, however, reads Eugenia's gender as an "either-or" situation. Frantzen, for example, views the transvestite saints as "switching" genders ("When Women Aren't Enough"), while Szarmach describes Eugenia's disguise as "inverted sexuality" explaining, "Eugenia's conversion of heart to Christianity requires a transformation of sex, *or at least the appearance of sex.* . . . Eugenia is repudiating her own sexuality, which is *de rigueur* for those who join 'sex-negative' Christianity."[41] Both Frantzen and Szarmach establish a gendered polarity in which the saint must be gendered either male or female, but not both; and, to be sure, sexual "switching" or "inversion" reiterates the hierarchical relation of male to female so explicitly stated in patristic writing. Szarmach's aside, "or at least the appearance of sex," is, I think, at the heart of the argument, because the concept of multiply layered gender reflects more accurately Ælfric's hermeneutics. Ironically, the surface that must be read beyond is, in this case, the masculine disguise, while the concealed inner truth is the essential female body. Rather than "switching" between gender identities, I would argue, the saint does not change her essential sexual identity, grounded in her female body, even if that body undergoes a material transformation (the loss of a breast or a change in hairstyle or clothing). While Christianity may in theory be "sex-negative" as Szarmach suggests, patristic views of gendered bodies are not.

The complex issue of Eugenia's gender identity can be traced in the scribal evidence of the two surviving manuscripts of Ælfric's Life of Eugenia, Otho B.x and Julius E.vii.[42] In both manuscript versions, Eugenia is referred to in grammatically feminine terms ("heo" and "mægð") both before and after she assumes her male disguise and joins the monastery. The grammatically feminine terms remain consistent even during two anxious moments of gender confusion: when she is elected abbot "þa gebroðra . . . nyston þæt heo wæs wimman swa þeah" [the brothers . . . did not know that she was still a woman] (32), and when Melantia tries to seduce her ("seo wydewe . . . com siððan gelome . mid leasum mode / to þam wlitegan mædene . wende þæt heo cniht wære" [afterwards the widow came frequently, with a deceitful mind, to that beautiful maiden and thought she was a young man] (32). The consistent use of feminine pronouns, in fact, throughout the scene with Melantia, makes the passage confusing to read. The first use of a masculine pronoun, "hine," for Eugenia, comes in Melantia's accusation, addressed to Eugenia's father. But as Szarmach has shown, when Eugenia faces her father during the trial, "the scribes of the Otho and Julius versions . . . cannot agree on how to present Eugenia's switching, the former considering her a 'he' and an 'abbot' while the latter considers her a 'she' and 'Eugenia'" ("Ælfric's Women Saints," 150). The confusion, I suggest, results from the cumulative layering of gender identities.

The layers of gender written onto Eugenia's body (she is biologically a woman, in male disguise, accused of acting like an "essential," sexualized male, and about to be exposed both socially and literally as a woman) causes the scribal confusion because of her multiple gender identities—each scribe must choose from the available options. The scribal confusion clears, however, and both refer to the saint as "Eugenia seo æþele fæmne," the noble woman, just as the layers are literally stripped away:

> . . . eugenia seo æþele fæmne .
> cwæð þæt heo wolde hi sylfe be-diglian .
> and criste anum hyre clænnysse healdan .
> on mægðhade wuniende . mannum uncuð .
> and forðy underfænge æt fruman þa gyrlan .
> wær-lices hades . and wurde ge-efsod .
> Æfter þysum wordum heo to-tær hyre gewædu .
> and æt-æwde hyre breost . þam breman philippe .
> and cwæð him to . þu eart min fæder .
> and þin gebædda claudia . gebær me to mannum .
> and ðas ðine gesætlan synd mine gebroðra .
> auitus . and særgius . and ic soðlice eom
> eugenia gehaten . þin agen dohtor .
> and ic for cristes lufe . forlæt eow ealle .
> and middan-eardlice lustas swa swa meox forseah .   (38)

[Eugenia, the noble woman, said that she wanted to keep herself secret and hold her chastity for Christ alone, dwelling in virginity, unknown to man, and therefore she had originally put on clothing in the manner of a man, and had her hair cut. After these words, she tore her clothing and showed her breast to the raging Philip, and said to him, 'You are my father and your wife Claudia gave birth to me, and those who are seated with you are my brothers, Avitus and Sergius, and I am truly called Eugenia, your own daughter, and I gave you all up for Christ's love and renounced the pleasures of the world just as if they were filth.]

Only the sight of Eugenia's bare breast permits her father and brothers to recognize her. Virginity itself (and more broadly, Christianity) has functioned as a protective enclosure for the saint, and the masculine disguise was the material manifestation of that spiritual space.

When the trial forces her to reveal the truth about herself, she exposes her bare breast (a literal truth) as a text to be read by the pagans; presumably it is the only kind of text they can read. Eugenia's breast (like Agatha's) is the site and sign of her essential female self, and the only self the pagans will recognize, since they only know her through the body. Tearing apart her robes and exposing her naked breast means leaving the enclosure of her masculine disguise and re-entering the realm of the body—a necessary sacrifice in order to protect herself from torture and death and to convert her family. Although Szarmach argues that, in the final trial scene, the wickedly sexual Melantia is contrasted to a "desexed Eugenia," (151) I would propose that we read Eugenia not as "desexed" but rather "resexed." Once she is re-figured in a variation of the original gender position she occupied at the narrative's outset, this *Life* then turns to a more "conventional" account of virgin martyrdom.[43]

After the climactic trial scene, the *Life* of Eugenia continues at some length. Although Eugenia founds a convent, and is atypically free from the demands of a pagan suitor, one of the virgins who joins her convent, Basilla, has just such a suitor, and thus the narrative follows the standard pattern: Basilla is martyred, and Eugenia too becomes the object of persecution, torture, and eventual martyrdom.

The representations of torture that occur towards the end of this text present many of the patterns of binding, imprisonment, and enclosure that we have seen in the previous virgin martyr narratives. Eugenia's torturers consistently devise strategies to rupture and thereby transform her literal body, without comprehending her spiritual self. The saint easily resists the superficial, earthly constraints placed on her body by the pagans. When Eugenia is dragged into a heathen temple, a kind of false enclosure, and ordered to worship Diana, the saint's prayers destroy the temple, thus proving its value-lessness. When the pagans hang a stone around her neck and throw her in a river, the stone breaks and she sits on the water's surface. She is put into hot baths, inside a burning oven, but her presence causes both oven and baths to cool down. She is put in a dark prison with no food, but Christ provides her with both light and food. The pattern is clear: each binding, fettering, or restraining structure the pagans impose on the saint is destroyed through her spiritual force. These false enclosures cannot contain the virgin; the power of virginity, based in interiority, will not be contained through literal force. Like

St. Agatha, Eugenia actually gains power from false enclosure, as narrow physical constraints provide spiritual release. No amount of punishment to the saint's body can affect that spiritual power.

Ælfric clearly believes in the power of virginity, and in the power virginity narratives can exert on their readers. Towards the end of his homily on the Book of Judith, Ælfric explains the homily's significance for his female reader (presumably a nun):

> Ic wylle eac secgan   min swustor,
> þæt mægðhad and clænnys   mycele mihte habbað
> swa swa we gehwær rædað   on martira þrowungum
> and on Vitas Patrum. . . .

> [I will also say, my sister, that virginity and chastity hold great power, just as we read elsewhere in the sufferings of the martyrs and the Lives of the Fathers. . . .][44]

The power of virginity comes from the closed, intact body, able to withstand easily attempts at rupture or penetration from without. Thus in female saints' lives, the principle narrative tension emerges in scenes of torture, when that *integritas* is threatened. The spatial metaphors of the virginal body resonate in Ælfric's hermeneutics, a system of interpretation that likewise depends upon the metaphors of depth and interiority to convey the process of finding spiritual meaning within the physical letters inscribed on a manuscript page. Like those physical letters, the saint's literal body operates in these *Lives* as the vehicle that conveys meaning. Like texts, saints' bodies carry the potentiality of spiritual meaning but require that a skilled interpreter read beyond their naked surfaces.

In many ways, of course, saints' bodies always matter. Saints' relics, for example—often parts of their bodies—have traditionally been an integral feature of the veneration of saints.[45] But the narrative functions of the saint's body before death, and during scenes of torture, have received little critical attention. Like all sacred texts, saints' bodies teach lessons; they contain mystical truths to be uncovered. Using Ælfric's own hermeneutics to analyze the bodies of saints permits us a more detailed understanding of the textual operations of the *Lives of Saints*. Reading these *Lives* through the lens of Ælfric's corporeal hermeneutics demonstrates how tangibly the body matters in these texts and confirms the extent to which the *Lives* of female virgin martyrs depend upon the carnal to produce and ensure deeper spiritual truths.

NOTES

1. All citations from the *Lives of Saints* are from W.W. Skeat, ed. and trans., *Ælfric's Lives of Saints*, EETS o.s. 76, 82, 94, 114 (London: Oxford University Press, 1881–1888; rpt. in two volumes, 1966). Citation from Vol. 1, 4–5. Subsequent citations by page number will be provided parenthetically within my text. Unless otherwise noted, translations are mine.

2. My purpose here is not to provide a source-study of Ælfric's *Lives of Saints*; several scholars have already done so admirably. See especially Peter Clemoes, "Ælfric," in *Continuations and Beginnings*, ed. E.G. Stanley (London: Thomas Nelson and Sons, Ltd., 1966), 176–209; Gopa Roy, "A Virgin Acts Manfully: Ælfric's *Life of St. Eugenia* and the Latin Versions," *Leeds Studies in English* 23 (1992): 1–27; Patrick Zettel, "Saints' Lives in Old English: Latin Manuscripts and Vernacular Accounts: Ælfric," *Peritia* 1 (1982): 17–37; and the introductions to Godden's and Pope's editions of Ælfric's Homilies, cited below, notes 16 and 18. For bibliography see Luke Reinsma, *Ælfric: An Annotated Bibliography* (New York: Garland, 1987). Rather, I am interested in reading the *Lives of Saints* as they might have been received within the specific cultural context of late Anglo-Saxon England, by audiences who themselves were not necessarily familiar with the source texts (as Ælfric's prefatory remarks make clear). Clemoes explains the "consistent plan" of Ælfric's work this way: "He did not merely assemble patristic homilies as Paul [the Deacon] had done, or compose homilies in Latin by refashioning material from various patristic sources as Haymo [of Auxerre] had done. Instead he made selections from the thought of a number of authorities and used the vernacular to re-express that thought. His sets of homilies were a planned attempt to provide England with a body of orthodox preaching in vernacular prose" ("Ælfric," 183). On Ælfric's unique prose style, see Anne Middleton, "Ælfric's Answerable Style: The Rhetoric of the Alliterative Prose," *Studies in Medieval Culture* 4 (1973): 83–91.

3. Although several recent essay collections examine the roles of bodies and genders in medieval culture, it is rare to find an essay on Anglo-Saxon literature in such a collection. Notable exceptions include Clare Lees, "Men and *Beowulf*," in *Medieval Masculinities*, ed. Clare Lees (Minneapolis: University of Minnesota Press, 1994): 129–148; Allen Frantzen, "When Women Aren't Enough," in Nancy Partner, ed., *Studying Medieval Women* (Cambridge, MA: Medieval Academy of America, 1993): 143–169; and Paul

Szarmach, "Ælfric's Women Saints: Eugenia," in Helen Damico and Alexandra Hennessey Olsen, eds., *New Readings on Women in Old English Literature* (Bloomington: Indiana UP, 1990): 146–157. Good general collections on medieval bodies and/or gender include Miri Rubin and Sarah Kay, eds., *Framing Medieval Bodies* (New York: St. Martin's Press, 1994); Linda Lomperis and Sarah Stanbury, eds., *Feminist Approaches to the Body in Medieval Literature* (Philadelphia: University of Pennsylvania Press, 1993); and Nancy Partner, ed. *Studying Medieval Women* (Cambridge, MA: Medieval Academy of America, 1993). The recently published collection edited by Paul Szarmach, *Holy Men and Holy Women: Old English Prose Saints' Lives and Their Contexts* (Albany: SUNY Press, 1996) will now undoubtedly be the starting point for anyone interested in Anglo-Saxon hagiography.

    4. Kathryn Gravdal, *Ravishing Maidens: Writing Rape in Medieval French Literature and Law* (Philadelphia: University of Pennsylvania Press, 1991), 22. Subsequent citations from Gravdal will appear parenthetically in my text.

    5. To be sure, in Ælfric and throughout medieval hagiography, there are many examples of male saints and martyrs who are tortured and killed for their faith. One crucial gender difference that I perceive, however, is that the male bodies are rarely stripped and publicly displayed at length, while the females nearly always suffer this display, or the extended threat of it, which amounts to nearly the same thing. In my analysis, however, I am interested in examining the lives of female saints in order to demonstrate the cultural and thematic continuities to be found in representations of the feminine and the ideology of female enclosure.

    6. Clemoes writes that "[a]llegorical exegesis was applied to scripture to extract from it what Ælfric called þæt gastlice andgit, the spiritual sense, as against þæt anfealde andgit, the literal, specifically historical meaning" ("Ælfric," 188). Yet it is much more common for Ælfric to pair "gastlice" with "lichamlice" in discussions of this type. Through use of the *Microfiche Concordance to Old English*, I have located three instances of the "anfealde" [one-fold]/"gastlice" pairing, but nearly two dozen instances of "lichamlice"/ "gastlice." The *phrase* "anfealde andgyt," the one-fold (or literal) understanding occurs quite frequently in Ælfric; but important for my argument here is the particular juxtaposition of "lichamlice" and "gastlice" as they relate to understanding and interpretation, and it is this pairing which Ælfric uses most often.

    7. *Dominica in Media Quadragessima* [The Homily on Midlent Sunday], in Peter Clemoes, ed., *Ælfric's Catholic Homilies, The First Series*. Early English Text Society supplementary series 17 (Oxford: Oxford University Press, 1997): 275–280, citation from 277. Abbreviations have been expanded in square brackets. Subsequent references to Clemoes' edition will appear within my text. Translations are my own.

8. Paul Szarmach, "Ælfric as Exegete," in *Hermeneutics and Medieval Culture*, ed. Patrick J. Gallacher and Helen Damico (Albany: State University of New York Press, 1989), 237–247; citations from 239.

9. In *Early English Devotional Prose and the Female Audience*, Elizabeth Robertson argues that Ælfric "eschews the literal in favor of the allegorical" (160) and that he considers "[t]he literal world [to be] unworthy of contemplation" (161). I would suggest instead that Ælfric's exegesis is more complicated: rather than "unworthy," Ælfric sees the literal as "insufficient"; as I shall demonstrate, in the *Lives of Saints*, as in the homilies, Ælfric views the literal as the necessary first stage in readers' spiritual progression. Thus I would argue that Ælfric exemplifies the "quotidian realism" that Robertson shows operating both in anonymous late Anglo-Saxon homilies and in twelfth- and thirteenth-century English devotional prose for women. In particular, Ælfric's *Lives* of female saints demonstrate a concern for the corporeal that aligns him quite closely with the later medieval literary traditions in England that Robertson identifies.

10. Augustine, Tractatus XXIV, *In Iohannis Evangelium Tractatus CXXIV*, edited by D. Willems. In *Opera* VIII. Corpus Christianorum Series Latina XXXVI (Turnhout: Brepols, 1954), 244. Trans. John W. Rettig, *Tractates on the Gospel of John 11–27*. The Fathers of the Church, vol. 79 (Washington D.C.: Catholic University of America Press, 1988), 232.

11. Augustine, Tractatus XXIV, 244; trans. Rettig, 232.

12. Augustine, Tractatus XXIV, 244; trans. Rettig, 232.

13. Of course elsewhere Augustine warns severely against any reading practice which is exclusively literal; the "death of the soul" [*mors animae*] will result when "that which is said figuratively is taken as though it were literal [and] understood carnally"; when "the understanding [is] subjected to the flesh in pursuit of the letter." *On Christian Doctrine*, ed. and trans. D.W. Robertson, Jr. (Indianapolis: Bobbs-Merrill, 1958) 84. See the discussion of this passage in chapter 3, above, p. 111.

14. The correlation and juxtaposition of *lichamlic / corporalis; gastlic / spiritalis* can likewise be found in Ælfric's *Grammar*, where this particular combination of terms appears to be his own device; Ælfric's source does not link these terms in this way. I am grateful to David Porter for bringing this to my attention.

15. ll. 36ff; 119ff; 126ff; 135ff; 140ff; 156ff; and 190. There are several other implicit references, as for example l. 287ff, where *gastlicum andgite* seems to imply its opposite. See also Szarmach, "Ælfric as Exegete," 243–244, for a discussion of these terms in this homily.

16. Malcolm Godden, ed., *Ælfric's Catholic Homilies: The Second Series*, Early English Text Society supplementary series 5 (London: Oxford University Press, 1979). Citation from 151. Translations are mine.

17. It should be noted that Ælfric also uses *lichamlic(e)* in a perfectly straightforward way to refer to things people do with their bodies; in *Nativitas Sancti Iohannis Baptistae*, The Homily on the Nativity of John the Baptist, for example, Ælfric explains, "Twa forhæfednysse cynn sindon: an lichamlic, oðer gastlic" (Clemoes, 385) [there are two kinds of abstinence, one bodily, the other spiritual]; in *Octabas et Circumcisio Domini*, he writes, "ða wearð he on þam eahteoþan dæge his gebyrdtide lichamlice ymbsniden" (Godden, 226) [then he was bodily circumcised on the eighth day after his birth]. These examples demonstrate that it is not simply through the juxtaposition of the terms that Ælfric conflates the literal with the bodily, but more precisely that the juxtaposition must occur within a discussion of reading, interpretation, and understanding.

18. *Dominica Quinta Post Pascha* [The Homily on the Fifth Sunday After Easter], in *Homilies of Ælfric: A Supplementary Collection*, ed. John C. Pope. Volume 1. EETS, o.s. 259 (London: Oxford University Press, 1967). Citation from 359. Translations are mine.

19. S.J. Crawford, ed., *The Old English Version of the Heptateuch, Ælfric's Treatise on the Old and New Testament and his Preface to Genesis*. Early English Text Society original series 160 (London: Oxford University Press, 1922). Citation from 74. Translations are mine.

20. Elaine Scarry, *The Body in Pain: The Making and Unmaking of the World* (New York and Oxford: Oxford University Press, 1985). Citations from Scarry will appear parenthetically in my text. Page duBois has shown that, for ancient Greek culture, the body (particularly the slave body) contained and concealed truth, so that only by means of torture could reliable truths be produced. See *Torture and Truth* (New York: Routledge, 1991).

21. See Jean Leclercq, *The Love of Learning and the Desire for God*, trans. Catharine Misrahi (New York: New American Library, 1961), 76–93. See also Mary Carruthers, *The Book of Memory: A Study of Memory in Medieval Culture* (Cambridge: Cambridge University Press, 1990): "Gregory the Great writes, 'We ought to transform what we read into our very selves, so that when our mind is stirred by what it hears, our life may concur by practicing what has been heard,'" 164. Here Carruthers is referring to the bodily practice of mouthing or murmuring the words as one reads so as to have a full bodily experience of reading; see also 167ff. for a discussion of readers' appropriate corporeal and emotional responses to what they read (or hear).

22. Leclercq, *Love of Learning*, 75.

23. Aelred of Rievaulx, *De Institutione Inclusarum*, in *Opera Omnia*, vol. 1 *Opera Ascetica*, ed. A. Hoste and C.H. Talbot. Corpus Christianorum Continuatio Mediaevalis I (Turnhout: Brepols, 1971), 663–664. Translation from Aelred of Rievaulx, *A Rule of Life for a Recluse*, trans. Mary Paul MacPherson.

In *The Works of Aelred of Rievaulx*, Vol. 1 (Spencer, MA: Cistercian Publications, 1971), 81.

24. Aphrodosia here fills a secondary role common to these narratives: the older, corrupt woman who, especially in her juxtaposition to the saint, represents all the traditional misogynist notions of women—particularly older women—such as insatiable sexuality, garrulousness, or grotesque corporeality.

25. Both meanings are attested in *The Dictionary of Old English*, though the more general rendering "to change" is more common. *S.v. awendan, (DOE)*. See also Ann E. Nichols, *"Awendan:* A Note on Ælfric's Vocabulary." *JEGP* 63 (1964): 7–13, for a discussion of Ælfric's use of this verb.

26. Similarly, in the early Middle English Life of St. Margaret (which has close affinities to Ælfric's *Lives*), St. Margaret also displays this kind of rhetorical skill in her responses to her torturer, a skill that she has and he does not. This saintly eloquence suggests a significant difference between stylized narratives of martyr torture and the real thing; as Scarry has argued, torture deconstructs or inhibits discourse, whereas in saints' lives, torture very frequently incites or enhances the saint's discursive role. On the Life of St. Margaret, see S.M.W. Withycombe, *"St. Margarete:* A Late Old English Perception of Feminine Sanctity," *Parergon* n.s. 10.2 (1992): 167–179.

The verbal eloquence and vigor which characterizes the female saints in English collections may be a typically English tradition. For example, Brigitte Cazelles has shown that, starting with the earliest vernacular hagiography in France, female saints are more typically characterized as passive and silent (*The Lady as Saint: A Collection of French Hagiographic Romances of the Thirteenth Century* [Philadelphia: University of Pennsylvania Press, 1991], 29). This is far from the case with Ælfric's female saints, or Juliana, who seemingly cannot be silenced.

27. Ælfric makes frequent use of the "opening" metaphor in his explanations of scriptural exegesis, for example:

We habbað anfealdlice gesæd eow nu þis godspel
and we willað geopnian eow þæt andgit nu   (Pope I, 46)

[Now we have told this gospel to you simply, and we will now open up to you its meaning].

28. Allen J. Frantzen, "When Women Aren't Enough," 160.

29. When Agatha's breast is restored, our gaze follows hers: "Æfter ðam gebede . beseah to hyre breoste . / and wæs þæt corfene breost . þurh crist ge-edstaðelod . / and ealle hire wunda wurdon gehælede . [After that prayer she looked at her breast, / and the breast that had been cut off was

restored through Christ, / and all her wounds were healed]" (trans. Skeat, 204–205). In describing the act of looking, Ælfric builds a place in the narrative, in a sense, into which the reader can locate her (or him) self. This sight likewise confirms the breast as the locus of her female identity.

30. See *Holy Feast and Holy Fast*, 270–275.

31. This aborted torture attempt is an example of a fairly common narrative strategy in saints' lives, in which the audience is almost invited to "see" the saint naked, before her nakedness is suddenly protected. Although the narrative typically works to prevent exposing the saint's nakedness, it nonetheless suggests that image, and thus the tension or dual perspective once again falls on the saint's literal body, emphasizing that readers should not be concerned with that body, even as the narrative creates the suspense that it will be displayed. The suggestion of display is nearly as important as the "real thing" and works didactically because the suggestion is often interrupted by a forceful reminder of the saint's true, i.e., spiritual, meaning.

32. Agatha's miracle of stopping Eutychia's hemorrhaging may have a special significance as a miracle done by a female saint to a woman; medieval medical theory saw women as excessively "moist," controlled by bodily fluids, and thus more apt to be controlled by lust. Agatha's miracle may have had the effect of reducing that "moistness" and thus the lustfulness which would be inherent in Eutychia's female body. For an overview of medieval medical views about the female body, see Elizabeth Robertson, "Medieval Medical Views of Women and Female Spirituality in the *Ancrene Wisse* and Julian of Norwich's *Showings*," in *Feminist Approaches to the Body in Medieval Literature*, ed. Linda Lomperis and Sarah Stanbury (Philadelphia: University of Pennsylvania Press, 1993), 142–167.

33. Aldhelm cites Augustine's *de Civitate Dei* I.18 to confirm this point: "unde Augustinus . . . eleganti prosae sententia promulgat dicens: *Ita non amittitur corporis sanctitas manente animi sanctitate etiam corpore oppresso, sicut amittitur sanctitas corporis violata animi puritate etiam corpore intacto*" ["Whence Augustine . . . declares in an elegant sentence of prose, saying, 'Thus the sanctity of the body is not lost provided that the sanctity of the soul remains, even if the body is overcome, just as the sanctity of the body *is* lost if the purity of the soul is violated, even if the body is intact'"]. Rudolph Ehwald, ed. *Aldhelmi Opera*. Monumenta Germaniae Historica Auctorum Antiquissimorum Vol. XV (Berlin: Weidmann, 1961), 319. Translation from Michael Lapidge and Michael Herren, eds. and trans., *Aldhelm: The Prose Works* (Cambridge and Totowa: Brewer/Rowman and Littlefield, 1979), 129. It is important to reiterate, however, that in practice, this idea does not always seem to be believed. Cf. the discussion by Jane Schulenburg, "Heroics of Virginity," and Chapter Three, above.

34. As Jane Chance has suggested, "the description of the [saint's] torture often veils with obvious sexual symbolism the act of intercourse. . . . [W]hen the naked Saint Lucia must be tortured, she is finally wounded in the stomach with an obviously phallic sword (p. 218). The virgin martyr becomes a type of the feminine soul joined with Christ to become a *miles Christi*. . . . Appropriately, then, the threat of seduction of the virgin martyr symbolically represents the Devil's adulterous assault on the feminine soul" (*Woman as Hero in Old English Literature* [Syracuse: Syracuse University Press, 1986], 56).

35. On the image of Christ as bridegroom in Old English literature, see Stephen Morrison, "The Figure of Christus Sponsus in Old English Prose," *Beiträge zur Deutschen Philologie* 58 (1984): 5–15. See also John Bugge, *Virginitas: An Essay in the History of a Medieval Ideal* (The Hague: Martinus Nijhoff, 1975); E. Ann Matter, *The Voice of My Beloved: The Song of Songs in Western Medieval Christianity* (Philadelphia: University of Pennsylvania Press, 1990); on the early (and mistaken) view that Ælfric used Ambrose as his source, see J.H. Ott, *Uber die Quellen der Heiligenleben in Ælfrics Lives of Saints I* (Inaugural Dissertation, Halle, 1892). It is now generally agreed by scholars that Ælfric's source was not Ambrose. See Zettel, "Saints' Lives in Old English"; and Bernadette Moloney, "Another Look at Ælfric's Use of Discourse in Some Saints' Lives" *English Studies 63* (1982): 13–19, especially 17. See also Robertson's discussion of this motif (and its benefits for the female virgin) in the Middle English prose treatise *Hali Meidenhad* (*Early English Devotional Prose and the Female Audience*, 81–93).

36. The imagery describes her relationship with Christ in conjugal terms, even as her language makes clear that the relationship is purely spiritual. In this way, her speech anticipates the affective movement in medieval women's spirituality which focused so intensely on the body of Christ and the religious woman's (nearly) physical relationship with that body. The union of her body with Christ's resembles the later medieval mystical understanding of *imitatio Christi* found in the writings of medieval women mystics discussed by Caroline Walker Bynum; as Bynum explains:

> 'Imitation' meant union—fusion—with that ultimate body which is
> the body of Christ. The goal of religious women was thus to
> realize the *opportunity* of physicality. They strove not to eradicate
> body but to merge their own humiliating and painful flesh with
> that flesh whose agony, espoused by choice, was salvation. Luxur-
> iating in Christ's physicality, they found there the lifting up—the
> redemption—of their own. (*Holy Feast and Holy Fast,* 246)

While the Life of St. Agnes does not demonstrate the same degree of physical identification seen in the works discussed by Bynum, it nonetheless shows an understanding of Christ through metaphors of the virgin's body.

37. The Life of St. Euphrosyne, an anonymous *vita* included in the *Lives of Saints* manuscript, Cotton Julius E.vii, likewise depicts a cross-dressing female saint. Although it is a fascinating narrative, I omit it from my discussion here because Euphrosyne is not tortured and martyred. The cross-dressing episode, however, offers a useful link to my discussion because it shows Euphrosyne being interpreted "literally"—that is, on the basis of surface appearance. See Paul Szarmach, "St. Euphrosyne: Holy Transvestite," in *Holy Men and Holy Women*, 353–365.

38. See John S. Anson, "The Female Transvestite in Early Monasticism: The Origin and Development of a Motif," *Viator* 5 (1974), 1–32; Szarmach, "St. Euphrosyne" (cited above), and "Ælfric's Women Saints: Eugenia," in *New Readings on Women in Old English Literature*, ed. Helen Damico and Alexandra Hennessey Olsen (Bloomington: Indiana University Press, 1990), 146–157.

39. In addition to the articles by Szarmach and Anson already cited, see Gopa Roy, "A Virgin Acts Manfully: Ælfric's Life of St. Eugenia and the Latin Versions," *Leeds Studies in English* 23 (1992), 2–27; Vern Bullough, "Transvestism in the Middle Ages," in *Sexual Practices and the Medieval Church*, ed. Vern L. Bullough and James Brundage (Buffalo: Prometheus Books, 1982), 43–54; and Frantzen, "When Women Aren't Enough."

40. Bullough, 45.

41. Szarmach, "Ælfric's Female Saints," 147–148, emphasis added.

42. See Skeat's textual notes, pp. 34–40. Szarmach, to my knowledge, is the only one to have discussed this interesting scribal confusion, in "Ælfric's Female Saints," 150. On the deficiencies in Skeat's edition (and suggestions for a much-needed new edition of the *Lives of Saints*) see Robert J. Alexander, "W.W. Skeat and Ælfric," *Annuale Mediaevale* 22 (1982): 36–53. Alexander does not address the textual variants I discuss here.

43. In his interesting analysis of the story of St. Eugenia, Anson argues that in transvestite saints' lives, "once their sex has been revealed, then women must die as martyrs under the cruelest tortures. . . . Once stripped of their disguises, they have no recourse save the destruction of their bodies for reattaining their unity with a male godhead" (28).

44. Homily on the Book of Judith, in *Angelsächsische Homilien und Heiligenleben*, ed. Bruno Assman; reprinted with a supplementary introduction by Peter Clemoes (Darmstadt: Wissenschaftliche Buchgesellschaft, 1964), 115. Translation mine.

45. As Michael Lapidge writes, "We should not imagine that the saints were conceived abstractly as disembodied spirits. Theirs was a physical and palpable presence: that is to say, the saint was physically present in each shrine insofar as that shrine contained a relic of his/her body—a bone, a fingernail, a lock of hair, whatever." See "The Saintly Life in Anglo-Saxon England," in *The Cambridge Companion to Old English Literature*, ed. Malcolm Godden and Michael Lapidge (Cambridge: Cambridge University Press, 1991), 243. On the cultural functions of relics, see Patrick Geary, *Furta Sacra: Thefts of Relics in the Middle Ages* (Princeton: Princeton University Press, 1978). See also Caroline Walker Bynum, *The Resurrection of the Body in Western Christianity, 200–1336* (New York: Columbia University Press, 1995). Bynum's book examines patristic and medieval attitudes about the body in terms of burial, resurrection, and the cult of saints. She skips, however, from the fourth to the twelfth centuries, bypassing Anglo-Saxon England entirely.

Christina of Markyate and Legacies of Enclosure

The author of the twelfth-century Latin life of Christina of Markyate well understood the myriad ways that the literal body of the saint could act as the vehicle for her spiritual triumph and, more pragmatically, for her authorized entry into sainthood. The *Life* of Christina traces its subject's spiritual and physical progress away from her family and into an anchoritic and, later, a monastic life. The *Life* is valuable for the study of post-Conquest Anglo-Saxon women, because Christina (originally named Theodora) is the daughter of an Anglo-Saxon nobleman, and at one point the Latin text even includes a late Old English phrase.[1] More importantly for our purposes, the *Life* of Christina provides some of the most detailed and unpleasant descriptions of physical enclosure in early medieval literature. Nonetheless, throughout the *Life*, monastic enclosure remains Christina's objective, and the text considers at length both literal and symbolic models of female containment. As a result it provides a fitting subject for the conclusion of this study, because it represents a point of convergence for many of the issues discussed here: Anglo-Saxon attitudes towards femininity; the relationship of women to textuality; the material conditions of female monasticism; the tensions between female confinement and autonomy. The *Life* bridges the gap, moreover, between Anglo-Saxon and later medieval cultures and reminds us of the many continuities to be explored between two historical periods that are too often viewed separately.

The descriptions of physical enclosure in *The Life of Christina of Markyate* are explicit and often graphic. When Christina first flees her family (who oppose her desire to become a nun), she finds protection with an anchorite, Alfwen, and spends nearly two years

173

hidden in a dark, narrow "cell" that "was closed and locked on all sides" ("carcer ille clausus [erat] et obstructus undique" Talbot, 98–99). But the most compelling description of her physical enclosure comes after Christina leaves that original anchorhold and is hidden in a small cell by Roger the Hermit. Because they are afraid of causing a scandal by living in such close proximity, Roger places Christina within a miserable confinement:

> In hoc ergo carcere Rogerus ovantem sociam posuit. et ligni robur pro hostio conveniens admovit. Et hoc eciam tanti ponderis erat. quod ab inclusa nullatenus admoveri sive removeri poterat. Hic igitur ancilla Christi coartata supra duram petram sedit usque ad obitum Rogeri. id est .iiii. annis. et eo amplius. Latens illos quoque qui cum Rogero simul habitabant. O quantas sustinuit illic incommoditates frigoris et estus. famis et sitis. cotidiani ieiunii. Loci angustia non admittebat necessarium tegumentum algenti. Integerrima clausula nullum indulgebat refrigerium estuanti. Longa inedia. contracta sunt et aruerunt sibi intestina. Erat quando pre ardore sitis naribus ebullire<n>t frusta coagulati sanguinis. Hiis omnibus illi erat intollerabilius. quod exire foras non nisi sero licebat. ad alia quedam necessaria que natura postulabat. Nimirum instante necessitate nequibat ipsa sibi aperire et Rogerus de more tardabat. ad illam venire. Itaque necesse fuit immobiliter eam in loco sedere. torqueri et tacere.

> [In this prison, therefore, Roger placed his happy companion. In front of the door he rolled a heavy log of wood, the weight of which was actually so great that it could not be put in its place or taken away by the recluse. And so, thus confined, the handmaid of God sat on a hard stone until Roger's death, that is, four years and more, concealed even from those who dwelt together with Roger. O what trials she had to bear of cold and heat, hunger and thirst, daily fasting! The confined space would not allow her to wear even the necessary clothing when she was cold. Through long fasting, her bowels became contracted and dried up. There was a time when her burning thirst caused little clots of blood to bubble up from her nostrils. But what was more unbearable than all this was that she could not go out until

the evening to satisfy the demands of nature. Even when she was in dire need, she could not open the door for herself, and Roger usually did not come till late. So it was necessary for her to sit quite still in the place, to suffer torments, and to keep quiet. . . .]   (Talbot, 102–105)

The intimacy of these details has suggested to many readers an autobiographical element to the *Life*; whether or not Christina herself dictated these events, we will never know. Certainly the text focuses to an unusual degree on the physical hardships of enclosure. These descriptions of suffering are centered on Christina's body, I believe, because the *Life* is attempting to sanctify its subject, and in the process it uses models Christina herself may have known: late Anglo-Saxon lives of female virgin martyrs.[2] By emphasizing corporeal experiences of enclosure and escape, confinement and release (themes that pervade this text), *The Life of Christina of Markyate* draws on the tradition of ideological enclosure that we have seen regularly featured in Old English literature about women. The descriptions of both physical and spiritual torments that Christina suffers throughout this text appear to be part of a systematic attempt to enter this female subject into the mainstream of Anglo-Saxon hagiography. As we have seen in the literature examined throughout this study, in this *Life*, enclosure operates as a trope, a necessary narrative condition for the construction of the female (religious) subject. The *Life* of Christina appropriates a number of plot devices from Anglo-Saxon saints' lives, including cross-dressing, gender confusion, imprisonment, and the threat of rape, as it attempts to write Christina into this literary tradition. As do other early medieval texts, this *Life* deploys both the material conditions and discursive practices of enclosure in its efforts to construct the female subject.

In the preceding chapters I have argued that both physical and ideological enclosure are centrally concerned with the regulation of the female body. In *The Life of Christina of Markyate*, too, Christina's body is continually subjected to real or threatened violence in ways that seem designed to evoke images of late Anglo-Saxon female virgin martyrs. But whereas the stylized lives and deaths of legendary martyrs may be difficult for readers to identify with fully, Christina's physical persecutions seem all too real, couched in what Elizabeth Robertson has called "quotidian realism."[3] The torture of virgin martyrs by pagan officials (often their own fathers) emerges in Christina's *Life* as violence done to her by her parents and by various church officials. In one scene, Christina's mother, frustrated by her daughter's refusal to marry, beats her:

> et que [Beatrix] non potuit filie victrix fieri: sategit vel probrosis illius penis saciari. Erat quando repente de convivio illam eduxit. et in secreciori loco crinibus arreptam quamdiu lassata est verberavit. Scissamque rursus introduxit coram convivantibus ad ludibrium. relictis in dorso eius verberum vestigiis que nunquam potuerunt ipsa superstite deleri.

> [{A}s {Beatrix} could not break her daughter's will, {she} tried to gain satisfaction from the shameful sufferings she inflicted on her. There was one time when on impulse she took her out from a banquet and, out of sight of the guests, pulled her hair out and beat her until she was weary of it. Then she brought her back, lacerated as she was, into the presence of the revellers as an object of derision, leaving on her back such weals from the blows as could never be removed as long as she lived.]   (Talbot, 74–75)

Certainly Ælfric's *Lives* of female saints do not personalize suffering in this way. But nevertheless, here we see a distinct plot structure drawn from those lives: the physical beating in reaction to the saint's resolve, paired with the public display and mockery of the saint's tortured body. Such public display is an integral feature of virgin martyr narratives, as these scenes expose what should remain private and enclosed: the virginal female body.

The *Life* of Christina also employs the narrative device of the cross-dressing saint as a means of evoking the tradition of virgin martyr legends. Again, the device seems intended to protect Christina's body from exposure. In traditional cross-dressing narratives, such as Ælfric's *Life* of St. Eugenia, the young woman disguises herself as a man in order to worship freely and to be safe from unwanted sexual advances. As we have seen, a number of scholars have recently argued that cross-dressing allowed the female saint to put off her womanhood and assume masculinity, a gender position that would put her closer to spiritual perfection. In Christina's case, the plot device of cross-dressing appears without its spiritual underpinnings; rather, here cross-dressing operates simply as a textual device that the narrator evidently deems important for constructing female sanctity.

Like Eugenia, Christina disguises herself as a man in order to escape her family and pursue her spiritual life. Yet the disguise—and the plot device—become somewhat muddled: because Christina does not want her family to see her in male clothing, she covers herself with a long cloak, thereby disguising the disguise. Her situation becomes problematic when a sleeve from the male disguise slips out from beneath the cloak, and she is almost "exposed" by her sister (90–92). Although the cross-dressing episode thus has some suspense, it has no narrative justification, since Christina must conceal the disguise—ostensibly meant to guard her chastity—from her family, the primary threat to her chastity. The cross-dressing convention functions merely as a generic device.

Representations of cross-dressing in a text such as the *Life* of St. Eugenia negotiate the saint's various gendered identities—that is, the layers or accretions of gender that envelop the saint. The *Life* of Christina does conform to this convention, even though it fails to integrate the plot device fully. After leaving her house doubly disguised, Christina walks to a nearby meadow for an arranged rendezvous with a servant who is helping her to escape:

> Premittensque sui noticiam [appo]sita manu fronti digitoque erecto. comitem et equos habuit [pa]ratos. Quorum unum arripiens: rubore perfus substit<it>. Quid fugitiva m[ora]ris? Quid sexum feminei vereris? [Vi]rilem animum indue. et more viri [in] equum ascende. Dehinc ab[iecta pusil]animitate: viriliter super equum [saliens] atque calcaribus eius latera [pungens] famulo dixit. Sequere me . . . .

> [And making herself known by raising a finger to her forehead, she got both her companion and the horses. And seizing hold of one of them, she paused, covered with embarrassment. Why delay, fugitive? Why do you respect your feminine sex? Put on manly courage and mount the horse like a man. At this she put aside her fears and, jumping on the horse as if she were a youth and setting spurs to his

flanks, she said to the servant: 'Follow me . . . .'] (Talbot, 92–93).

The masculine clothing presents Christina with a very practical kind of gender anxiety. Her hesitation before mounting the horse "like a man" ("more viri") exposes the gender confusion inherent in the image of the cross-dressed saint. What begins as a forceful gesture— seizing the horse—quickly shifts to uncertainty. Christina seems surprised that, dressed as a man she should be expected to act like one. The unusual intervening voice ("Quid fugitiva m[ora]ris? Quid sexum feminei vereris?" "Why delay, fugitive? Why do you respect your feminine sex?") suggests that putting on a masculine disguise is not sufficient for masculinity; manly courage is also required. The voice reminds Christina and her readers of a primary function of hagiographic cross-dressing: to overcome feminine weakness through masculine strength. Yet the passage also reveals Christina struggling with the mandates of female enclosure, as it suggests her anxiety at leaving the ideological and cultural "enclosure" of femininity and adopting masculine behavior—even though, paradoxically, such behavior will ultimately protect her.

When Christina finally arrives at the anchorhold, she imme-diately puts on a religious habit (Talbot, 92). The masculine disguise (now forgotten) was thus a transitional vehicle bringing her both literally and spiritually to her life as an anchorite. The disguise (like the anchorite's clothing) allowed Christina to envelop herself quite literally in layers of feminine sanctity. The author of Christina's *Life* seems to have recognized that, in saints' lives, a masculine disguise can itself act as a kind of enclosure, providing both freedom to wor-ship and protection from sexual threats.

This threat of sexuality, the danger that the female body might be penetrated either literally by a man or spiritually by the devil, is yet another way in which this text promotes the ideology of enclo-sure, which views the female body as itself an enclosed space that must also be enclosed. After the death of Roger the Hermit, Christina is ordered by the archbishop to live under the protection of a man identified only as "a certain cleric" ("cuidam clerico," Talbot, 112– 115), evidently a man of some social and political power. Their rela-tionship is initially chaste:

Sed hoc diu non [pat]iens diabolus castitatis inimicus [de]
ipsorum securitate et domestica conver[sac]ione nactus
opportunitatem. laten[ter] prius surrepsit et callide. et post
pau[lo] heu fortiter illos aggressus est impugnare. Et ignita
iacula mittens tanta virtute institit. quod viri fortitudinem
penitus expugnavit. virginis autem et variis titillacionibus
carnem. cogi[tac]ionibus impetivit animum. nunquam
[tamen] ab ea prevaluit extorquere con[sensum].

[But the devil, the enemy of chastity, not brooking this for
long, took advantage of their close companionship and
feeling of security to insinuate himself first stealthily and
with guile, then later on, alas, to assault them more openly.
And, loosing his fiery darts, he pressed his attacks so vigor-
ously that he completely overcame the man's resistance. But
he could not wrest consent from the maiden, though he
assailed her flesh with incitements to pleasure and her mind
with impure thoughts.]   (Talbot, 114–115)

The descriptions of Christina's struggle with her own sexual desire
extend for several pages, as again a practical realism grounds the
traditional virgin martyr motif. The image of the devil sending his
fiery arrows to penetrate the virginal flesh of Christians is deeply
evocative of the same image in the Old English *Juliana* (discussed in
Chapter Three). There, the devil explains how the process works:

>   . . . ic ærest him
> þurh eargfare   in onsende
> in breostsefan   bitre geþoncas
> þurh mislice   modes willan,
> þæt him sylfum   selle þynceð
> leahtras to fremman   ofer lof godes,
> lices lustas.   (403b–409a)

[. . . I first send into [the Christian], through a flight of
arrows, bitter thoughts into his mind, through various
desires of his heart, so that he thinks it better for himself to
perform vices, lusts of the body, over the praise of God].

The devil's methods are exemplified by Christina's own desire for the cleric, and she works hard to discipline herself against the penetration of those fiery darts. The sexual nature of the devil's assault is directly linked within the text to the cleric's relentless attempts to molest Christina sexually. Throughout this extended episode, explicit rape metaphors threaten the integrity of the closed, impermeable female body.

The situation is resolved in an extraordinary way when Christ visits Christina, taking pity on her for her long struggle against her own desire:

> Accipiens itaque virgo puerum in manibus: gracias agens astrinxit sibi ad pectus. Et inestimabili de[lectacione] nunc et virginali illum in suo tenebat sinu. nunc intra se immo per ipsam cratam pectoris [apprehen]debat intuitu. Quis eruc[tabit memo]riam abundancie suavitatis qua [leta]batur mancipium ex hac dignacio[ne] sui conditoris? Ex tunc ille lib[idinis] ardor ita extinctus defecit. quod nun[quam] postea reviviscere potuit.

> [So the maiden took Him in her hands, gave thanks, and pressed Him to her bosom. And with immeasurable delight she held Him at one moment to her virginal breast, at another she felt His presence within her even through the barrier of her flesh. Who shall describe the abounding sweetness with which the servant was filled by this condescension of her creator? From that moment the fire of lust was so completely extinguished that never afterwards could it be revived.]   (Talbot, 118–119)

Thus the threat of illicit sexual penetration of the virginal female body is alleviated by the spiritual penetration of that body by Christ, who likewise alleviates Christina's sexual desire. This action ensures that Christina's body emulates the Virgin Mary's as Christ enters and occupies the bodily enclosure, while at the same time ensuring that the body remains sealed and impenetrable through the spiritual power such an action confers.

The primary importance of the sealed virginal body, and the homologies between this body and the enclosed site of the anchorhold, are the hallmarks of much female anchoritic and spiritual literature from the twelfth century onwards. The best-known of these texts, the *Ancrene Wisse*, has been shown by scholars to be a carefully constructed, self-enclosing text, the narrative structures of which embody its message. The opening and closing books, 1 and 8, of *Ancrene Wisse* concern the "outer rule," that is, the anchoresses' guidelines for life in the external world. These books enclose books 2 through 7, which concern the "inner rule," that is, the interior spiritual comportment of the anchoress.[4] The explicit ideology of female containment, in which the anchoress's cell becomes her tomb, would seem to offer a stable and impossibly secure enclosure for women, with no likelihood of release. Yet as feminist scholars have shown, the very insistence on enclosure in such texts necessitates the possibility of release.[5] Anchoritic texts insist so forcefully on female enclosure, in other words, because the possibility of penetrating the boundaries of cell and body is so real. As Sarah Beckwith has recently argued, in *Ancrene Wisse* "inner" and "outer" are mutually dependent categories, and the text's female subject is produced at the boundary of the two: "For it is, of course, precisely the distinction between what is on the inside and what is on the outside that constitutes the individual body's sense of its own integrity."[6] Similarly, Jocelyn Wogan-Browne has argued that *Ancrene Wisse* is "itself a body model, structuring the anchoress's physical and spiritual existence as a series of enclosures: her cell and body enclosing her heart and soul, her heart 'God's chamber.' . . . . Contained and containing, the recluse's body-boundaries are as intensely regulated as those of the cell itself, and form a frontier across which significant egresses and entrances may occur."[7] The spatial dimensions these scholars have identified in the anchoritic literature bear a striking resemblance to many of the multiply-enclosed women of Old English literature. Juliana and Ælfric's female saints, as we have seen, neatly illustrate this concept: the female saint encloses Christ in her heart even as she is enclosed within a variety of imprisoning structures. The speakers of the Old English female elegies, likewise physically enclosed, struggle to escape that confinement by opening up and exploring those "inner" chambers.

It is not surprising, of course, that texts such as the *Ancrene Wisse*, whose mission is largely to promote female containment, should find ways of imaging and reinforcing such containment through narrative, structural, and ideological means. The proliferation of enclosure practices in the twelfth and thirteenth centuries, and the concomitant anxieties concerning the permeability of the boundaries of enclosures (whether body or cell), have been linked to a number of philosophical, theological, and cultural ideas that emerged in the twelfth century: a new emphasis on the individual, the rise of affective piety, an increase in the numbers of women both in commercial and in religious life.[8] This period shows evidence of increasingly strict regulations on female enclosure coincident with growing numbers of women entering religious and especially anchoritic life.[9] Yet as we have seen in the preceding chapters, the cultural thematics of enclosure was prevalent in a number of key vernacular works that predated *Ancrene Wisse* and its related texts.

Within Anglo-Saxon England, models of literal and figurative female enclosure predominate in cultural representations of women. And just as boundaries serve as particular sites of tension in later texts, they similarly reveal anxieties in Old English texts. In the elegies, although they are contained physically, the female speakers willingly explore their own physical desires and emotions, opening up the *hord-cofa*, a "site" the Wanderer is unwilling to examine. In *Beowulf*, the episode featuring Grendel's Mother continually negotiates boundaries: through Beowulf's penetration of the mere; through Grendel's Mother's own attempted (and failed) penetration of Beowulf's body; even through her ability to wander outside of her own domestic space. This simultaneous concern with enclosures, with that which they enclose, and with the boundary between inside and outside plays out structurally in *Beowulf's* many frames and ring structures, some version of which literally surrounds every woman in the poem. Finally, the tensions found at the boundary of enclosure and enclosed shape our readings of the female bodies of Saints Juliana, Agatha, Agnes, Lucy, and Eugenia. When *The Life of Christina of Markyate* "reads" (or perhaps "translates") these or similar lives, it shows an understanding of the conventions by which late Old English texts constructed their female subjects by means of both physical and ideological enclosure.

The emphasis on anchoritism and enclosure in *The Life of Christina of Markyate* has traditionally served to align it with other twelfth and thirteenth century anchoritic texts. Yet in many ways, this *Life* reveals the deep influence of Anglo-Saxon literature about women. The *Life* displays the traces of reading and textuality that likewise mark much of the earlier literature: its "reading" of Old English representations of women is demonstrated through its appropriation of enclosure motifs, and through its desire to enter its subject, Christina, into this long tradition of women's literary history. It does so by means of a thematic that, as we have seen, acts as a powerful gender marker in Old English literature: female enclosure.

The present study has not only located within Old English literature an important site of earlier models of female enclosure; it also hopes to suggest that this trope is important for a broader understanding of the gender operations of later medieval literature. In addition, it has aimed to present a model for finding continuities in women's literature of the early and later Middle Ages. Although female enclosure does not remain static throughout the Middle Ages (and it may shift around even within certain texts, as it does in *The Life of Christina of Markyate*), it nonetheless provides a cultural framework that can help us understand some of the ways that early medieval literature represented women and femininity. In examining the affinities between early and later texts, we can also use the enclosure motif to examine the textualizing processes of the later works, as they write and revise the words and the worlds that have preceded them. The outpouring of women's literature and spirituality so often associated with the later Middle Ages finds a powerful precursor in the literary models of female enclosure in Anglo-Saxon England.

NOTES

1. See Christopher Holdsworth, "Christina of Markyate," in *Medieval Women*, ed. Derek Baker (Oxford: Basil Blackwell, 1978): 185–204, for a good comprehensive overview of the *Life* of Christina. See also Ruth Karras, "Friendship and Love in the Lives of Two Twelfth–Century English Saints" (*Journal of Medieval History* 14 [1988]: 305–320); and Thomas Head, "The Marriages of Christina of Markyate" (*Viator* 21 [1990]: 75–101. *The Life of Christina of Markyate* is edited and translated by C.H. Talbot (Oxford: Clarendon, 1959); rpt. Medieval Academy Reprints for Teaching 39 (Toronto: University of Toronto Press, 1998). All citations and translations from the *Life* will refer to the MART edition. The Old English phrase, "[my]n sunendaege dohter" is spoken by Roger the hermit and addressed to Christina. The narrator points out that Roger spoke to her "in English": "Et ad virginum . . . ait anglico sermone" (Talbot, 106).

2. Christina herself was evidently familiar with Anglo-Saxon saints' lives. Holdsworth and others have argued that the St. Albans Psalter was originally made for Christina's private use. In addition to an Old French version of the Life of St. Alexis, the Psalter contains clear evidence of Christina's familiarity with Anglo-Saxon hagiography, as its calendar records entries for Saints Amalburga, Æthelthryth, Frideswide, Hild, and others. See Jocelyn Wogan-Browne, "Saints' Lives and the Female Reader," *Forum for Modern Language Studies* 27 (1991): 314–332, especially p. 316. Wogan-Browne additionally argues that the St. Juliana recorded in the Psalter's calendar is the same saint as in Cynewulf's verse life (see p. 330 n. 15). See also Otto Pächt, C.R. Dodwell, and Francis Wormald, eds., *The St. Albans Psalter* (London: Warburg Institute, 1960). On Christina's relationship to the Psalter, see Madeline H. Caviness, "Anchoress, Abbess, and Queen: Donors and Patrons or Intercessors and Matrons?" in *The Cultural Patronage of Medieval Women*, ed. June Hall McCash (Athens and London: University of Georgia Press, 1996): 105–154, especially pp. 107–113.

3. See Elizabeth Robertson, *Early English Devotional Prose*, 3 and *passim*.

4. See Beckwith, "Passionate Regulation," 807–813; Price, "Inner and Outer," Linda Georgianna, *The Solitary Self: Individuality in the* Ancrene Wisse (Cambridge: Harvard University Press, 1981), 20–27; and Robertson, *Early English Devotional Prose*, 57ff. There is a rich body of feminist scholarship on *Ancrene Wisse* and the related texts of the Katherine and Wooing Groups. Unfortunately, the texts and their critical history fall just outside the scope of my study, and I will not be able to discuss them in detail here. At the risk of stating the obvious, I would simply point out the immense importance of the motifs of physical, spiritual, and ideological enclosure in the texts of the Wooing and Katherine Groups, and suggest that these enclosure motifs are critical for constructing the gendered identities of their female subjects. For the text of Ancrene Wisse, see *Anchoritic Spirituality: Ancrene Wisse and Associated Works*, trans. Savage and Watson (New York: Paulist Press, 1991); and J.R.R. Tolkien, *The English Text of the Ancrene Riwle: Ancrene Wisse: Edited from MS Corpus Christi College Cambridge 402*, EETS o.s. 249 (Oxford, 1962).

5. See Jocelyn Price, "Inner and Outer," and Beckwith, "Passionate Regulation."

6. "Passionate Regulation," 809; Beckwith also cites this relevant passage from Judith Butler: "Bodily contours and morphology are not merely implicated in an irreducible tension between the psychic and the material but are that tension. Hence the psyche is not a pre-given grid through which the pre-given body appears" (*Bodies That Matter* [London: Routledge, 1993], 65); cited in Beckwith at 822, n. 28.

7. "Chaste Bodies: Frames and Experiences," in *Framing Medieval Bodies*, ed. Miri Rubin and Sarah Kay (New York: St. Martin's, 1994): 27.

8. Space prohibits anything more than this brief and over-simplified glance at twelfth-century currents of thought. These have in any event been well-documented by other scholars. See Georgianna, *The Solitary Self;* Colin Morris, *The Discovery of the Individual, 1050–1200;* Robertson, *Early English Devotional Prose;* Caroline Walker Bynum, *Jesus as Mother: Studies in the Spirituality of the High Middle Ages* (Berkeley: University of California Press, 1982); on the proliferation of enclosure in the twelfth and thirteenth centuries, see Ann K. Warren, *Anchorites and Their Patrons in Medieval England* (Berkeley and Los Angeles: University of California Press, 1985).

9. See Schulenburg, "Strict Active Enclosure," and Warren, 18ff.

Bibliography

PRIMARY SOURCES

Acta S. Julianae. Ed. William J. Strunk. Reprinted in *The Juliana of Cynewulf.* Boston: D.C. Heath, 1904.

Aelred of Rievaulx. *De Institutione Inclusarum.* In *Opera Omnia* I. Opera Ascetica. Ed. A. Hoste and C.H. Talbot. Corpus Christianorum Continuatio Mediaevalis I. Turnhout: Brepols, 1971.

———. *A Rule of Life for a Recluse.* Trans. Mary Paul MacPherson. In *The Works of Aelred of Rievaulx.* Vol. 1. Spencer, MA: Cistercian Publications, 1971.

Aldhelm. *De Virginitate.* In *The Prose Works,* edited and trans. by Michael Lapidge and Michael Herren. Cambridge: D.S. Brewer, 1979.

———. *De Virginitate.* In *Opera.* Ed. Rudolph Ehwald. Monumenta Germaniae Historica 15. Berlin-Charlottenburg: Weidman, 1961.

Allen, Michael J. and Daniel Calder. *Sources and Analogues of Old English Poetry.* Cambridge: D.S. Brewer, 1976.

Amt, Emilie, ed. *Women's Lives in Medieval Europe: A Sourcebook.* New York: Routledge, 1993.

Ancrene Wisse: Guide for Anchoresses. Ed. and trans. Hugh White. London: Penguin, 1993.

The Anglo-Saxon Poetic Records. 6 Volumes. Edited by George Philip Krapp and Elliot Van Kirk Dobbie. New York: Columbia University Press, 1931–1953.

Assman, Bruno, ed. *Angelsächsische Homilien und Heiligenleben.* Reprinted with a supplementary introduction by Peter Clemoes. Darmstadt: Wissenschaftliche Buchgesellschaft, 1964.

Attenborough, F.L., ed. and trans. *The Laws of the Earliest English Kings.* Cambridge: Cambridge University Press, 1922.

Augustine. *City of God.* Trans. Henry Bettenson. London: Penguin, 1972; rpt. 1984.

187

——. *De Doctrina Christiana.* In *Opera* IV.i. Ed. Joseph Martin. Corpus Christianorum Series Latina XXXII. Turnhout: Brepols, 1962.

——. *In Iohannis Evangelium Tractatus CXXIV.* Ed. D. Willems. In *Opera* VIII. Corpus Christianorum Series Latina XXXVI. Turnhout: Brepols, 1954.

——. *On Christian Doctrine.* Trans. D.W. Robertson. Indianapolis: Bobbs-Merrill, 1958.

——. *Tractates on the Gospel of John 11–27.* Trans. John W. Rettig. The Fathers of the Church, vol. 79. Washington D.C.: Catholic University of America Press, 1988.

Beowulf. Translated by E. Talbot Donaldson. Edited by Joseph E. Tuso. New York: Norton, 1975.

Caesarius of Arles. *Regulae Monasticae.* In *Opera Varia.* Edited by D. Morin. Maretioli, 1942.

[Chadwick], Nora Kershaw. *Anglo-Saxon and Norse Poems.* Cambridge: Cambridge University Press, 1922.

Clemoes, Peter, ed. *Ælfric's Catholic Homilies, The First Series.* Early English Text Society supplementary series 17. Oxford: Oxford University Press, 1997.

Colgrave, Bertram and R.A.B. Mynors, eds. and trans. *Bede's Ecclesiastical History of the English People.* Oxford: Clarendon, 1969.

Crawford, S.J., ed. *The Old English Version of the Heptateuch, Ælfric's Treatise on the Old and New Testament and his Preface to Genesis.* Early English Text Society original series 160. London: Oxford University Press, 1922.

Deshman, Robert. *The Benedictional of Æthelwold.* Princeton: Princeton University Press, 1995.

Emerton, Ephraim, ed. and trans. *The Letters of Saint Boniface.* New York: Norton, 1940, 1976.

Godden, Malcolm, ed. *Ælfric's Catholic Homilies: The Second Series.* Early English Text Society supplementary series 5. London: Oxford University Press, 1979.

Jerome, Saint. *Epistulae.* Ed. I. Hilberg. Corpus Scriptorum Ecclesiasticorum Latinorum. Vols. 54–56. 3 volumes. Vienna: Verlag der Österreichischen Akademie der Wissenschaften, 1996.

——. *The Principle Works of St. Jerome.* Trans. W.H. Fremantle. *A Select Library of the Nicene and Post-Nicene Fathers of the Christian Church.* Second series 6. Grand Rapids: Eerdmans, 1954.

Klaeber, Fr., ed. *Beowulf and the Fight at Finnsburg.* 3rd ed. Lexington MA: D.C. Heath, 1950.

Klinck, Anne L. *The Old English Elegies: A Critical Edition and Genre Study.* Montreal: McGill-Queen's University Press, 1992.

Kornexl, Lucia, ed. *Die* Regularis Concordia *und ihre altenglische Interlinearversion.* Munich: Wilhelm Fink Verlag, 1993.

Leslie, R.F. *Three Old English Elegies.* Manchester: Manchester University Press, 1961.

Millett, Bella and Jocelyn Wogan-Browne, eds. *Medieval English Prose for Women: From the Katherine Group and Ancrene Wisse.* London: The Clarendon Press, 1990; rpt. 1992.

Pächt, Otto, C.R. Dodwell, and Francis Wormald, eds. *The St. Albans Psalter.* London: The Warburg Institute, 1960.

Petroff, Elizabeth Alvilda, ed. *Medieval Women's Visionary Literature.* Oxford: Oxford University Press, 1986.

Pope, John C., ed. *Homilies of Ælfric: A Supplementary Collection.* 2 Volumes. Early English Text Society original series 259. London: Oxford University Press, 1967.

Raffel, Burton, trans. *Poems from the Old English.* Lincoln: University of Nebraska Press, 1964.

Savage, Anne and Nicholas Watson, trans. *Anchoritic Spirituality:* Ancrene Wisse *and Associated Works.* New York and Mahwah: Paulist Press, 1991.

Skeat, W.W., ed. and trans. *Ælfric's Lives of Saints.* Early English Text Society original series 76, 82, 94, 114. London: Oxford University Press, 1881–1888. Reprinted in two volumes, 1966.

Skeat, W.W. ed. *The Gospel According to Saint Matthew.* Cambridge: Cambridge University Press, 1887.

Smith, A.H. ed. *The Parker Chronicle.* London: Methuen, 1935.

Symons, Thomas, ed. and trans. *Regularis Concordia Anglicae Nationis Monachorum Sanctimonialumque.* [The Monastic Agreement of the Monks and Nuns of the English Nation.] London: Thomas Nelson and Sons, 1953.

Talbot, C.H., trans. *The Life of St. Leoba, by Rudolph, Monk of Fulda.* In *Medieval Women's Visionary Literature,* edited by Elizabeth Alvilda Petroff, 106–114. New York: Oxford University Press, 1986.

Talbot, C.H., ed. and trans. *The Life of Christina of Markyate: A Twelfth Century Recluse.* Oxford: The Clarendon Press, 1959. Rpt. Medieval Academy Reprints for Teaching 39. Toronto: University of Toronto Press, 1998.

Tangl, M., ed. *Die Briefe des Heiligen Bonifatius und Lullus.* 2nd ed. Monumenta Germaniae Historica. Epistolae Selectae I. Berlin: Weidmann, 1955.

Tolkien, J.R.R., ed. *The English Text of the Ancrene Riwle: Ancrene Wisse: Edited from MS Corpus Christi College Cambridge 402.* Early English Text Society original series 249. Oxford: Oxford University Press, 1962.

Waitz, G., ed. *Vita Leobae Abbatissae Biscofesheimensis Auctore Rudolfo Fuldensi.* Monumenta Germaniae Historica. Scriptores 15, part 1. Hannover, 1887; rpt. Stuttgart: Anton Hiersemann, 1992.

Whitelock, Dorothy, ed. *English Historical Documents c. 500–1042.* English Historical Documents 1. New York: Oxford University Press, 1955.

Woolf, Rosemary, ed. *Juliana.* London: Methuen, 1955.

SECONDARY SOURCES

Alexander, Robert J. "W.W. Skeat and Ælfric." *Annuale Mediaevale* 22 (1982): 286–315.

Alfano, Christine. "The Issue of Feminine Monstrosity: A Reevaluation of Grendel's Mother." *Comitatus* 23 (1993): 1–16.

Anson, John. "The Female Transvestite in Early Monasticism: The Origin and Development of a Motif." *Viator* 5 (1974): 1–32.

Baker, Peter S., ed. Beowulf: *Basic Readings.* New York and London: Garland, 1995.

Baker, Peter. "The Ambiguity of *Wulf and Eadwacer.*" *Studies in Philology* 78 (1981): 39–51.

———. "*Wulf and Eadwacer*: A Classroom Edition." *Old English Newsletter* 16.2 (1983): appendix 1–8.

Bartlett, Adeline Courtney. *The Larger Rhetorical Patterns in Anglo-Saxon Poetry.* New York: Columbia University Press, 1935.

Bateson, Mary. "Origin and Early History of Double Monasteries." *Transactions of the Royal Historical Society* n.s. 13 (1899): 137–98.

Baum, Paull F. "The *Beowulf* Poet." *Philological Quarterly* 39 (1960): 389–399; rpt. in *An Anthology of* Beowulf *Criticism,* edited by Lewis E. Nicholson, 353–365. Notre Dame and London: University of Notre Dame Press, 1963).

Beckwith, Sarah. "Passionate Regulation: Enclosure, Ascesis, and the Feminist Imaginary." *South Atlantic Quarterly* 93.4 (1994): 803–824.

Belanoff, Patricia. "Women's Songs, Women's Language: *Wulf and Eadwacer* and *The Wife's Lament.*" In *New Readings on Women in Old English Literature,* edited by Helen Damico and Alexandra Hennessey Olsen, 193–203. Bloomington: University of Indiana Press, 1990.

Bennett, Helen. "Exile and the Semiosis of Gender." In *Class and Gender in Early English Literature: Intersections,* edited by Britton Harwood and Gillian Overing, 43–58. Bloomington: University of Indiana Press, 1994.

———. "The Female Mourner at Beowulf's Funeral: Filling in the Blanks/ Hearing the Spaces." *Exemplaria* 4.1 (1992): 35–50.

———. "From Peace Weaver to Text Weaver: Feminist Approaches to Old English Literature." In *Twenty Years of the "Year's Work in Old English Studies,"* edited by Katherine O'Brien O'Keeffe. *Old English Newsletter Subsidia* 15 (1989): 23–42.

Bennett, Judith. "Feminism and History." *Gender and History* 1.3 (1989): 251–272.

———. "Medieval Women, Modern Women: Across the Great Divide." In *Culture and History, 1350–1600: Essays on English Communities, Identities, and Writing*, edited by David Aers, 147–175. New York and London: Harvester Wheatsheaf, 1992.

Biddick, Kathleen. "Genders, Bodies, Borders: Technologies of the Visible." In *Studying Medieval Women*, edited by Nancy F. Partner, 87–116. Cambridge: Medieval Academy of America, 1993.

Bjork, Robert. "*Sundor æt Rune*: The Voluntary Exile of the Wanderer." *Neophilologus* 73 (1989): 119–129.

Bloomfield, Josephine. "Diminished by Kindness: Frederick Klaeber's Rewriting of Wealhtheow." *JEGP* 93.2 (1994): 183–203.

Bolton, W.F. "'The Wife's Lament' and 'The Husband's Message': A Reconsideration Revisited." *Archiv* 205 (1969): 337–351.

Bonjour, Adrien. *The Digressions in* Beowulf. Oxford: Blackwell, 1950.

Boswell, John. *The Kindness of Strangers: The Abandonment of Children in Western Europe from Late Antiquity to the Renaissance*. New York: Pantheon, 1988.

Bosworth, Joseph. *An Anglo-Saxon Dictionary*. 1898; rpt. Oxford: Oxford University Press, 1976. Supplement by T. Northcote Toller. London: Oxford University Press, 1966.

Brown, Peter. *The Body and Society: Men, Women and Sexual Renunciation in Early Christianity*. New York: Columbia University Press, 1988.

———. *The Cult of the Saints*. Chicago: University of Chicago Press, 1981.

Bugge, John. *Virginitas: An Essay in the History of a Medieval Ideal*. The Hague: Martinus Nijhoff, 1975.

Bullough, Vern. "Transvestism in the Middle Ages." In *Sexual Practices and the Medieval Church*, edited by Vern L. Bullough and James Brundage, 43–54. Buffalo: Prometheus Books, 1982.

Butler, Judith. *Gender Trouble: Feminism and the Subversion of Identity*. New York: Routledge, 1990.

Bynum, Caroline Walker. *Jesus as Mother: Studies in the Spirituality of the High Middle Ages*. Berkeley: University of California Press, 1982.

———. *Holy Feast and Holy Fast: The Religious Significance of Food to Medieval Women*. Berkeley: University of California Press, 1987.

———. *The Resurrection of the Body in Western Christianity, 200–1336*. New York: Columbia University Press, 1995.

Calder, Daniel. *Cynewulf*. Boston: Twayne, 1981.

Carruthers, Mary. *The Book of Memory: A Study of Memory in Medieval Culture*. Cambridge: Cambridge University Press, 1990.

Castelli, Elizabeth. "'I Will Make Mary Male': Pieties of the Body and Gender Transformation of Christian Women in Late Antiquity." In *Body Guards:*

The Cultural Politics of Gender Ambiguity, edited by Julia Epstein and Kristina Straub, 29–49. New York: Routledge, 1991.

Caviness, Madeline H. "Anchoress, Abbess, and Queen: Donors and Patrons or Intercessors and Matrons?" In *The Cultural Patronage of Medieval Women*, edited by June Hall McCash, 105–154. Athens and London: University of Georgia Press, 1996.

Cazelles, Brigitte. *The Lady as Saint: A Collection of French Hagiographic Romances of the Thirteenth Century*. Philadelphia: University of Pennsylvania Press, 1991.

Chance, Jane. *Woman as Hero in Old English Literature*. Syracuse: Syracuse University Press, 1986.

Chase, Colin, ed. *The Dating of* Beowulf. Toronto: University of Toronto Press, 1981. Rpt. Toronto Old English Series 6. Toronto: University of Toronto Press, 1998.

Clanchy, Michael. *From Memory to Written Record: England 1066–1307*. 2nd ed. Oxford: Blackwell, 1993.

Clemoes, Peter. "Ælfric." In *Continuations and Beginnings*, edited by E.G. Stanley, 176–209. London: Thomas Nelson and Sons, Ltd., 1966.

Copeland, Rita. "Why Women Can't Read: Medieval Hermeneutics, Statutory Law, and the Lollard Heresy Trials." In *Representing Women: Law, Literature, and Feminism*, edited by Susan Sage Heinzelman and Zipporah Batshaw Wiseman, 253–286. Durham: Duke University Press, 1994.

Crane, Susan. *Gender and Romance in Chaucer's Canterbury Tales*. Princeton: Princeton University Press, 1994.

Curry, Jane L. "Approaches to a Translation of the Anglo-Saxon *The Wife's Lament*." *Medium Ævum* 35 (1966): 187–198.

Daichman, Graciela. *Wayward Nuns in Medieval Literature*. Syracuse: Syracuse University Press, 1986.

Damico, Helen. Beowulf's *Wealhtheow and the Valkyrie Tradition*. Madison: University of Wisconsin Press, 1984.

Desmond, Marilynn. "The Voice of Exile: Feminist Literary History and the Anonymous Anglo-Saxon Elegy." *Critical Inquiry* 16 (1990): 572–590.

The Dictionary of Old English, edited by Antonette diPaolo Healey, et al. Toronto: Pontifical Institute for Mediaeval Studies, 1986–. (Fascicles published to date: D, C, B, Æ, A, E.)

Dinshaw, Carolyn. *Chaucer's Sexual Poetics*. Madison: University of Wisconsin Press, 1989.

Doane, A.N. "Heathen Form and Christian Function in 'The Wife's Lament." *Mediaeval Studies* 28 (1966): 77–91.

Dockray-Miller, Mary. "The Masculine Queen of *Beowulf*." *Women and Language* 21 (1998): 31–38.

Dronke, Peter. *Women Writers of the Middle Ages.* Cambridge: Cambridge University Press, 1984.

―――. *The Medieval Lyric.* London: Hutchinson, 1968.

duBois, Page. *Torture and Truth.* New York: Routledge, 1991.

Duden, Barbara. "A Repertory of Body History." In *Fragments for the History of the Human Body.* Vol. 3. Edited by Michel Feher, et al, 471–578. New York: Urzone, 1989.

Elkins, Sharon K. *Holy Women of Twelfth Century England.* Chapel Hill: University of North Carolina Press, 1988.

Elliot, Dyan. *Spiritual Marriage: Sexual Abstinence in Medieval Wedlock.* Princeton: Princeton University Press, 1993.

Enright, Michael J. *Lady With a Mead-Cup: Ritual, Prophecy, and Lordship in the European Warband from La Tène to the Viking Age.* Dublin: Four Courts Press, 1996.

Evans, G.R. *The Language and Logic of the Bible.* Cambridge: Cambridge University Press, 1984.

Fee, Christopher. "Beag & Beaghroden: Women, Treasure, and the Language of Social Structure in *Beowulf.*" *Neuphilologische Mitteilungen* 97 (1996): 285–294.

Feher, Michel, et al., eds. *Fragments for the History of the Human Body.* 3 Vols. New York: Urzone, 1989.

Fell, Christine. "Saint Æðelþryð: A Historical-Hagiographical Dichotomy Revisited." *Nottingham Medieval Studies* 38 (1994): 18–34.

―――. "Some Implications of the Boniface Correspondence." In *New Readings on Women in Old English Literature,* edited by Helen Damico and Alexandra Hennessey Olsen, 29–43. Bloomington: Indiana University Press, 1990.

―――. *Women in Anglo-Saxon England.* Oxford: Blackwell, 1984.

Finke, Laurie A. *Feminist Theory, Women's Writing.* Ithaca: Cornell University Press, 1992.

Foucault, Michel. *The Archaeology of Knowledge.* Trans. A.M. Sheridan Smith. New York: Pantheon Books, 1972.

Frantzen, Allen. *Desire for Origins: New Language, Old English, and Teaching the Tradition.* New Brunswick and London: Rutgers University Press, 1990.

―――. "When Women Aren't Enough." *Speculum* 68.2 (1993): 445–471. Reprinted in *Studying Medieval Women,* edited by Nancy F. Partner, 143–169. Cambridge: Medieval Academy of America, 1993.

Frese, Dolores Warwick. "*Wulf and Eadwacer:* The Adulterous Woman Reconsidered." *Notre Dame English Journal* 15.1 (1983): 1–22. Reprinted in *New Readings on Women in Old English Literature,* edited by Helen

Damico and Alexandra Hennessey Olsen, 273–291. Bloomington: Indiana University Press, 1990.

Geary, Patrick J. *Furta Sacra: Thefts of Relics in the Central Middle Ages.* Princeton: Princeton University Press, 1978.

Georgianna, Linda. *The Solitary Self: Individuality in the Ancrene Wisse.* Cambridge, MA: Harvard University Press, 1981.

Gilchrist, Roberta. "Community and Self: Perceptions and Use of Space in Medieval Monasteries." *Scottish Archaeological Review* 6 (1989): 55–64.

———. *Gender and Material Culture: The Archaeology of Religious Women.* New York and London: Routledge, 1994.

———. "The Spatial Archaeology of Gender Domains: A Case Study of Medieval English Nunneries." *Archaeological Review From Cambridge* 7.1 (1988): 21–28.

Gravdal, Kathryn. "Chrétien de Troyes, Gratian, and the Medieval Romance of Sexual Violence." *Signs* 17 (1992): 558–585.

———. *Ravishing Maidens: Writing Rape in Medieval French Literature and Law.* Philadelphia: University of Pennsylvania Press, 1991.

Green, Martin. "Introduction." In *The Old English Elegies: New Essays in Criticism and Research,* edited by Martin Green. Rutherford: Fairleigh Dickinson University Press, 1983.

———. "Time, Memory, and Elegy in *The Wife's Lament.*" In *The Old English Elegies: New Essays in Criticism and Research,* edited by Martin Green, 123–132. Rutherford: Fairleigh Dickinson University Press, 1983.

Greenfield, Stanley. "*Wulf and Eadwacer*: All Passion Pent." *Anglo-Saxon England* 15 (1986): 5–14.

Greenfield, Stanley B. and Daniel G. Calder. *A New Critical History of Old English Literature.* New York: New York University Press, 1986.

Griffiths, Gwen. "Reading Ælfric's Saint Æthelthryth as a Woman." *Parergon* 10.2 (1992): 35–49.

Hansen, Elaine Tuttle. *The Solomon Complex: Reading Wisdom in Old English Poetry.* Toronto: University of Toronto Press, 1988.

Head, Pauline. *Representation and Design: Tracing a Hermeneutics of Old English Poetry.* Albany: SUNY Press, 1997.

Head, Thomas. "The Marriages of Christina of Markyate." *Viator* 21 (1990): 75–101.

Hermann, John P. *Allegories of War: Language and Violence in Old English Poetry.* Ann Arbor: University of Michigan Press, 1989.

———. "Why Anglo-Saxonists Can't Read: Or, Who Took the Mead out of Medieval Studies." *Exemplaria* 7 (1995): 9–26.

Hieatt, Constance B. "Envelope Patterns and the Structure of *Beowulf.*" *English Studies in Canada* 1 (1975): 249–265.

Higley, Sarah Lynn. *Between Languages: The Uncooperative Text in Early Welsh and Old English Nature Poetry.* University Park: Penn State University Press, 1993.

Holdsworth, Christopher. "Christina of Markyate." In *Medieval Women*, edited by Derek Baker, 185–204. Oxford: Basil Blackwell, 1978.

Hollis, Stephanie. *Anglo-Saxon Women and the Church.* Woodbridge, Suffolk: The Boydell Press, 1992.

Horner, Shari. "The Vernacular Language of Rape in Old English Literature and Law: Views from the Anglo-Saxon(ist)s." In *Sex and Sexuality in Anglo-Saxon England: Essays in Memory of Daniel G. Calder.* Edited by Robert Bjork, Carol Braun Pasternack, and Lisa Weston. Forthcoming.

———. "Women's Literacy and Female Textuality in Old English Poetry." Ph.D. Diss. University of Minnesota, 1992.

Howe, Nicholas. "The Cultural Construction of Reading in Anglo-Saxon England." In *The Ethnography of Reading*, edited by Jonathan Boyarin, 58–79. Berkeley: University of California Press, 1993.

Innes-Parker, Catherine. "Sexual Violence and the Female Reader: Symbolic 'Rape' in the Saints' Lives of the Katherine Group." *Women's Studies* 24 (1995): 205–217.

Irigaray, Luce. *This Sex Which is Not One.* Trans. Catherine Porter. Ithaca: Cornell University Press, 1985.

Irvine, Martin. *The Making of Textual Culture: "Grammatica" and Literary Theory 350–1100.* Cambridge: Cambridge University Press, 1994.

———. "Medieval Textuality and the Archaeology of Textual Culture." In *Speaking Two Languages: Traditional Disciplines and Contemporary Theory in Medieval Studies*, edited by Allen J. Frantzen, 181–210. Albany: State University of New York Press, 1991.

Irving, Edward. *Rereading* Beowulf. Philadelphia: University of Pennsylvania Press, 1989.

Jager, Eric. "Speech and the Chest in Old English Poetry: Orality or Pectorality?" *Speculum* 65 (1990): 845–859.

Jensen, Emily. "*The Wife's Lament's* Eorðscræf: Literal or Figurative Sign?" *Neuphilologische Mitteilungen* 91 (1990): 449–457.

John, Eric. "*Beowulf* and the Margins of Literacy." *Bulletin of the John Rylands University Library of Manchester* 56 (1973–4): 388–422. Reprinted in *Beowulf: Basic Readings*, edited by Peter Baker, 51–77. Garland: New York, 1995.

Jombart, Emile and Marcel Viller. "Clôture." *Dictionnaire de Spiritualité, ascétique, et mystique, doctrine et histoire.* Vol. 2. Paris: Beauchesne, 1953.

Karras, Ruth. "Friendship and Love in the Lives of Two Twelfth-Century English Saints." *Journal of Medieval History* 14 (1988): 305–320.

Kiernan, Kevin. "Grendel's Heroic Mother." *In Geardagum* 6 (1984): 25–27.

Klinck, Anne L. "Female Characterisation in Old English Poetry and the Growth of Psychological Realism: *Genesis B* and *Christ I.*" *Neophilologus* 63 (1979): 597–610.

Knowles, David and R. Neville Hadcock. *Medieval Religious Houses: England and Wales.* 2nd ed. London: Longman, 1971.

Lapidge, Michael. "The Saintly Life in Anglo-Saxon England." In *The Cambridge Companion to Old English Literature*, edited by Malcolm Godden and Michael Lapidge, 243–263. Cambridge: Cambridge University Press, 1991.

———. "The Study of Latin Texts in late Anglo-Saxon England I: The Evidence of Latin Glosses." In *Latin and the Vernacular Languages in Early Medieval Britain*, edited by Nicholas Brooks, 99–140. Leicester: Leicester University Press, 1982.

Leclercq, Jean. *The Love of Learning and the Desire for God.* Trans. Catharine Misrahi. New York: New American Library, 1961.

Lees, Clare A. "At a crossroads: Old English and feminist criticism." In *Reading Old English Texts*, edited by Katherine O'Brien O'Keeffe, 146–169. Cambridge: Cambridge University Press, 1997.

———. "Men and *Beowulf.*" In *Medieval Masculinities: Regarding Men in the Middle Ages*, edited by Clare Lees, 129–148. Minneapolis: University of Minnesota Press, 1994.

Lees, Clare A., ed. *Medieval Masculinities.* Minneapolis: University of Minnesota Press, 1994.

Lees, Clare A. and Gillian R. Overing. "Birthing Bishops and Fathering Poets: Bede, Hild, and the Relations of Cultural Production." *Exemplaria* 6.1 (1994): 35–65.

Lehmann, Ruth P.M. "The Metrics and Structure of *Wulf and Eadwacer.*" *Philological Quarterly* 48 (1969): 151–165.

Lench, Elinor. "*The Wife's Lament*: A Poem of the Living Dead." *Comitatus* 1 (1970): 3–23.

Lerer, Seth. *Literacy and Power in Anglo-Saxon Literature.* Lincoln: University of Nebraska Press, 1991.

Leyerle, John. "The Interlace Structure of *Beowulf.*" *University of Toronto Quarterly* 37 (1967): 1–17.

Liuzza, Roy Michael. "On the Dating of *Beowulf.*" In Beowulf: *Basic Readings*, edited by Peter S. Baker, 281–302. New York and London: Garland, 1995.

Lochrie, Karma. "Gender, Sexual Violence, and the Politics of War in the Old English *Judith.*" In *Class and Gender in Early English Literature*, edited by Britton J. Harwood and Gillian R. Overing, 1–20. Bloomington: Indiana University Press, 1994.

————. *Margery Kempe and Translations of the Flesh.* Philadelphia: University of Pennsylvania Press, 1991.

Lomperis, Linda and Sarah Stanbury, eds. *Feminist Approaches to the Body in Medieval Literature.* Philadelphia: University of Pennsylvania Press, 1993.

Lucas, Angela. "The Narrator of *The Wife's Lament* Reconsidered." *Neuphilologische Mitteilungen* 70 (1969): 282–297.

Maclean, Ian. *The Renaissance Notion of Woman: A Study in the Fortunes of Scholasticism and Medical Science in European Intellectual Life.* Cambridge: Cambridge University Press, 1980.

Mandel, Jerome. *Alternative Readings in Old English Poetry.* New York: Peter Lang, 1987.

Matter, E. Ann. *The Voice of My Beloved: The Song of Songs in Western Medieval Christianity.* Philadelphia: University of Pennsylvania Press, 1990.

McKitterick, Rosamond. *The Carolingians and the Written Word.* Cambridge: Cambridge University Press, 1989.

Menzer, Melinda J. "*Aglæcwif* (*Beowulf* 1259A): Implications for -*Wif* Compounds, Grendel's Mother, and Other *Aglæcan.*" *English Language Notes* 34 (September 1996): 1–6.

A Microfiche Concordance to Old English. Compiled by Richard L. Venezky and Antonette diPaolo Healey. Newark, Del.: University of Delaware Press, 1980.

Middleton, Anne. "Ælfric's Answerable Style: The Rhetoric of the Alliterative Prose." *Studies in Medieval Culture* 4 (1973): 83–91.

Miles, Margaret. *Carnal Knowing: Female Nakedness and Religious Meaning in the Christian West.* Boston: Beacon Press, 1989.

Mitchell, Bruce and Fred C. Robinson. *A Guide to Old English.* 5th ed. Oxford: Blackwell, 1992.

Moloney, Bernadette. "Another Look at Ælfric's Use of Discourse in Some Saints' Lives." *English Studies* 63 (1982): 13–19.

Morris, Colin. *The Discovery of the Individual, 1050–1200.* New York: Harper & Row, 1973.

Morrison, Stephen. "The Figure of Christus Sponsus in Old English Prose." *Beiträge zur Deutschen Philologie* 58 (1984): 5–15.

Mulvey, Laura. *Visual and Other Pleasures.* Bloomington: Indiana University Press, 1989.

Nichols, Ann E. "*Awendan*: A Note on Ælfric's Vocabulary." *JEGP* 63 (1964): 7–13.

Niles, John. Beowulf: *The Poem and Its Tradition.* Cambridge, MA: Harvard University Press, 1983.

————. "Locating *Beowulf* in Literary History." *Exemplaria* 5.1 (1993): 79–109.

O'Keeffe, Katherine O'Brien. *Visible Song: Transitional Literacy in Old English Verse.* Cambridge: Cambridge University Press, 1990.

Olsen, Alexandra Hennessey. "Cynewulf's Autonomous Women: A Reconsideration of *Elene* and *Juliana.*" In *New Readings on Women in Old English Literature,* edited by Helen Damico and Alexandra Hennessey Olsen, 222–232. Bloomington: University of Indiana Press, 1990.

———. "Inversion and Political Purpose in the Old English *Judith.*" *English Studies* 63 (1982): 289–293.

Ong, Walter. *Orality and Literacy: The Technologizing of the Word.* London: Routledge, 1982.

Orton, Peter. "An Approach to *Wulf and Eadwacer.*" *Proceedings of the Royal Irish Academy* 85 (1985): 223–258.

Osborne, Marijane. "The Text and Context of *Wulf and Eadwacer,*" in *The Old English Elegies: New Essays in Criticism and Research,* edited by Martin Green, 174–189. Rutherford: Fairleigh Dickinson University Press, 1983.

Ott, J.H. *Über die Quellen der Heiligenleben in Ælfrics Lives of Saints I.* Inaugural Dissertation, Halle, 1892.

Overing, Gillian R. *Language, Sign and Gender in* Beowulf. Carbondale: Southern Illinois University Press, 1990.

Page, R.I. "The Study of Latin Texts in late Anglo-Saxon England II: The Evidence of English Glosses." In *Latin and the Vernacular Languages in Early Medieval Britain,* edited by Nicholas Brooks, 141–165. Leicester: Leicester University Press, 1982.

Page, William, et al., eds. *The Victoria History of the Counties of England.* London: St Catherine Press, 1908–.

Parks, Ward. "Ring Structure and Narrative Embedding in Homer and *Beowulf.*" *Neuphilologische Mitteilungen* 89 (1988): 237–251.

Partner, Nancy F., ed. *Studying Medieval Women.* Cambridge: Medieval Academy of America, 1993.

Pasternack, Carol Braun. *The Textuality of Old English Poetry.* Cambridge: Cambridge University Press, 1995.

Pope, John C. "Second Thoughts on the Interpretation of 'The Seafarer.'" *Anglo-Saxon England* 3 (1974): 75–86; rpt. in *Old English Shorter Poems,* ed. Katherine O'Brien O'Keeffe (New York: Garland, 1994), 213–229.

Power, Eileen. *Medieval English Nunneries (ca. 1275–1535).* Cambridge: Cambridge University Press, 1922.

Price, Jocelyn G. "The *Liflade of Seinte Iuliene* and Hagiographic Convention." *Medievalia et Humanistica* n.s. 14 (1986): 37–58.

———. "'Inner' and 'Outer'" Conceptualizing the Body in *Ancrene Wisse* and Aelred's *De Institutione Inclusarum.*" In *Medieval English Religious and Ethical Literature: Essays in Honour of G.H. Russell,* edited by Gregory Kratzmann and James Simpson, 192–208. Cambridge: D.S. Brewer, 1986.

Probyn, Elspeth. *Sexing the Self: Gendered Positions in Cultural Studies*. New York: Routledge, 1993.

Reinsma, Luke. *Ælfric: An Annotated Bibliography*. New York: Garland, 1987.

Renoir, Alain. "Christian Inversion in *The Wife's Lament*." *Studia Neophilologica* 49 (1977): 19–24.

———. "Point of View and Design for Terror in *Beowulf*." *Neuphilologische Mitteilungun* 63 (1962): 154–167.

———. "A Reading Context for 'The Wife's Lament.'" In *Anglo-Saxon Poetry: Essays in Appreciation*, edited by Lewis E. Nicholson and Dolores Warwick Frese, 224–241. Notre Dame: Notre Dame University Press, 1975.

Renoir, E. "Clôture Monastique." *Dictionnaire d'Archéologie Chrétienne et de Liturgie*. Vol. 3. Paris: Librairie Letouzey et Ané, 1914.

Ridyard, Susan J. *The Royal Saints of Anglo-Saxon England*. Cambridge: Cambridge University Press, 1988.

Robertson, Elizabeth. *Early English Devotional Prose and the Female Audience*. Knoxville: University of Tennessee Press, 1990.

———. "Medieval Medical Views of Women and Female Spirituality in the *Ancrene Wisse* and Julian of Norwich's *Showings*." In *Feminist Approaches to the Body in Medieval Literature*, edited by Linda Lomperis and Sarah Stanbury, 142–167. Philadelphia: University of Pennsylvania Press, 1993.

———. "The Rule of the Body: The Feminine Spirituality of the *Ancrene Wisse*." In *Seeking the Woman in Late Medieval and Renaissance Writings: Essays in Feminist Contextual Criticism*, edited by Sheila Fisher and Janet E. Halley, 109–134. Knoxville: University of Tennessee Press, 1989.

Robinson, Fred C. "*Beowulf*." In *The Cambridge Companion to Old English Literature*, edited by Malcolm Godden and Michael Lapidge, 142–159. Cambridge: Cambridge University Press, 1991.

———. Beowulf *and the Appositive Style*. Knoxville: University of Tennessee Press, 1985.

Rollason, David. *Saints and Relics in Anglo-Saxon England*. Oxford: Blackwell, 1989.

Roy, Gopa. "A Virgin Acts Manfully: Ælfric's *Life of St. Eugenia* and the Latin Versions." *Leeds Studies in English* 23 (1992): 1–27.

Rubin, Gayle. "The Traffic in Women: Notes on the 'Political Economy' of Sex." In *Toward an Anthropology of Women*, edited by Rayna R. Reiter, 157–210. New York and London: Monthly Review Press, 1975.

Rubin, Miri and Sarah Kay, eds. *Framing Medieval Bodies*. New York: St. Martin's Press, 1994.

Scarry, Elaine. *The Body in Pain: The Making and Unmaking of the World*. New York and Oxford: Oxford University Press, 1985.

Schafer, Ursula. "Two Women in Need of a Friend: A Comparison of *The Wife's Lament* and Eangyth's Letter to Boniface," in *Germanic Dialects:*

Linguistic and Philological Investigations, edited by Bela Brogyanyi and Thomas Krommelbein, 491–524. Amsterdam and Philadelphia: John Benjamins, 1986.

Schneider, Claude. "Cynewulf's Devaluation of Heroic Tradition." *Anglo-Saxon England* 7 (1978): 107–118.

Schrader, Richard. *God's Handiwork: Images of Women in Early Germanic Literature*. Westport: Greenwood Press, 1983.

Schulenburg, Jane Tibbetts. "The Heroics of Virginity: Brides of Christ and Sacrificial Mutilation." In *Women in the Middle Ages and Renaissance: Literary and Historical Perspectives*, edited by Mary Beth Rose, 29–72. Syracuse: Syracuse University Press, 1986.

———. "Strict Active Enclosure and its Effects on the Female Monastic Experience (500–1100)." In *Medieval Religious Women Volume 1: Distant Echoes*, edited by John A. Nichols and Lillian Thomas Shank, 51–86. Kalamazoo: Cistercian Publications, 1984.

———. "Women's Monastic Communities, 500–1100: Patterns of Expansion and Decline." *Signs* 14.2 (1989): 261–92. Rpt. in *Sisters and Workers in the Middle Ages*, edited by Judith M. Bennett, Elizabeth A. Clark, Jean F. O'Barr, B. Anne Vilen, and Sarah Westphal–Wihl, 208–239. Chicago: University of Chicago Press, 1989.

Scott, Joan Wallach. *Gender and the Politics of History*. New York: Columbia University Press, 1988.

Scragg, Donald G. "The Nature of Old English Verse." In *The Cambridge Companion to Old English Literature*, edited by Malcolm Godden and Michael Lapidge, 55–70. Cambridge: Cambridge University Press, 1991.

Sedgwick, Eve Kosofsky. *Between Men: English Literature and Male Homosocial Desire*. New York: Columbia University Press, 1985.

Sklute, L. John. "*Freoðuwebbe* in Old English Poetry." In *New Readings on Women in Old English Literature*, edited by Helen Damico and Alexandra Hennessey Olsen, 204–210. Bloomington: University of Indiana Press, 1990.

Smalley, Beryl. *The Study of the Bible in the Middle Ages*. Notre Dame: Notre Dame University Press, 1964.

Spamer, James. "The Marriage Concept in *Wulf and Eadwacer*." *Neophilologus* 62 (1978): 143–144.

Spelman, Elizabeth. "Woman as Body: Ancient and Contemporary Views." *Feminist Studies* 8 (1982): 109–131.

Stevick, Robert. "Formal Aspects of *The Wife's Lament*." *JEGP* 59 (1960): 21–25.

Stock, Brian. *The Implications of Literacy: Written Language and Models of Interpretation in the Eleventh and Twelfth Centuries*. Princeton: Princeton University Press, 1983.

Swanton, M.J. "'The Wife's Lament' and 'The Husband's Message': A Reconsideration." *Anglia* 82 (1964): 269–290.

Szarmach, Paul, ed. *Holy Men and Holy Women: Old English Prose Saints' Lives and Their Contexts.* Albany: State University of New York Press, 1996.

Szarmach, Paul. "Ælfric as Exegete." In *Hermeneutics and Medieval Culture,* edited by Patrick J. Gallacher and Helen Damico, 237–247. Albany: State University of New York Press, 1989.

———. "Ælfric's Women Saints: Eugenia." In *New Readings on Women in Old English Literature,* edited by Helen Damico and Alexandra Hennessey Olsen, 146–157. Bloomington: Indiana University Press, 1990.

———. "The Recovery of Texts." In *Reading Old English Texts,* edited by Katherine O'Brien O'Keeffe, 124–145. Cambridge: Cambridge University Press, 1997.

———. "St. Euphrosyne: Holy Transvestite." In *Holy Men and Holy Women,* edited by Paul Szarmach, 353–365. Albany: State University of New York Press, 1996.

Taylor, Keith P. "*Beowulf* 1259a: The Inherent Nobility of Grendel's Mother." *ELN* 31 (1994): 13–25.

Tonsfeldt, H. Ward. "Ring Structure in *Beowulf.*" *Neophilologus* 61 (1977): 443–452.

Tripp, Jr., Raymond P. "The Narrator as Revenant: A Reconsideration of Three Old English Elegies." *Papers on Language and Literature* 8 (1972): 339–361.

Walker-Pelkey, Faye. "*Frige hwæt ic hatte*: *The Wife's Lament* as Riddle." *Papers on Language and Literature* 28 (1992): 242–266.

Warren, Ann K. *Anchorites and Their Patrons in Medieval England.* Berkeley and Los Angeles: University of California Press, 1985.

Wemple, Suzanne Fonay. *Women in Frankish Society: Marriage and the Cloister 500–900.* Philadelphia: University of Pennsylvania Press, 1981.

Wentersdorf, Karl. "The Situation of the Narrator in the Old English *Wife's Lament.*" *Speculum* 56.3 (1981): 592–516. Rpt. in *Old English Shorter Poems: Basic Readings,* edited by Katherine O'Brien O'Keeffe, 357–392. New York: Garland, 1994.

Whitelock, Dorothy. "The Audience of *Beowulf.*" Reprinted in *From Bede to Alfred,* by Dorothy Whitelock, 1–111. London: Variorum Reprints, 1980.

———. "The Interpretation of 'The Seafarer,'" in *Old English Literature: Twenty-Two Analytical Essays,* edited by Martin Stevens and Jerome Mandel, 198–211. Lincoln: University of Nebraska Press, 1968.

Withycombe, S.M.W. "*St. Margarete*: A Late Old English Perception of Feminine Sanctity." *Parergon* n.s. 10.2 (1992): 167–179.

Wittig, Joseph. "Figural Narrative in Cynewulf's *Juliana.*" *Anglo-Saxon England* 4 (1975): 37–55.

Wogan-Browne, Jocelyn. "Chaste Bodies: Frames and Experiences." In *Framing Medieval Bodies*, edited by Miri Rubin and Sarah Kay, 24–42. New York: St. Martin's, 1994.

———. "Rerouting the Dower: The Anglo-Norman Life of St. Audrey by Marie (of Chatteris?)." In *Power of the Weak: Studies on Medieval Women*, edited by Jennifer Carpenter and Sally-Beth MacLean, 27–56. Urbana: University of Illinois Press, 1995.

———. "Saints' Lives and the Female Reader." *Forum for Modern Language Studies* 27.4 (1991): 314–322.

Woolf, Rosemary. "Saints' Lives." In *Art and Doctrine: Essays on Medieval Literature*, edited by Heather O'Donoghue, 219–244. London: Hambledon, 1986.

———. "*The Wanderer, The Seafarer*, and the Genre of *Planctus*." In *Anglo-Saxon Poetry: Essays in Appreciation*, edited by Lewis Nicholson and Dolores Warwick Frese, 192–207. Notre Dame: Notre Dame University Press, 1975.

Wormald, Patrick. "The Uses of Literacy in Anglo-Saxon England and its Neighbors." *Transactions of the Royal Historical Society* 5th ser. 27 (1977): 95–114.

Yorke, Barbara. "'Sisters Under the Skin'? Anglo-Saxon Nuns and Nunneries in Southern England." *Reading Medieval Studies* 15 (1989): 95–117.

Zettel, Patrick. "Saints' Lives in Old English: Latin Manuscripts and Vernacular Accounts: Ælfric." *Peritia* 1 (1982): 17–37.

Index